Get Started in Computing

Image credits

Teach Yourself®

Get Started in Computing

Moira Stephen

For UK order enquiries: please contact Bookpoint Ltd, 130 Milton Park, Abingdon, Oxon OX14 4SB. Telephone: +44 (0) 1235 827720. Fax: +44 (0) 1235 400454. Lines are open 09.00–17.00, Monday to Saturday, with a 24-hour message answering service. Details about our titles and how to order are available at www.teachyourself.com

For USA order enquiries: please contact McGraw-Hill Customer Services, PO Box 545, Blacklick, OH 43004-0545, USA. Telephone: 1-800-722-4726. Fax: 1-614-755-5645.

For Canada order enquiries: please contact McGraw-Hill Ryerson Ltd, 300 Water St, Whitby, Ontario L1N 9B6, Canada. Telephone: 905 430 5000. Fax: 905 430 5020.

Long renowned as the authoritative source for self-guided learning – with more than 50 million copies sold worldwide – the Teach Yourself series includes over 500 titles in the fields of languages, crafts, hobbies, business, computing and education.

British Library Cataloguing in Publication Data: a catalogue record for this title is available from the British Library.

Library of Congress Catalog Card Number: on file.

First published in UK 2010 by Hodder Education, part of Hachette UK, 338 Euston Road, London NW1 3BH.

First published in US 2010 by The McGraw-Hill Companies, Inc.

Previously published as Teach Yourself Basic Computer Skills

The Teach Yourself name is a registered trade mark of Hodder Headline.

Typeset by MPS Limited, A Macmillan Company.

Printed in Great Britain for Hodder Education, an Hachette UK Company, 338 Euston Road, London NW1 3BH, by CPI Cox & Wyman, Reading, Berkshire RG1 8EX.

The publisher has used its best endeavours to ensure that the URLs for external websites referred to in this book are correct and active at the time of going to press. However, the publisher and the author have no responsibility for the websites and can make no guarantee that a site will remain live or that the content will remain relevant, decent or appropriate.

Computer hardware and software brand names mentioned in this book are protected by their trademarks and are acknowledged.

Hachette UK's policy is to use papers that are natural, renewable and recyclable products and made from wood grown in sustainable forests. The logging and manufacturing processes are expected to conform to the environmental regulations of the country of origin.

Impression number   10 9 8 7 6 5 4 3 2 1

Year   2014 2013 2012 2011 2010

Contents

Welcome to *Get Started in Computing*

Get Started in Computing is for anyone who wants to learn how to make good use of their PC. It doesn't assume that you are a complete novice – there are very few of those left! You have probably used a PC a little – and can steer the mouse and use the keyboard (at least a bit).

You may have done a little with one application – perhaps tried the Internet, sent an email or played a game – and now want to get to grips with more. You may even be thinking of taking a basic qualification in IT. This book will get you off to a good start with Windows, Word, Excel, Access, PowerPoint, the Internet and email.

The book starts by looking at **security**! Maybe not exactly where you want to dive in – but take your time and read it. Using a PC is one thing – but looking after your computer, yourself and your data is *really* important. The more you use a computer, the more you will come to depend on it – so find out what might threaten your security – and how to minimise the risks of getting caught out.

Chapter 2 goes on to help you get started **using your PC and working in Windows**. You will be taken on a tour of your PC environment (*Windows 7* in this case). Starting with switching on, through personalizing your desktop (everyone likes their favourite picture on their desktop!), finding help when you need it, managing your folders and files and installing software.

Chapter 3 introduces **system maintenance** and suggests things that you can do to help make sure our computer stays healthy – and things that you will need a technician to help with. It also discusses health and safety issues, licensing and the Data Protection Act.

Chapter 4 covers features that are pretty standard across the **Microsoft Office applications**, such as creating, saving, printing, closing and opening files. Other topics include basic formatting options, moving and copying text and data, spell checking, searching, clip art and drawing. This is a good chapter to keep referring back to as you use your applications.

Word is introduced in Chapter 5. You will learn how to create and manipulate basic documents, format using tabs and indents, create and edit tables, use styles and templates, perform a mail merge and create and format graphs.

In Chapter 6 you will find out how to unleash the power of **Excel**. As you create and format your worksheets, you will find out how to build formulas, use functions and create and format graphs.

The **Access** database package is introduced in Chapter 7. You will learn how to create tables and input and edit data. You will also find out how to create forms and use them for data input, manipulate your data by sorting and querying, and present your data effectively using reports.

Chapter 8 will teach you how to create effective presentations using Microsoft **PowerPoint**. You will find out how to add text, tables, pictures, charts and other objects to your slides. You will also learn how to add special effects and present the finished product.

Chapter 9 introduces you to the **Internet**. You will learn how to locate websites, surf the Net, customize your browser and manage your Favorites.

And finally, in Chapter 10 we look at **email**. You will find out how to send and reply to e-mails, send attachments and manage your messages.

Each chapter has some questions at the end of it – so you can check what you have learnt.

If you are working towards an IT User certificate at beginner or intermediate level, you will find that this book complements your studies very well.

I hope you enjoy *Teach Yourself Get Started in Computing*, and make good use of your new skills.

Moira Stephen
2010

Only got one minute?

OK. You need to learn how to use a computer – but you are really short on time. And you're really not sure where you should start.

Well, first of all decide what you want to use your computer for. Do you need to send e-mails? Or research something on the Internet? Or be able to type up a letter or report?

Decide what you want to do first (no-one can learn to do everything at once) and start with that - and ignore the rest for the time being. Get the hang of one thing at a time – if you are too ambitious you will get bogged down. Once you can do a one thing, the next thing is a bit easier.

Once you get going you can find out how to customize your desktop, and – very important – how to organize your files. You will be saving files and should learn how to set up folders and organize them properly. It might be for your reports and letters, or your holiday photos from your camera – but life is so much easier if you can find things once you've filed them away.

Organizing your e-mail messages into folders is a good idea too – and the principle is the same – whether it is documents or emails.

It's also vital to learn how to protect your system from viruses, keep your data safe and generally look after yourself and your PC. The more you use your PC, the more it hurts when something goes wrong – so get savvy on what to watch out for and what to try to avoid.

But the main thing is to start with something you really want to be able to do – whether it is researching your next holiday on the Internet, e-mailing your aunt in Australia or creating a report for a course you are doing – then it all becomes more meaningful.

5 Only got five minutes?

The fact that you are reading this suggests that you are looking for something to help you make better use of your computer. This is a get started book – so I guess you are either a near beginner, or someone who has muddled on for a while using a PC, and has decided it is perhaps time to learn a bit more about it. You don't want a huge volume to plough through – they look too intimidating and time consuming. And you want something in plain English – because computer speak just isn't really your language! So this book has caught your eye.

Computers are very versatile things. Lots of people say they 'use a computer' – but this can mean so many things that you will need to dig deeper if you want to find out what they actually mean. What do they do with it? Do they make music with it? Create websites? Teach? Enter order details on it? Manage patient records? Analyze statistics? Prepare accounts? Write blogs on it?

There are so many things that you can do with a computer!!

So you need to decide what *you* want to do with *your* computer – and then learn how to do it.

You will certainly need to get to grips with the range of computer applications that are probably the most widely used at a personal and business level – those in the Microsoft Office suite. The applications are Access (database), Excel (spreadsheet), Outlook (e-mail), PowerPoint (presentation graphics) and Word (word processing). There's also Internet Explorer (web browser) and Windows Outlook (e-mail software).

Windows 7 is the operating system (that creates the environment that you work within on your computer) and you will need guidance on looking after yourself, your computer and your data.

Teaching yourself is easier when you have a reason for wanting to learn something. For example, you might be preparing for a job interview and have been asked to give a presentation. This sounds like a very good reason to learn to use PowerPoint! Or you may have children and grandchildren who have moved away and you want to be able to e-mail them. When you have a reason for learning something, it is easier to stick with it and see it through.

Whatever your motivation, stick with whatever application you are trying to learn for a while – so that you really start to get to grips with it – before you move on to something else. That way you will see a measureable difference in your ability and confidence.

Learning to use a computer is like learning a language or learning to drive a car – you need to practice. And regular practice is much better than trying to do a marathon session and then do nothing for a couple of weeks.

And don't forget – being able to use a computer can open doors to many other things – social, educational and professional. So don't hold back – go for it! And it should be fun – so enjoy!

1

User IT security

In this chapter you will learn:
- *how to protect your PC from computer viruses*
- *about information security*
- *about threats to networked systems*
- *how to keep your data safe*

1.1 System performance security

SPAM

Spam is one of the biggest culprits when it comes to security breaches affecting the performance of your IT system. Spam is usually in the form of e-mail but it can also be sent through IMS (instant messaging systems), mobile phones, on-line gaming, etc. Spam happens when people/organizations do mass mailings to random e-mail addresses to try and engage the recipient in some activity.

The only way to be sure of getting no spam is to stop using electronic communications.

Spam usually tries to:

▶ *Sell you something*
▶ *Ask you to invest in something (or some other con to relieve you of your funds)*

> ▶ *Ask you to confirm some personal/confidential information about yourself (bank account number, pin number, etc.).*

Anti-spam software is often installed on company IT systems to try and stop the spam getting through to the organization. The anti-spam software analyses the message and rejects it if it looks like spam.

However, it is a balancing act – the only sure way to stop all spam is to block everything – and that isn't really an option. So inevitably, some spam will get through and land in your Inbox.

So how do you know if a message is spam?

It can be difficult at times – so use your common sense. If something looks too good to be true – it probably is.

What should you do with spam? Depending on what it is and whether you are at work or at home, you could:

> ▶ *Forward the message to your IT security/helpdesk if this is what your company asks you to do with such communication.*
> ▶ *Try to contact the organization some other way to check things out. You could try phoning them, or e-mail them (but not as a reply to the message you are suspicious of).*
> ▶ *Search the Internet to see if anyone else is getting similar stuff. You won't be the only one getting it if it is spam.*
> ▶ *Delete it – if it is something important whoever sent it will try to contact you again.*

Spam is a system performance security issue because of the volume of it that gets sent – it takes a lot of IT resources to try and identify and stop it.

MALICIOUS PROGRAMS (MALWARE)

A malicious program is software that is designed to get loaded into your computer system without you knowing it is there. It is usually done with the intention of causing some kind of damage to your system.

Malicious software installs itself without you knowing!

Viruses, worms, Trojans, spyware, adware and rogue diallers are all examples of malicious programs.

This type of software is often spread in e-mail attachments, or in files that are downloaded from the Internet and or from pirate copies of software.

Viruses are the most commonly reported type of malware, but there are others.

A virus, once on your computer, can spread through your disks, memory and files and cause all sorts of damage – and many viruses can spread across computer networks and bypass security systems. Viruses are often sent in e-mail attachments – so don't open attachments from unknown sources.

Diagnosing a virus

Things that might indicate that you have a virus include:

- ▶ *Your computer running unusually slowly*
- ▶ *Unusual error messages*
- ▶ *Strange screen activity*
- ▶ *Files and/or folders changing their name*
- ▶ *Programs crashing.*

There could be other reasons for these symptoms, but if you experience them, suspect a virus.

Protection is better than cure

To help protect your system from viruses you should ensure that your software is up-to-date (by installing updates as required) and install anti-virus software, e.g. Norton or McAfee. Once you have installed your virus checker you must keep it up to date (most anti-virus software suppliers download updates to your system as they become available). You need to keep the anti-virus software up to date because new viruses appear all the time – and the anti-virus software suppliers keep updating their software to deal with the new viruses that appear. You must run the anti-virus software regularly to make sure that your system is clean – you can usually set it to run automatically at a specific time of day.

Norton is popular, but there are many others, e.g. McAfee and AVG Antivirus.

To help protect your system from viruses

- ▶ *Install reliable anti-virus software on your computer, and update it regularly*
- ▶ *Use the anti-virus software to scan your system for viruses regularly*
- ▶ *Use the anti-virus software to scan any removable disks before you open files on them*
- ▶ *Scan any files downloaded from the Internet before you open them – viruses are often transmitted in attachments to e-mails*
- ▶ *Install only genuine software from reputable sources*
- ▶ *Don't open e-mails from sources that you don't recognize*
- ▶ *Don't open attachments to e-mails from sources that you don't recognize.*

Any messages, files, software and attachments that you receive from unknown sources should be treated with caution. Ask your IT security person to check them, or run your virus checker on them, or delete them.

Other terms you may encounter when discussing or reading about viruses include:

Worm   A program which actively transmits itself over a network to infect other computers

Trojan horse	A piece of software which appears to perform a certain action, but in fact, performs another.
Spyware	A type of malware that spies on you and collects information about you (e.g. name, ID, password), your computer and/or Internet browsing habits without your consent. You should install anti-spyware software on your computer to help protect your system.
Adware	Software that automatically plays, displays, or downloads advertisements to your computer after software is installed on it or while the application is being used.
Rogue diallers	Rogue diallers (sometimes called Trojan Horse diallers), are programs that make phone calls from your computer. They are installed on your computer without your knowledge and they dial up to expensive premium rate phone numbers or international numbers. In most cases, dial-up access users are unaware that their computer is dialling up to these numbers until they receive a big phone bill.

Infiltration

A hacker is someone who focuses on the security mechanisms of computer and network systems. A hacker isn't an authorized user but they try to find ways of infiltrating a system. Hackers try to access your computer systems by evading or disabling any security measures that you have in place. They are usually programmers who either hack into systems for kicks, or for more sinister purposes.

Most reporting of computer hackers is that of hackers breaking into IT systems with the intention of causing damage – spying, stealing information and data, deleting files or corrupting systems in some way. However, some organizations employ hackers to test their security systems. These hackers are not criminals but are employed to try and find weaknesses in the organization's IT security so that it can be improved.

To help protect a system against hackers you should install a firewall.

The firewall will check all messages entering and leaving your system – and if they don't meet the security criteria set for the firewall they will be blocked.

It makes sure that no program on your computer tries to connect to the Internet without your consent, and that no one can download things to your PC without you knowing.

A firewall can be hardware or software – and every computer with access to the Internet should have one!

Hoaxes

Hoaxes can take the form of virus hoaxes, chain letters, scams, false alarms, misunderstandings and scares. They can be really annoying – and sometimes a bit worrying. You are bound to receive a hoax from time to time. The trick is being able to tell the difference between a hoax and something that is real.

Beware of hoaxes. If an e-mail tells you to delete a file – you should probably check it out first!

Sometimes it is obvious it is a hoax – perhaps a chain letter telling you that you need to send it on to 10 other people or you will get a wart on the end of our nose! Just delete it – anything that happens to your nose will be purely coincidental.

Others are worth checking out – particularly virus hoaxes. You might receive an e-mail saying that a virus is due to be activated within the next 24 hours, and to protect your computer you need to delete a certain file from your system. Don't do it – check it out. Report it to your IT department to see if they know anything about it. Or check the Internet – you can usually find out whether or not they are genuine.

Virus hoaxes are more than just an annoyance as they may result in some users ignoring all virus warning messages – thinking it is just a hoax. And this is not a good idea either.

Virus writers can use known hoaxes to their advantage – perhaps attaching a virus to the original hoax – so always be on your guard.

1.2 Information security

IDENTITY/AUTHENTICATION

The information on your IT system can be at risk from unauthorized users. It is therefore important that you can identify yourself to your IT system, so that it knows who you are and what you are allowed to do on the system.

When working in a networked environment you will have a User ID and a password to access the system. These are used to identify you so that appropriate rights are made available to you while you work. These rights give you access to the drives that you need to use as well as read and/or write access to files.

Keep your password a secret!

There are various levels of password protection available to help ensure that authorized users only can access the system and open and edit the files held on it.

Passwords are sometimes called PINs – Personal Identification Numbers.

User-level

Password protection can be assigned at a user level (through the operating system) so that only authorized users can access the system. With this type of password protection, the computer will pause as it boots up and you need to enter your user identification and password before you can go any further.

Choose your passwords carefully!

Don't use things like a name someone can associate with you (e.g. your own name or your child's), your date of birth or 'password'.

Use a mixture of letters and numbers that you can remember but that you think it will be difficult for someone to guess, e.g. 1wng2a4c

Don't tell anyone your password.

Change your password regularly.

Many systems have a minimum length of password e.g. 8 characters.

FILES

If you have files on the system that you don't want other users to be able to view or edit, you may be able to password protect the individual files (most modern applications allow you to do this).

By using the password protection features available, the following security features could be available on a networked PC:

- ▶ *A password to access the system*
- ▶ *A password to access a file*
- ▶ *A password to allow editing of a file.*

Change your password regularly.

Different users can have different levels of security clearance assigned to them, allowing different users access to different parts of the system and its files.

To change your Windows password

1 *Open the* Control Panel *(Start, Control Panel).*
2 *Go to* User Accounts and Family Safety.
3 *Click* Change your Windows Password *in* User Accounts.
4 *Click* Create a password/Change your password.
5 *Complete the dialog box.*
6 *Click* Create/Change password.

USB/Flash drives

You can also protect the contents of some memory sticks by assigning a password to them. The contents can only be viewed if you supply the correct password.

Confidentiality

It is important that you keep your password/PIN confidential – don't tell anyone what it is. Then no-one can log on to the system pretending to be you.

Don't write your password or PIN number down – you don't want anyone else finding it and being able to use it.

You should always respect the confidentiality of any information that you have access to. This means that if you have access to a file at work you should not go and discuss it with your friends when you are out later. You can discuss it with work colleagues who also have access to it – but it is not something that should be treated as general knowledge.

To help ensure that no-one accesses your computer when you are not at your desk, always log off, or lock your system. This will prevent anyone accessing data if they don't have permission to do so.

Identity theft

Spam e-mails are often also phishing scams!

Phishing is an attempt to criminally and fraudulently acquire sensitive information, such as usernames, passwords and credit card details, by pretending to be a trustworthy source (eBay, PayPal and online banks are common targets of phishing scams).

You may receive e-mails that look like they have come from your bank or credit card company suggesting that you click here to contact them and confirm your details.

Don't – banks and credit card companies don't use e-mails to collect or confirm sensitive/confidential data! If you receive this type of e-mail you are probably being targeted by a 'phishing' scam where someone is trying to collect your details. If they succeed, they will pretend to be you and may withdraw money from your account, or buy goods online using your details.

E-mails are not a secure way of sending messages – they can easily be intercepted! So don't send confidential information via e-mail. Bank account details, pin numbers – in fact any information that you don't want to fall into the wrong hands – should be transmitted in some other way e.g. a secure link to your bank.

1.3 Technology security

NETWORKS

Local Area Network (LAN)

A LAN is made up of computers connected together by cables or wireless in the same room or building. The computers are in close proximity (local) to each other and the network is owned and controlled by the organization. PCs can share peripherals. e.g. printer or scanner over a LAN. They can also share application and data files easily and they can communicate using e-mail (provided e-mail software is installed). They can also share a link to the Internet.

WLAN (Wireless Local Area Network)

A WLAN is a local area network where the devices use wireless technology, e.g. WiFi or Bluetooth, to communicate.

A *hotspot* is a location where high-speed Internet access is available to anyone with a WiFi enabled computer, through a Wireless Local Area Network (WLAN) access point. Many handheld and laptop computers are WiFi enabled. WiFi is a standard that allows your PC to access a WLAN, which in turn may allow access to the Internet and your e-mail. Many PDAs are fitted with this standard.

Wide Area Network (WAN)

Computers connected over a long distance are part of a WAN. Large organizations may use a WAN to connect their offices in different parts of the country. The WAN could use leased lines (perhaps from BT or Mercury) for the exclusive use of the organization.

Internet

The Internet is a huge WAN. Computers from all over the world are linked together to form the Internet. You can access the World Wide Web via the Internet, send e-mails, access your company computer system and transfer files, etc.

The Internet is also used as a collaborative tool where groups of people who are remote from each other can share information, research findings, etc. Web logs (blogs), forums and discussion groups, social networks like Bebo and Facebook and instant messaging, e.g. MSN are all accessed via the Internet.

Intranet

An *intranet* is a private network that uses Internet features to give access to your company data. When using the company Intranet, it *looks* and feels like the Internet to the user, but the pages are internal to the organization. The information is displayed on Web style pages, and hyperlinks allow the user to jump from place to place, but the data will be held on a company server, with access limited to company employees.

Extranet

An *extranet* is a private network that uses the Internet technology and the public telecommunication system to securely share part of a business's information or operations with suppliers, customers, or other businesses. An extranet can be viewed as part of a company's intranet that is extended to users outside the company. Users can log into the extranet over the Internet by entering their username and password.

SECURITY CONSIDERATIONS

When connecting to the Internet you can use a *private* or *public* network.

At work, your IT staff will deal with securing the Internet connection so that only those with appropriate permissions and rights can use the connection.

Over 50% of people admit to having used someone else's wireless Internet without permission.

PRIVATE

At home, you might be the person responsible for managing your own Internet connection. You could have several wireless devices at home e.g. laptop, PDA, etc. that you want to have Internet access. You will most probably set up *one* Internet connection from your main/host computer and allow the other wireless devices to share it.

But you don't want *everyone* round about with wireless using your connection – just your friends and family. To ensure that other wireless users, e.g. neighbours, don't use your wireless connection you should secure it. You would be surprised how many connections are not secure. If you try picking up a wireless connection in any residential area you will probably find several – and it's quite likely that some are unsecured.

If you don't secure your connection, then anyone with a WiFi enabled device will be able to pick up your network signal and will be able to access the Internet using your connection.

At best, you may never know and nothing untoward will come from it. At worst the piggy backer will be able to monitor your Internet activity and they will be able to access any site they wish and download anything they want. This could be a relatively minor inconvenience, e.g. if your Internet connection slows down because they are downloading lots of stuff – or it could end up pretty serious and get you into trouble, because whatever they are accessing or downloading, will point to you.

You need to install a *wireless router* to allow your wireless devices to connect to the Internet using the same connection as your main PC.

Top Tips!

Keep your system up to date

Check that you have up-to-date anti-virus, security patches, and client firewall software. This will help to protect your wireless network by stopping malware-based connections to it.

Use encryption

Wireless routers give you the option of encrypting your data, so bank details and passwords can't be intercepted. Wi-Fi Protected Access (WPA and WPA2) is a much stronger encryption system for securing your communications than WEP, which can be easily cracked by hackers.

Use a password

Set up a password for your wireless internet connection. Choose a strong password for securing your network – don't use the one that came with your Wi-Fi router or anything that would be easy to guess. The devices using your secure connection will need to know the password before being allowed to use it.

(Contd)

Don't broadcast your wireless network name (SSID).

The name of your wireless network should not be broadcast to passers-by. Choose a hard-to-guess SSID to make life harder for Wi-Fi hackers. Don't name your wireless network 'home', 'wireless' or 'internet' – those are the first ones that people will guess. SSIDs can be a mixture of alpha and numeric characters – maximum size 32 characters.

Use MAC address filtering

A MAC (Media Access Control) address is a unique identifier for network interface cards or network adapters – and each wireless device will have one. You need to set up a list of the MAC addresses that you want to allow to use your connection on your router, e.g. those in your home. The feature is normally turned off when the router is shipped so you need to enable it. This isn't a complete solution – but it will certainly stop most piggy backers.

Restrict Internet access to certain hours

Some wireless routers allow you to restrict Internet access to certain times of the day so if you know you are at work between 9–5, Monday to Friday, schedule your router to disable access between those hours.

PUBLIC

Hotspots in coffee shops and airports use a *public* wireless network. When you try to connect your laptop to a public network, it will show as an 'unsecured wireless connection'. There are a few precautions that you should take when using a public network.

Sites that you give credit card details to should be secure – watch for https://

If you are going to transmit confidential information e.g. your credit card details, *ALWAYS* look for an https:// web address in the address bar. An https:// address indicates a link to a secure site and your personal information is protected, even on an unsecured connection. This type of connection is usually considered secure enough for sending your credit card number, etc. The data sent to an https:// address is encrypted before it is transmitted, so no-one can make any sense of it unless they know the encryption code.

At a public hotspot, the greater risk is potentially from someone near you that can see the numbers that you type on your keyboard! So watch out for people peeking over your shoulder!

Another security risk at a public hotspot involves other computers that are also connected to the same unsecured network. Network attacks can be made through them and they may be able to connect to your computer – and possibly download information from your hard drive.

The best solution here is to have a firewall on your computer. Firewalls guard against these incoming attackers. It is also good practice not to stay connected to unsecured networks for too long at a time as you can then become a target for attack.

So always run a good firewall program if you are connected to an 'unsecured wireless network' and disconnect when not using the link.

Think security!

When setting up your Internet connection you will need to log in to your router or network device to secure it and identify the authorised users. Initially, you will be given a default login and password, e.g. UserID: NewUser; Password: password. You should change the password to something else that others will not guess easily so that they can't login and change your settings.

You should also change your Internet Security Settings to reduce the risk of other users accessing your network. You can do this from Internet Explorer – Tools, Options, Security.

CONNECTIVITY

We have already mentioned Wifi – a standard used for wireless networking. Another widely used technology is Bluetooth.

Bluetooth lets devices with a Bluetooth chip communicate by radio instead of cables – things like your computer, monitor, mouse, keyboard, PDA could have a Bluetooth chip.

It has two main benefits:

▶ *You don't need cables*
▶ *You can easily synchronize information between devices.*

To get Bluetooth devices to communicate, you just need to place them near each other.

When a Bluetooth device detects another one nearby it automatically links up to it – you don't need to configure anything or use cables. As long as the Bluetooth devices are within range of each other – about 10 metres – they can connect.

Infra-red is similar but for infra-red devices to communicate they need to have 'line of sight'. Like most TV remotes, or controls for overhead projectors. With Bluetooth you don't need 'line of sight' – they can find each other as long as they are close enough.

Bluetooth makes communication between devices easy for the average user who isn't particularly technical when it comes to computers. And it makes communication between devices quick and easy.

Think of your digital camera. Until recently (and it still is the case with mine), to get your pictures from your camera to your computer and/or printer you had to connect the camera to the computer using a cable. You could then copy your pictures over and print them. With Bluetooth you can sit your camera down close to your computer and copy the pictures or print them – no cables required.

Bluetooth isn't intended to replace office computer networks.
It sends data much slower – at around 1Mb per second – compared
with proper wireless networks that communicate at 10–54 Mbps.

The main benefits of Bluetooth are:

▶ *It is cable free – so you could get an Internet connection
through it from your laptop (even if your Bluetooth device
is in your rucksack).*
▶ *It you have Bluetooth on your computer, monitor, printer,
keyboard, mouse – you could have your computer and printer
in one part of the house and your keyboard, mouse and
monitor in another.*
▶ *Synchronizing things like the address book, calendar and task
list on your computer, mobile or PDA is much easier – they
can sync without even asking you!*

Bluetooth is great, but how secure is it??

Bluetooth uses the 2.45 GHz radio band which it shares with cordless
phones and microwave ovens! To be secure, Bluetooth devices
constantly change the radio frequency that they are using to help
prevent eavesdropping. Also, every Bluetooth device has an individual
ID and before they can swap data, you have to enter a PIN number
to authorize the connection. This is to stop passers-by hooking up to
your machines! That said, once you have set up the connection your
devices can remember them and this can be a security risk.

Check your settings

The Bluetooth settings on your device should be adjusted to
prevent the risk of unauthorized access to the device by others.

PORTABLE DEVICES

ICT devices are becoming increasingly portable – laptops are
smaller and lighter, notebooks are about the size of the average
novel, PDAs, mobile phones and multimedia players are so small
that they can easily be slipped into your pocket.

Portable devices are particularly vulnerable to being stolen – or getting lost or forgotten.

We carry more of these devices around with us much of the time – and as the amount of storage available on them continues to increase, we have more information, bigger databases, more detailed spreadsheets, music and photographs on them than ever before.

A telephone can have many names and numbers on it, as well as photographs, contact addresses, calendar appointments and task lists. Multimedia players could contain your complete music and DVD collection, your laptop or notebook could contain lots of important files, reports and figures, as well as company databases.

To reduce the security risks:

▶ *Be careful not to lose them – don't leave them on the bus or in the coffee shop.*
▶ *Beware of thieves – be discrete – you don't want to become a target for the opportunist!*
▶ *If you leave them in your car – lock them in the boot so they are out of sight.*
▶ *At home, don't leave them in the garden, or where a passer-by can see them.*

A thief will probably just hope to sell the device on and make a quick profit – but if the data on it is valuable to you, or confidential to your organization, the loss of the data will have far more serious consequences than the loss of hardware.

1.4 Guidelines and procedures

Your organization will have guidelines and procedures that should be followed to help maintain IT security.

You will often be told where to find these at your induction. Most companies will publish the guidelines on their Intranet, or put them in the staff handbook, or display them on posters.

You should become familiar with your company guidelines and procedures and follow them at all times.

If you are unsure of what a procedure means, or need anything explained to you further, you should be able to approach either your line manager or the IT department (or whoever is responsible for the guidelines).

There may be security checks that you are required to carry out. These will vary from organization to organization – so find out what should happen where you work.

If you become aware of any IT security threats or breaches, you should know who to report your concerns to – perhaps your line manager, or the IT security manager.

1.5 Privacy

Your company will also have a privacy policy. This policy will help explain how the company plans to ensure the privacy of the data that it holds, and how it will comply with the Data Protection Act.

A privacy policy will provide information to customers on how their personal data is handled.

Some companies will publish their privacy policy so customers can view it. You can read the BBC's policy at http://www.bbc.co.uk/privacy/

A privacy policy will explain things like:

- *What information the company may collect about you*
- *How the organization will use information collected about you*
- *When the company will use your details to contact you*
- *Whether the company will disclose your details to anyone else*
- *Your choices regarding the personal information you have provided to the organization*
- *The use of cookies on the company's website and how you can choose not to accept these.*

You should know your company's privacy policy and follow the guidelines in it so that you make correct use of the data that you hold.

DATA PROTECTION ACT

The Data Protection Act (1984, updated 1998) states that users of personal data relating to living, identifiable individuals should be registered with the **Data Protection Registrar**. The users of the personal data should then adhere to The Codes of Practice and Data Protection Principles set out within the Act.

The rules that must be followed by all organizations keeping personal data on individuals are listed here. The personal data must be:

- *Obtained lawfully*
- *Held securely*
- *Used only for the purpose stated to the Data Protection Registrar (or compatible purposes)*
- *Adequate, relevant and not excessive in relation to the purpose for which it is held*
- *Accurate and kept up to date*
- *Deleted when it is no longer required*

▶ *Available to individuals so that they can access and check the information that is held on them.*

As most organizations hold personal data – on customers, employees, suppliers, patients, etc. most organizations (even small ones) must be registered with the Data Protection Registrar.

Part of the organization's privacy policy will state how it plans to ensure it abides by these rules.

1.6 Data security

SECURITY

Increased use and reliance on computers has resulted in a need for users to be aware of threats to the security of equipment and information. It is also vitally important the users take appropriate steps to reduce the danger from these threats.

Your computer equipment and the data on it are very important resources. It is therefore important that you look after them and take precautions to ensure that, should anything happen to them, you can recover from the situation.

Hardware can be protected through insurance policies – if your PC is stolen or damaged you can take precautions to ensure that you will be able to replace it. You can help minimize the risks to your hardware by ensuring that you lock your office/room and close the windows when you leave. Security cables can also be used to lock your computer and hardware down – this not only deters thieves from running off with your hardware, but it will help keep your data safe too.

Your software will most probably have been installed from CD, and if it becomes corrupted in any way you should be able to re-install it from your original disks (you should make sure that these are kept in a safe place).

However, protecting your *data* needs a bit more thought. Threats to your data include:

▶ *Power cuts (where any unsaved data will be lost)*
▶ *Serious hardware fault*
▶ *Physical damage (perhaps as a result of flood or fire)*
▶ *Infection by a computer virus*
▶ *Theft or other malicious act*
▶ *Data corruption – the data on your disk becoming unreadable – perhaps as the result of a hardware fault, or virus*
▶ *Accidental damage by the user – a file deleted by mistake; a laptop left in the coffee shop.*

Lost files on a home computer may cause some inconvenience, but on a business machine the effect of losing data could ruin an organization.

BACKUPS

To minimize the effect of such incidents, you should *back up* the data on your HDD (hard disk drive) regularly. You may just back up important files to a flash drive/USB pen, CD-R or CD-RW, or you may back up the whole drive to a DVD or external hard drive.

In a business situation, back-ups may be done every few hours, or at the end of each day, week, etc. – it depends on the organization and how much the files change in a period of time. In many organizations, data is backed up overnight when most people aren't at work and the process is usually at least partially automated.

The set of media containing the backups is called the *backing store*. Ideally, the backing store should be kept *off site* – at a different location to the computer with the original data – or at least in a different room and ideally in a different building altogether.

An external hard drive.

Backups must be removable!

DO NOT back up your data to another location on the same computer that the original data is on. If the computer is stolen or damaged you will probably lose both the original and the backup data. Back up to an external device, and store it away from the main system. Or backup to an on-line storage facility.

Storage

All backup media should be kept in an environment that is thief proof and flood and fire proof. A safe or vault is often used. Ideally more than one set of backup media should be kept.

The storage devices for a backing store need to be large enough to hold all the files that are considered crucial to the operation of the organization. Specialized storage devices such as tape-streaming machines can be used, or CD-R or multi-gigabyte HDDs may be used.

For a home PC user, a flash drive, CD-R or CD-RW can be used for backing up your data. Exactly how often you back up will vary from individual to individual – but if you've just spent hours working a project on your PC, it's a good idea to back up the files before you finish work.

And always store your software securely – then if your hardware gets stolen or damaged, you can always install the software on another system.

TEST

1 ICT security covers three main areas. What are they?

2 You think that you have received some spam. What might give you this impression?

3 Suggest two ways of dealing with spam.

4 How do you install malware?

5 Suggest three ways of preventing a virus from attacking your computer system.

6 What makes portable IT devices a security risk?

7 How can you improve the security of your Internet connection?

8 Name two documents often issued by companies to staff using IT equipment.

9 Identify three threats to data security.

10 Why should you back up your computer data?

How did you do?
You can find the answers at the back of the book.

2

Using your computer and operating system

In this chapter you will learn:
- *how to start, stop and restart a PC*
- *about the Windows Desktop*
- *how to use the online Help*
- *about file management*
- *how to find files and identify file types*
- *how to compress and extract files*
- *about WordPad*

2.1 Start, stop and re-start your PC

SWITCHING ON

Where's the switch???
The location of the switches on a PC varies from model to model. Have a look at yours and try to find them. The switch on the main unit (the box containing the hard drive, CPU, etc.) will be somewhere on the front of the unit. The switch for the VDU (if it has one) will also normally be on the front of the unit.

1 *Ensure that your PC is plugged in and the power is switched on at the socket.*
2 *Press the on/off button on the main unit.*

3 *Switch on the monitor (if necessary – with some PCs, the monitor goes on and off with the main unit).*

4 *Wait for a few seconds until the Welcome screen appears. If your PC has several users, the user names will be displayed.*

5 *Click on your user name to log on.*

6 *Enter your password if prompted.*

7 *If you are the PC's only user, steps 5 and 6 will be bypassed.*

8 *Your screen will display the Desktop.*

If it doesn't work...

Check that:

▶ *The cables are inserted into the back of the units properly.*

▶ *The computer is plugged in.*

▶ *It is switched on at the wall.*

▶ *The brightness control hasn't been turned down (there should be a control somewhere on your screen).*

▶ *The screen saver hasn't just blanked the screen (move the mouse and wait a few seconds to see if your PC wakes up!).*

▶ *If none of the above work – you might need to get some help!*

SHUT DOWN OR LOG OFF THE COMPUTER

When you have finished using your computer you might want to switch it off altogether, or leave it on so that someone else can use it.

If you have finished using the computer for a while (and you don't share it with anyone who may want to use it soon) you should shut it down – don't just switch it off (if you do Windows may not close properly, and this could cause problems in the future).

To shut down your computer:

1 **Close** *all your files and programs.*

2 *Click the* **Start** *button on the Taskbar.*

3 *Click* **Shut down.**

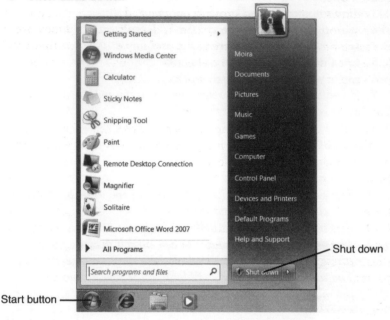

Start button

Shut down

Click what?

In this book, 'click' means use the left mouse button, 'right-click' means click the right button and 'double-click' means click the left button twice, rapidly.

If you share your computer and have finished working on it, you could use one of the following options to close your session but still leave the computer on, ready for someone else to use. Click the arrow next to Shut down to display the options.

Switch User

This allows you to suspend your programs and documents, and allows another user to use the system. It doesn't matter if they use the same programs as you were using, and any documents that you leave open will not normally be affected (although there may be problems if another user tries to work on them).

Log Off

This option closes any open programs but leaves the PC running so someone else can use it. It is a good option if you have finished working on the PC for a while, but know others will be using it before you get back.

Lock

Lock suspends your programs and locks your account. Anyone who tries to access your account will be asked for the password (there is no point using this if you don't have your account password-protected).

Sleep

Sleep shuts down the screen and drives, but leaves the memory intact. This mode leaves the PC ready to jump into action again quickly, but reduces the power consumption considerably. It is a good option if everyone has finished using the PC for a while, but you want to be able to have it up and running again quickly when you get back to it.

Avoid excess wear

Turning a computer off and on too often can wear out some of the circuits and components more quickly – so rather than switch it on and off several times a day, let it sleep if you know you'll be gone for an hour or two!

DEALING WITH CRASHES

There may be times when your computer refuses to do anything –
this is a crash. Your computer may have crashed if:

▶ *The busy symbol appears (the small spinning disk) and refuses
to go away (don't be too impatient with it – it really might just
be busy).*
▶ *The mouse and keyboard have no effect – the PC doesn't
respond to anything you try with them.*
▶ *The screen display isn't right, e.g. part of a dialog box is left
displayed when you have closed it.*

If this happens you could try this:

1 *Press* [Ctrl]-[Alt]-[Delete].
   The following options will be displayed:
      Lock this computer
      Switch User
      Log off
      Change a password
      Start Task Manager
2 *Select* **Start Task Manager**.

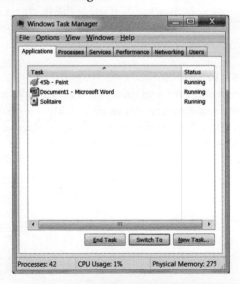

3 *At the Task Manager dialog box, select the* **Applications** *tab. If a program has crashed, it should be at the top of the list with* **Not responding** *next to it.*

4 *Select the application and click* **End Task.**

5 *If no programs are identified as Not responding, close the dialog box and wait a while longer – Windows might just sort itself out.*

If things don't sort themselves out, you may have to restart your computer some other way.

If the PC is responding to the mouse:

1 *Click the* **Start** *button, then the* **arrow** *to the right of the* **Shut down** *button.*

2 *Select* **Restart.**

If the mouse is not working:

1 *Press the* **Restart** *button on your PC (usually located on the front of your system box).*

If all attempts to restart the computer fail, switch it off (either at the on/off switch, or at the wall if that fails) and try again!

Look after yourself!!

Once you start using a computer – whether at work or at home – you will be surprised how much time you end up sitting in front of that screen! Follow the health and safety guidelines in Section 3.3.

2.2 System information

Your computer will most likely consist of:

- ▶ *A unit that contains the Central Processing Unit, Random Access Memory, modem, a hard disk, a CD-RW or DVD drive (or a combined drive)*
- ▶ *Keyboard*
- ▶ *Mouse*
- ▶ *Visual Display Unit*
- ▶ *Printer*
- ▶ *Speakers, to listen to your favourite music while you work!*

You can get details of these components and others in the System Information area. These may be useful if you are speaking to a technical or support person (perhaps to discuss some problem, or an upgrade). They might ask you how much memory it has, or what size the hard disk is, or what processor it has.

To display your system information:
1 *Open the* **Start menu.**
2 *Choose* **All Programs.**
3 *Open* **Accessories.**
4 *Select* **System Tools.**
5 *Click on* **System Information.**

The System Summary will give you high-level information on your system with details of the operating system name and version and the amount of random access memory (RAM) that your computer has.

You can open the sub-categories, e.g. Hardware Resources, Components, Software Environment, to display more detailed information about your system.

You might need this information if you are talking to an engineer.

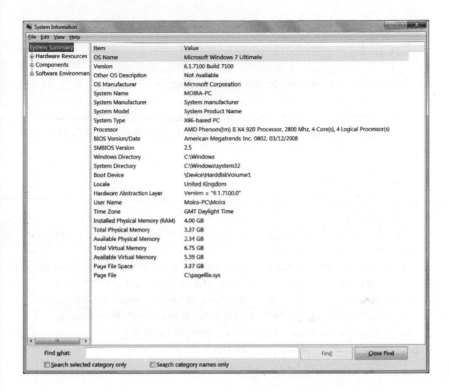

2.3 Set up

There are various settings that you can adjust to customize Windows and personalize your working environment. Some of the more popular settings are discussed in this section, e.g. Themes, desktop colour, screen saver, time and date, the volume of your speakers and gadgets. Experiment with them.

Personalization

Many of the options are accessed from the Personalization dialog box. To access the Personalization options:

1 *Right-click on the Desktop background.*
2 *Choose* **Personalize** *from the shortcut menu.*

THEMES

A theme is a group of options – the Desktop Background, Window Color, Sounds and Screen Saver – saved under the one name. You can change them all at once by selecting a new theme. There are several standard themes to choose from, e.g. Windows 7 or a Slide Show, e.g. Architecture or Landscapes – or you can create your own.

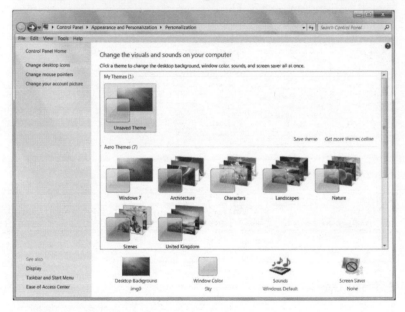

To select a standard theme:

1 *Select the theme required e.g. Architecture or Landscapes – just click on it.*
2 *Close the dialog box.*

To customize a theme:

1 *Select the theme you want to start from.*
2 *Choose the area that you wish to customize, e.g. Desktop Background, Window Color, Sounds or Screen Saver – see below.*

Save a theme:
When you customize the individual elements a new unsaved theme is created.

If you wish to save the theme so that you can apply it whenever you wish, click **Save theme** and give the theme a name.

It will be listed under **My Themes** and can be applied like any other.

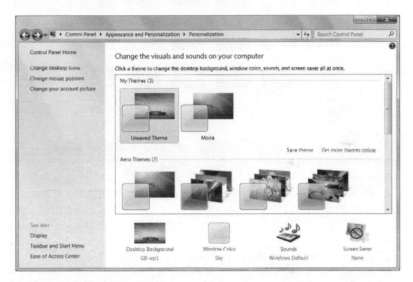

Delete a theme:
If you have saved a theme and then decide that you no longer want it you can delete it.

1 *Right-click on the theme.*
2 *Click* **Delete theme.**

Desktop Background
1 *Click* **Desktop Background.**
2 *Specify the* **Picture Location.**
3 *Select the picture required – click on it.*
Or

4 *Hold down* [Ctrl] *and click on each picture required to create a slide show.*

Or

5 *Click* **Select all**.
6 *Select the* **Picture position** *from the drop-down list.*
7 *If creating a slide show, set the time interval that you want to change the picture.*
8 *If you want your slide show pictures displayed at random rather than in sequence click the* **Shuffle** *checkbox.*
9 *Click* **Save changes.**

Window Color

1 *Click* **Window Color.**
2 *Select the colour required.*
3 *Select/deselect* **Enable transparency** *as required.*
4 *Set the* **Color intensity** *using the slide control – click and drag with the mouse.*
5 *Click* **Save changes.**

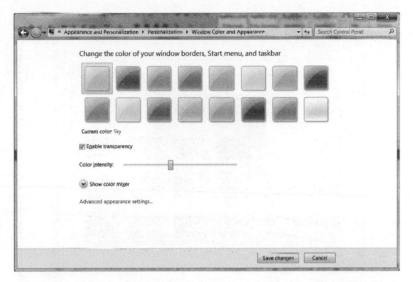

Advanced options for other window elements are available in the **Advanced appearance settings...**

Screen Saver

A screen saver is a moving image that displays on the screen if the computer is left inactive for a while. It is mainly used for effect these days as many new monitors have an energy-saving feature that turns them off if they have been inactive for a given period of time.

1 *Click* **Screen Saver** *in the Personalization window.*
2 *Click the drop-down arrow and select a saver from the list.*

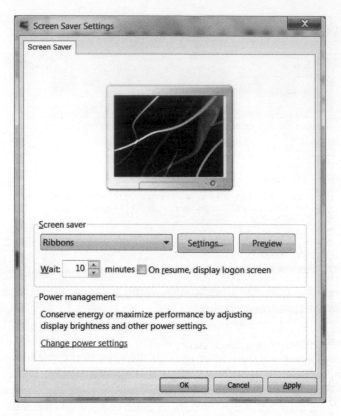

3 Click **Settings**, *adjust the options as required and click* **OK**.
4 *Increase or decrease the Wait time as required (somewhere between 2 and 10 minutes is fine).*
5 *To check your settings, click* **Preview**.
6 *Click* **Apply** *(if you want to keep the dialog box open) or* **OK**.

Sounds

Sounds are those noises that you hear when Windows wants to warn you about something – perhaps something is unavailable, or your have forgotten to save a file, or a new e-mail has arrived. The sounds options in Personalize are used to change or customize Sound Schemes. You can switch the individual sounds on or off, and choose which sound to use in what situation, in the Sound dialog box.

1 *Click* **Sounds** *in the Personalization window.*

2 *Select the Sound Scheme you wish to use.*
3 *Click* **OK.**

To customize a scheme:
  1 *Choose a Sound Scheme from the list.*
  2 *Select the event that you want to change the setting for.*
  3 *Choose a sound from the Sounds – use* **None** *to switch it off.*
  4 *Click* **Test** *to check out the sound effect.*
  5 *To save your new scheme, click* **Save As...** *and give it a name.*
  6 *Click* **OK** *to close the* **Sound** *dialog box.*

DISPLAY SETTINGS

Text size

The options in this area allow you to change the size of text on the Taskbar, Start menu, Dialog boxes, etc. to make it easier to read what is on the screen.

To change text size:
1 *Click* **Display** *in the Personalization window.*
2 *Choose* **Smaller**, **Medium** *or* **Larger**.
3 *Click* **Apply**.

You will be prompted to log off as the settings will be applied the next time you log on.

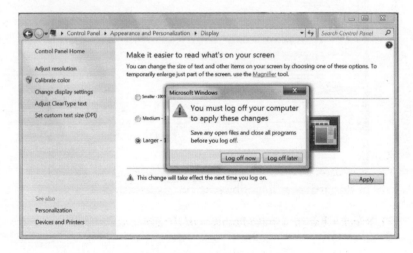

Resolution

You can also change the screen resolution. The higher the resolution the greater the number of pixels (dots of light) used to create the images on your screen. The higher the resolution the more you can see on screen at the one time.

1 *Click* **Display** *in the personalization window.*
2 *Select* **Adjust resolution**.

3 *Select the Display, Resolution and Orientation options required.*
4 *Click* **OK.**

Mouse

You can also customize the mouse settings. There are a couple of tabs in this area that might be particularly useful.

1 *Click* **Change Mouse Pointers** *in the Personalization window.*
2 *On the* **Buttons** *tab in the* **Mouse Properties** *dialog box:*
   ▷ *Button configuration – makes the right button the main one (intended for left-handed users, although most left-handed people I know leave the left button set as the primary one).*
   ▷ *Double-click speed – set it to suit your click speed.*
   ▷ *ClickLock – useful if you have difficulty in holding down* **[Ctrl]** *when you drag.*

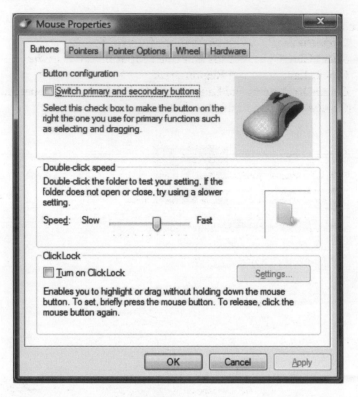

3 *On the Pointer Options tab:*

▷ *Motion – lets you specify how quickly the pointer moves in relation to mouse movement – slower is easier to control.*

▷ *Visibility – trails make the pointer easier to see, and if you have problems seeing where it is on screen,* **Show Location of pointer when I press the Ctrl key** *may be useful (although moving the mouse usually draws your attention to it).*

Keyboard

By default your keyboard language is most likely to be English. If others use the keyboard and their primary language is not English you can adjust the keyboard settings according to the language required.

To add a language:

1 *Click the* **Start** *button and choose* **Control Panel.**
2 *Select* **Change keyboards and other input methods** *in the* **Clock, Language and Region** *area.*
3 *On the* **Keyboards and Languages** *tab click* **Change Keyboards...**
4 *On the* **General** *tab, click* **Add...**

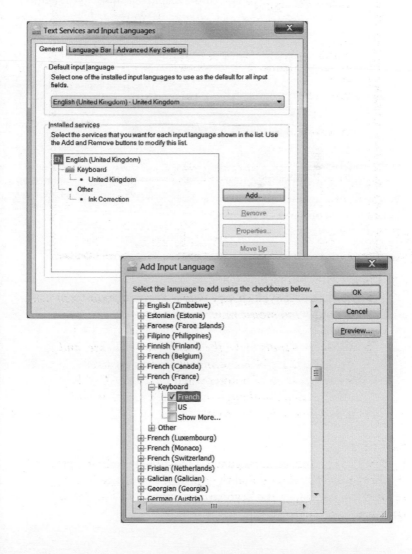

5 *Scroll through and select the language and options.*

6 *Click* **OK** *to add the language.*

7 *Click* **OK** *at the* **Text Services and Input Languages** *dialog box to confirm your selection.*

8 *Click* **OK** *again at the* **Regional and Language Options** *dialog box.*

> *The Language bar should be displayed in the Notification area of the Taskbar. To change the keyboard layout click the bar and select the language from the list.*

Date and Time

At the far right of the Taskbar you will see the clock. If you move your mouse pointer over the clock, the current date will appear.

You can easily switch the clock display on or off.

1 *Right-click on the clock and choose* **Properties**.

2 *Set the clock behaviour to on or off*

3 *Click* **OK**.

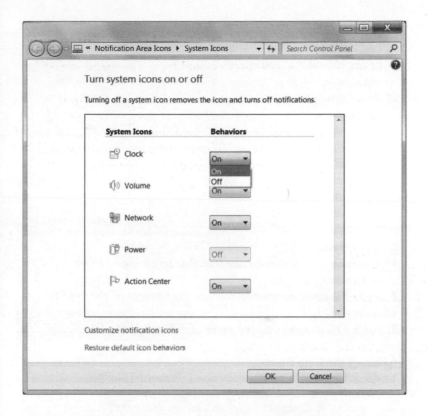

The date and time displayed on your clock should be accurate. If not, you can easily correct it (or change the time zone if needed).

1 *Click the Clock icon in the Notification Area.*
2 *Select* **Change Date and Time Settings...**
3 *At the Date and Time dialog box, select the* **Date and Time** *tab, and click* **Change Date and Time...**
4 *At the Date and Time Settings dialog box... (read on)*

To set the date:
1. *Click the arrows at the top of the calendar to change months.*
2. *Select the date.*

To set the time:
1. *Double-click on the part of the time to change – hours, minutes or seconds.*
2. *Type the value or use the arrows to the right of the field to change it.*
3. *Click* **OK** *to return to the* **Date and Time** *dialog box.*

To change the time zone:
1. *Click* **Change Time Zone** *on the Date and Time tab.*

2. *Choose the time zone from the drop-down list.*
3. *Select the checkbox to have your clock changed automatically when the clocks change each spring/autumn.*
4. *Click* **OK**.

You can also access the Date and Time dialog box from the Control Panel, using the menu sequence **Start > Control Panel > Clock, Language and Region > Date and Time.**

Volume

The volume settings of your audio equipment may be controlled by adjusting the volume on your hardware, or through software.

If the volume icon is present in the Notification Area:

1 *Click the* **Volume Control** *button on the Taskbar.*
2 *Drag the slider up or down to set the volume.*
Or
▶ *Click the* **Mute** *icon to silence the speakers.*
3 *Click anywhere on screen to close the control.*

The volume of System Sounds – those Windows makes to warn you about something, e.g. closing an application without saving the file – can be adjusted independently of the music volume.

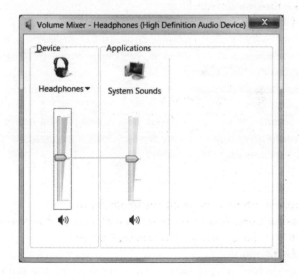

1 *Click the* **Volume Control** *button on the Taskbar.*
2 *Click* **Mixer** *below the slide control to open the* **Volume Mixer**.
3 *Set the volume for your* **Devices** *and* **Applications**.
4 *Close the Volume Mixer window.*

You can display the Volume Mixer dialog box from the Control Panel using the sequence: **Start > Control Panel > Hardware and Sound > Adjust System Volume** (under Sound).

GADGETS

Gadgets are mini applications that you can add to your Desktop. Some of the gadgets are really quite useful – I like the weather and newsfeed headlines – others are just for fun. Take a look and see what you think!

The gadgets are normally displayed on the right of the Desktop.

To add gadgets to the desktop:
1 *Right-click on the Desktop.*
2 *Click* **Gadgets...**
3 *At the Gadget gallery, double-click on the gadget you want to add (you can also get more gadgets online) – or drag the gadget onto the desktop*
4 *Close the Gadget gallery.*

▶ *If you move the mouse pointer over a gadget you will notice a mini toolbar that contains tools: Close, Larger size/smaller size, Options and Drag gadget.*

To remove a gadget:
1 *Move the mouse pointer over the gadget.*
2 *Click the* **Close** *tool.*

Customize a gadget
If the Options tool is there when you move your mouse pointer over a gadget, it can be customized. Not all can.

1   *Move the mouse pointer over the gadget.*
2   *Click the* **Options** *tool.*
3   *Customize the gadget as required – the options vary depending on the gadget.*
4   *Click* **OK** *to confirm your changes, or* **Cancel** *to close the dialog box without changing anything.*

To move a gadget:
1   *Move the mouse pointer over the* **Drag** *gadget tool.*
2   *Click and drag the handle to reposition the gadget.*

2.4 Install and uninstall programs

INSTALL

Software is normally very easy to install.

Your software will be supplied on a CD, and installing this software is a relatively easy procedure.

1   *Insert the CD into your CD drive.*
2   *Follow the instructions on the screen.*

If the CD does not start the setup process automatically, check the package for instructions.

Ensure that you purchase your software from a reputable supplier. Pirate software is illegal, and may be a source of computer viruses.

UNINSTALL

If you want to remove an application from your computer don't just find and delete its folder – this will not remove all traces of the application. If an application isn't removed properly it will still appear in the Start menu and it may conflict with other applications that are running on your computer and give you problems at a later date.

To uninstall an application:

1 *Go to the Control Panel.*
2 *Click* **Uninstall a program** *in the* **Programs** *area.*
3 *Select the program you wish to uninstall.*
4 *Click* **Uninstall** *on the toolbar (this button says* **Uninstall/change** *for some applications).*
5 *Follow the prompts.*

2.5 The Desktop

The Desktop is the name given to the background area of the screen. In concept, it is just like a physical desktop – it is where you keep the things you need to do your work, e.g. your clock and calculator, and where you create and edit your documents.

The Desktop consists of:

▶ *The* **background,** *which may be a flat colour, a picture, a web page or a pattern – you can customize it as you wish.*

- **Icons** – *the little graphics that usually do something when you click or double-click on them.*
- **Shortcuts** – *icons which give you quick access to your applications and other areas of your system.*
- **Taskbar** – *the bar along the bottom of the screen. It contains the Start button at the left. It also display the names of any applications that are open and probably a clock (at the far right in the Notification area). The Taskbar can be customized, so the one on your PC may be slightly different from the example shown.*
- **Notification area** – *at the right-hand side of the Taskbar. It may display System icons, e.g. the clock, volume and network and other icons like new e-mail notification.*
- **Clock** – *usually displayed in the notification area on the Taskbar.*
- **Start button** – *used to launch your applications, access the Help and Support Centre and locate recently-used files.*
- **Application windows** – *when you run an application, e.g. Word, it is displayed in a window. This may fill the screen, or it may be resized so that some of the Desktop can be seen behind it.*
- **Application buttons** – *displayed on the Taskbar when an application is running.*
- **Gadgets** – *displayed on your Desktop e.g. a clock, currency converter, weather reports.*

The Desktop can be customized to suit your preference.

DESKTOP ICONS

The desktop icons can be switched on and off, moved around the Desktop or sorted into your preferred order, or change their appearance. These options are all controlled from the shortcut menu that is displayed when you right-click on the Desktop.

To toggle the display of the Desktop icons:
1 *Right-click on your Desktop (or press the [**Application**] key on your keyboard – usually beside the right [**Ctrl**] key).*
2 *Point to **View** in the shortcut menu.*
3 *Click on **Show Desktop Icons**.*

With the Desktop Icons displayed, you can select from a range of view options (also listed in the Desktop shortcut menu, under View) – Large Icons, Medium Icons and Small Icons. Try them out to see which you prefer.

Arranging the icons on your Desktop

The icons on the Desktop can be placed where you want them – simply drag and drop them with the mouse. The position indicator (a big horizontal I-beam) shows where the icon will move to.

The icons are usually arranged at the left of your Desktop. This is what happens when the Auto Arrange option is on. If you wish to align them along the top, or around a picture, you can switch this off and drag the icons anywhere on the Desktop.

To toggle the Auto Arrange option:
1 *Right-click on your Desktop.*
2 *Point to* View *and click* Auto Arrange icons.

Align to Grid

The Desktop has an invisible grid that the icons align with. This helps keep them tidy by lining them up neatly on your Desktop.

To switch this option on and off:
1 *Right-click on your Desktop.*
2 *Point to* View *and click* Align icons to Grid.

Sort the icons
If you want Windows to arrange the icons on the Desktop and position them automatically you can sort them.

1 *Right-click anywhere on the Desktop.*
2 *Point to* Sort By.
3 *Click* Name, Size, Item type *or* Date modified.

You should pay attention to the icons on the Desktop and those in the dialog boxes, e.g. Computer, or on the Status bar so that you can recognize files, folders, shortcuts, etc. at a glance.

Desktop shortcuts
If you use an application, folder or file regularly, you could create a shortcut to it on your Desktop so that you can access it quickly.

To create a shortcut:
1 *Ensure that your Desktop is visible behind the Start menu or the Computer window.*
2 *Locate the application file, folder or file that you wish to create a shortcut to (either in the Start menu, or in the Computer window).*
3 *Right-click on the application, folder or file and drag it onto the Desktop.*

4 *Release the mouse button.*
5 *At the shortcut menu, click* **Create Shortcuts here.**

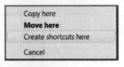

6 *The shortcut will appear on your Desktop.*

Any time that you want to access the application, folder or file, all you need to do is double-click the shortcut icon on the Desktop.

To remove a shortcut from your Desktop:
1 *Select it (click on it).*
2 *Press* [**Delete**].

The application, folder or file will not be deleted, but the shortcut to it is. Note that a Desktop shortcut always has a little arrow on it – this lets you know that it is a shortcut and not the application or folder itself.

2.6 Using windows

THE START MENU

The Start menu can be used to launch the applications on your computer, locate recently-used documents, and open the Help and Support Centre, etc.

To open the Start menu, click the Start button.

At the left of the Start menu, we have:

- ▶ *A list of frequently-used programs.*
- ▶ *The **All Programs** button (see below).*
- ▶ *Search programs and files field*

On the right of the Start menu, we have:

▶ *The name of the user who is logged on (at the very top).*
▶ *At the top, links to libraries in which files are stored.*
▶ *In the middle, links to Games and Computer.*
▶ *At the bottom, the Control panel, Devices and Printers,
   Default Programs and Help and Support Centre.*

Along the bottom of the Start menu are the shutdown options
discussed above.

All Programs
The All Programs option displays a list of all the applications
installed on your computer (not just the frequently-used ones).

1 *Click on* **All Programs** *(or point to it and wait). A list of
  programs and folders containing programs will be displayed
  (and the All Programs button changes to the Back button so
  you can return to the top level of the Start menu).*

2 *To open a folder containing programs, e.g.* **Accessories,** *click on the folder's name.*

3 *To start a program, e.g. WordPad, click on the program name.*

WORKING WITH WINDOWS

The applications that you work with will be displayed on your screen in a window. Each application will be in its own window – and the window can be manipulated independently to any other windows that are open.

It is important that you can recognize, name and know the purpose of the different parts of a window so that you can work effectively with your system.

▶ *You could open WordPad to have a look at the layout of a typical Window. Click* **Start** *select* **All Programs,** *then* **Accessories,** *then* **WordPad.**

The window below is fairly typical, and shows the main areas that you will find on most, if not all, windows.

The main areas in this window are labelled here:

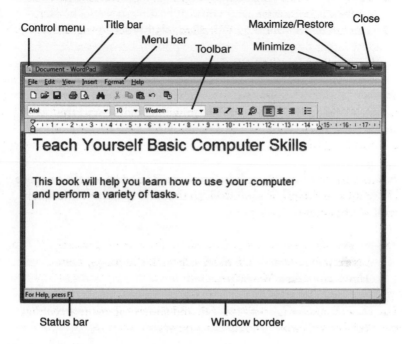

Control menu   Title bar   Maximize/Restore   Close
                Menu bar   Minimize
                            Toolbar

Maximize/restore down

If a window is maximized it fills the whole screen – you cannot see any Desktop area or other windows behind it. If a window is not maximized, you will see some Desktop area behind it.

▶ *You can toggle between windows being maximized or not by clicking the* **Maximize/Restore Down** *button (or by double-clicking the window Title bar).*

Minimize/restore

When you minimize a window, perhaps to see the Desktop or another application window, it is only visible as a Taskbar button.

▶ *Click the* **Minimize** *button to minimize a window.*
▶ *To restore a minimized window click on its name on the Taskbar.*

Resize

If a window is not maximized you will be able to see its border. You can resize the window by dragging its border to make the window larger or smaller. The mouse pointer becomes a double-headed arrow when it is over a window border.

Move

Windows that are not maximized can be moved around the desktop. Drag the Title bar of a window to move it.

Scroll bars

Some windows have scroll bars on them. You use the scroll bars to move up and down (or right and left) to display information that can't be fitted onto the screen.

Close

- ▶ *To close a window, click the* **Close** *button in the top right corner.*
- ▶ *Have a look at some other windows and see if you can identify the different areas.*
- ▶ *Try Computer (also referred to as Windows Explorer). This displays the drives and libraries on your system (see Section 2.9).*

1 *Click the* **Start** *button.*
2 *Select* **Computer.**

Have a look also at Paint (click the sequence, **Start > All Programs > Accessories > Paint**) or Solitaire (**Start > All Programs > Games > Solitaire**) and identify the areas in the window.

In Microsoft Office 2007, many of the applications, e.g. Word, Excel, PowerPoint and Access have a Ribbon, with groups and tabs on it – this area will be discussed in Section 2.7.

Moving between open windows

If you have several windows open you can easily move from one window to another.

- ▶ *Click on the title of the window you wish to move to on the Taskbar.*

Or

▶ *Hold down* [Alt] *and press* [Tab].

If you keep [Alt] down and press [Tab] repeatedly, a miniature of the open windows will be displayed and you will move from one to the other each time you press [Tab]. When the one you require is selected in the display of miniatures, release the keys. The selected window will be displayed.

2.7 Ribbon and menu bars

In most of the newer applications e.g. Microsoft Office 2007, the application window has the Ribbon along the top. This is used to choose options like formatting, page layout, table layout, etc. You can learn more about the Ribbon is Chapter 4.

In other applications a menu bar is used.

The menu bar is displayed at the top of many windows. You can use this to access every command in the program. You can open the menu and select options using the mouse or the keyboard.

1 *Click on the menu name to display the options in that menu.*
2 *Click on the menu item you wish to use.*
Or
3 *Once any menu is open, press the* [Left] *or* [Right] *arrow keys to move from one menu to another, then the* [Up] *or* [Down] *arrow keys to highlight an option, then press* [Enter].

To close a menu without selecting an item from the list:
▶ *Click the menu name again.*
Or
▶ *Click anywhere off the menu list.*
Or
▶ *Press* [Esc].

In addition to the menus, many of the features can be accessed using the toolbars or keyboard shortcuts.

2.8 Dialog boxes

Dialog boxes are where you interact with your software. You can define settings, select options and give instructions through them. The contents of dialog boxes vary – some contain lots of information, others are quite sparse, but the basic structure is pretty standard. The key elements are introduced here.

- ▶ **Tabs** – *if a dialog box contains a lot of information it may be arranged on several tabs. Simply click on each tab to display the information it holds.*
- ▶ **Text box** – *you can type information into a text field.*
- ▶ **Checkbox** – *allows you to select/deselect an option. A checked box is selected, a blank one is deselected.*
- ▶ **Radio button** – *these are usually in groups, and you can choose one option in the group.*
- ▶ **Drop-down list** – *click the down arrow then click the option you want. Used when there are a limited number of things to choose from, but more than would display well using radio buttons or checkboxes. You can sometimes choose more than one option if you hold down* [Ctrl] *as you select.*
- ▶ **OK** – *to confirm your selections and close the dialog box.*
- ▶ **Apply** – *to confirm your selections, but keep the box open.*
- ▶ **Cancel** – *to cancel your selections and close the dialog box.*

2.9 File management

Computer displays the *disk drives* and other *hardware* connected to your computer.

Your files – documents, pictures, music and videos – and the applications on your system – Word, Excel, Access, etc. are held on the disks on your computer.

You can display the different disk drives on your computer using the **Computer** window.

To open the Computer window:
1 *Click* Start.
2 *Select* Computer.

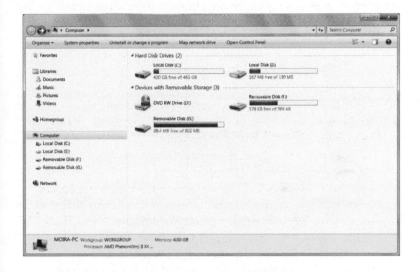

The drives are named using letters of the alphabet

▶ *Your local hard disk is C:*
▶ *Your DVD drive is probably D:*

You may have other disks e.g. additional hard disk drives, removable drives e.g. a USB Pen/Flash drive or network drives. On the computer illustrated here there are two hard drives, one DVD and two USB drives.

Your computer drives can be displayed in different ways depending on the *view* that is selected. You can change the view using the **Change your view** tool on the toolbar.

To select a view option for your Window

  1 *Click the drop-down arrow beside the* **Change** your view *tool.*
  2 *Select the view option required.*

The computer window has several panes on it – **Navigation,
Details** and **Preview** – and you can switch them on or off as
you wish.

  1 *Display the* **Organize** *list.*

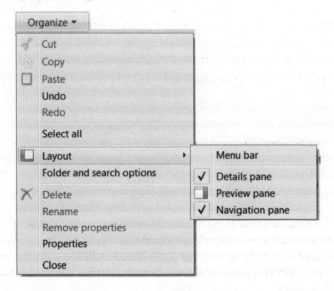

  2 *Choose* **Layout** *and then click the pane required to switch it
     on and off.*

STORAGE DEVICES

Hard disk drive: Most computers will usually be sold with a hard
disk drive (HDD) built into them. The hard disk will contain your
computer programs and your data.

You can buy additional HDDs to increase your storage space –
and you can get either drives that fit inside your PC or ones that

plug into your PC but sit outside the unit as a peripheral. External drives are usually more expensive than internal ones, and the cost of a drive increases with its capacity. Typically, HDDs store between 80 Gb and 320 Gb.

Network drive: A drive on a computer network. It may be an actual drive, or a logical drive – a section of a physical drive.

Compact disk (CD or CD-ROM): These have been used on PCs for several years. They are ideally suited for storing information that doesn't need updating often, e.g. application packages (you buy the next version if you want to change it), encyclopaedias, e.g. Encarta, clip art, etc. In addition to storage capacity, increased speed of access is another benefit of CDs.

You can also get CDs that you can write to, in the same way as to a HDD. There are two types of these: CD-R (Recordable) and CD-RW (ReWriteable). With a CD-R you can use the disk to record information once only – once you've recorded something on it you can't re-record. With a CD-RW you can record, and re-record, as often as you want – the disks are reusable. Both have a capacity of 650–750 Mb.

Digital Versatile Disks (DVDs): DVDs are also popular. You can store audio, video or computer program data on a DVD. CD-ROMs can be used in a DVD drive, but a DVD disk will not operate in a CD drive. DVD-R (recordable) is also available. They can hold 4–5 Gb of data.

USB flash drive: A small, lightweight, removable, rewriteable storage device integrated with a USB connector so you can plug it into your computer. They are about the size of a small highlighter pen. Their storage capacity varies considerably from 128 Mb up to several Gb.

Memory card: A memory or flash memory card is a storage device used with digital cameras, hand-held and mobile computers, telephones, music players, video game consoles, etc. They offer high re-recordability, power-free storage, small format and rugged specifications.

Online file storage: Sometimes referred to as a file hosting service or online media centre. The service is specifically designed to host static content, typically large files that are not web pages.

The storage devices discussed above are sometimes referred to as secondary storage.

Units of measurement

Bits, bytes, kilobytes, megabytes and gigabytes are the units used to describe the storage capacities on computers e.g. memory and disk size.

The measurements most often used are kilobytes (KB), megabytes (MB) and gigabytes (GB).

Unit of measurement	
1 bit	The amount of storage space needed to hold either a 1 or 0 in memory.
1 Byte	Is equal to 8 bits. Every letter or number, e.g. a, 2, z, ?, m, is made up of 8 bits (one byte), so each letter or number takes up one byte of storage space.
1 Kilobyte (KB) – 1024 bytes	You'll often see file sizes quoted in KB. Display your library in Details view, or look at the Details pane when you have a file selected.
1 Megabyte (MB) – about 1 million bytes – 1024 kilobytes.	Memory size is usually quoted in MB – a PC will typically have between 256 and 750 Mb of memory (although more can be added if required). CDs usually hold 650 or 750 MB. USB pens often have their storage capacity quoted in MB – although some will hold several GB.
1 Gigabyte (GB) – about 1 billion bytes – 1024 Megabytes.	DVDs and hard disk sizes are usually quoted in GB – on new PCs the hard disk could have several hundred GB of storage available. A DVD will hold 4–5 GB of data.

2.10 Libraries, folders and files

You may be able to save your files on several different drives – local, removable, networked, etc.

If you are sharing documents with others that use your computer system, using the *Public* folder or a shared network drive will mean that they can access the files easily when they are logged on. The advantage of online storage in Public folders and shared drives is that you can share access to files with other users.

It is important that you can manage your files efficiently within the storage areas that you use. This means that you should be able to set up folders to organize your documents so that you can find them again. Depending on circumstances, you might want a folder for your school, college or university work. Or you might want a folder for all files related to your hobby, travel arrangements, home accounts – it is really up to you to decide how best to organize things for yourself.

It is important that you give sensible names to your folders and files. The names should describe the contents of the folder, e.g. your college work folder could be called *College Work*. Inside this you could have a separate folder for each subject you are studying, e.g. *Computing*, *Maths*, and *Marketing*. If you give your files sensible names (and don't leave them called things like *Doc1*, *Doc2*, *Doc3*, etc.) – you should be able to find your work again quite easily.

NAVIGATION AND DETAILS

Libraries
Your files – documents, music, pictures and videos – are stored in **Libraries** on the disk drives.

You can access the Libraries from the **Navigation pane** in the Computer window – simply click the library required near the top of the Navigation pane.

You can also display your libraries from the Start menu.

The files in your Libraries can be organized into Folders,
e.g. documents could be organized into *Work* and *Personal*. Your
Personal folder may contain other folders so you can organize your
documents further, e.g. *Golf Club*, *Finances*, *PTA files*, etc.

Your *Pictures* library could have folders for different holidays or
occasions, e.g. *Japan 2009*, *Clare's Graduation*, etc.

To display the contents of a folder:
> ▶ *Select it in the* **Navigation pane** *– the contents will be
>   displayed in the* **File list pane.**

To expand/collapse the folders/subfolders in the *Navigation pane*:
> ▶ *Click the arrow to the left of the folder name.*

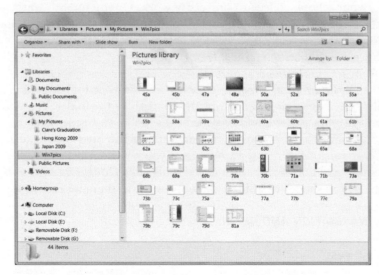

The *path* to the folder whose contents you are looking at is
displayed in the **Address bar** at the top of the Computer window.

You can backtrack quickly to any folder in the path by clicking on its name.

Details Pane

At the bottom of the window you will see information on the folder or file you have selected in the **Details Pane**.

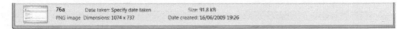

- ▶ *If you select a folder, it will tell you how many files are in it.*
- ▶ *If you select a file in the Details pane, it will display details about the file, e.g. name, dimensions, size and date created.*

Previewing a file

Previewing a file lets you take a look at what is in it without actually opening it. You can preview a file using the **Preview pane**.

1 *Display the* **Organize** *options.*
2 *Choose* **Layout** *and then click* **Preview pane** *to display the pane (it is on the right side of the window).*
3 *Click on the file you wish to preview. The contents will be displayed in the Preview pane.*

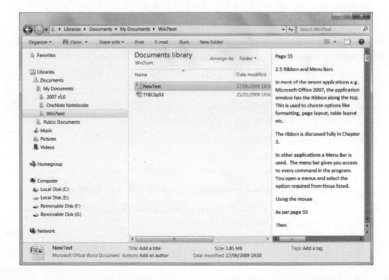

SELECTING FILES/FOLDERS

To select an individual file or folder:
▶ *Click on it.*

To select several files or folders that are next to each other:
1 *Click on the first one.*
2 *Hold down* [Shift].
3 *Click on the last one you want to select.*

To select several non-adjacent files or folders:
1 *Click on the first one.*
2 *Hold down* [Ctrl].
3 *Click on each of the other files/folders required.*

To create a new folder:
1 *Select your* **Documents Library** *(or the folder that you wish to make a folder within).*
2 *Click* **New Folder** *on the toolbar.*
3 *Type in the folder name.*
4 *Press* [Enter].

WORKING WITH FOLDERS AND FILES

You can copy, move, rename and delete folders and files to tidy up your files system if necessary.

You can easily rename any folder or file if you consider the current name unsuitable.

To rename a folder or file:
1 *Select the folder or file.*

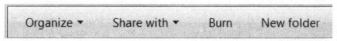

2 *Click* **Organize** *and then* **Rename**.
3 *Type in the new name for the folder or file.*
4 *Press* [Enter].

To move a folder or file:
1 *Select the folder or file.*
2 *Click* **Organize** *and then* **Cut.**
3 *Open the folder that you want to move it to.*
4 *Click* **Organize** *and then* **Paste.**

To copy a folder or file:
1 *Select the folder or file.*
2 *Click* **Organize** *and then* **Copy.**
3 *Open the folder that you want to move it to.*
4 *Click* **Organize** *and then* **Paste.**

DELETING FILES AND FOLDERS

This is a two-step process. When you delete a folder or file it is placed in the Recycle Bin. You can empty the Recycle Bin at any time, or, if you have deleted something and then realize that you should not have, you can restore it from the Recycle Bin.

To delete a folder or file:
1 *Select the folder or file.*
2 *Click* **Organize** *and then* **Delete.**
Or
3 *Press* [Delete].
4 *Click* **Yes** *to confirm the deletion at the prompt.*

Recycle Bin
The Recycle Bin is displayed on your Desktop.

To open the Recycle Bin:
▶ *Double-click the Recycle Bin on the Desktop.*

To restore a folder or file from the Recycle Bin:
1 *Select the folder or file(s).*
2 *Click* **Restore this item** *(if no item is selected, this option is* **Restore all items***). The item will be removed from the Recycle Bin and returned to the folder it was deleted from.*

To restore all items that are in the Recycle Bin:
1 *Click* Restore all items.

To empty the Recycle Bin:
1 *Click* Empty the Recycle Bin.

Backups

A very important way of trying to ensure the security of your data is to back it up. This means that you take a copy of any important data – anything that you can't afford to lose.

Companies usually have automated backup procedures where the data is backed up every few hours, or overnight. If you are working at home, or in a small business, it will probably be up to you to remember to back up your data.

You should regularly copy any data files that are important to a removable storage device, e.g. USB pen, external hard drive, or CD. On a home computer, the usual backup device is now a CD-RW. It is cheap, and stores 650–700 Mb of data. If you have quite a few files to back up, you can set up a Backup routine – see *Backup* in the Help system.

2.11 Searching and sorting

If you are well organized, and put all your files in the right folders, you should never need to search them out! However, if you do have difficulty remembering where you saved a file, you can use the Search feature to help you find it.

1 *Select the drive, library or folder to search in the Navigation pane (the search feature will search all subfolders within it).*
2 *Click in the Search field and start typing a keyword that you know is in the file – try to pick something significant.*

3 *Windows will start filtering your list of files almost immediately, and will keep filtering it down as you type. A list of the files that match your criteria will be displayed.*

4 *Once you've found the file that you're looking for, double-click on it to open it, or take a note of its location.*

If your search does not return the folder or file required you can try again by entering something else in the Search field.

Searching the results

At the end of the search results list are several options that you can explore to help you find the file required.

▶ *Click* **Libraries, Homegroup, Internet, Computer** *or* **File Contents** *to search those locations using the current search criteria.*

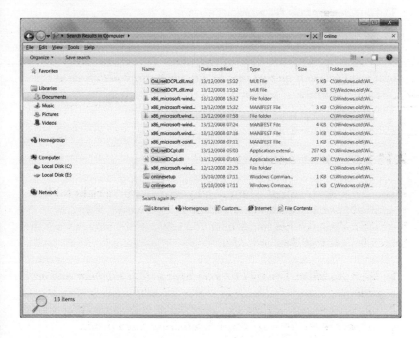

Other search options
When you click in the Search field, a list of the most recent searches will be displayed.

▶ *Click on one to re-use it.*

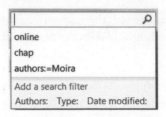

You can also add a search filter – Authors:, Type: or Date modified:

1 *Click the option required.*
2 *Select or specify your preferences.*
3 *Authors: You will be presented with a list of the file authors to choose from.*
4 *Type: You will be presented with a list of the file types in the current library or folder.*

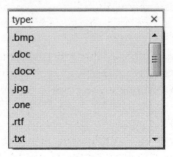

5 *Date modified: You will be presented with a calendar and date options.*

Wildcards

When searching for files and folders, you can use wildcards to represent individual characters or strings of characters that may be variable from file to file.

?   is used to represent an individual character.
*   is used to represent a string of characters.

For example, to search for all the files on a drive or in a folder that had 'report' in the filename – but you could not be sure where the word might come in the filename:

In the filename field, enter *report*. This would return all files that had 'report' somewhere in the name, e.g. End of term report, Report on marketing trends, Monthly report from Joe.

A search for 'Chapter ?' would return Chapter 1, Chapter 2, Chapter 3, etc.

SORTING

You can quickly sort the list of files in a folder in a variety of ways – ascending or descending order, or sorted by name, size, type or date modified.

To sort your file list:
1 *Display the list using the Details option.*
2 *Click the heading at the top of the column that you want to sort on – the list will be sorted into ascending order on that column.*
3 *Click the column heading again – the list will be sorted into descending order on that column.*

You can also arrange the contents of your libraries in a variety of ways – try the **Arrange by:** options in the Library pane.

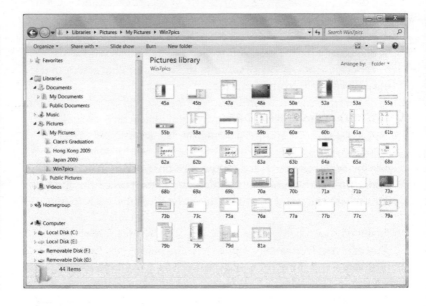

FILE TYPES

Different file types are created by different applications. You can identify the different files types from the icons beside the filenames, e.g.

PowerPoint

 Word

 Excel

 Access

 Bitmap

or by the extension at the end of the filename (if it is displayed).

To toggle the display of the file extension from Computer:
1 *Open the* **Tools** *menu and choose* **Folder Options...**
2 *Select the* **View** *tab.*
3 *Scroll through the options until you find the* **Hide extensions for known file types** *checkbox.*
4 *Select or deselect the checkbox as required.*
5 *Click* **OK**.

Common file extensions:

Application	Extension	File type
Access 2007	accdb	Database
Excel 2007	xlsx	Spreadsheet
PowerPoint 2007	pptx	Presentation graphics
Word 2007	docx	Word processing
Access 97–2003	mdb	Database
Excel 97–2003	xls	Spreadsheet
PowerPoint 97–2003	ppt	Presentation graphics
Word 97–2003	doc	Word processing
Paint	bmp	Image file
Publisher	pub	Desktop publishing
WordPad*	rtf	Text

*and other text/basic word processing applications

(Contd)

Other file types that you are bound to meet include:

Audio (e.g. mp3, wma)
Video (e.g. avi, wmv)
Web pages (htm, html)
Images (e.g. gif, jpg, png)
Portable document format (pdf)
Compressed files (e.g. zip)
Temporary files (tmp)
Executable files – ones which start programs (e.g. excel.exe).

2.12 Other useful options

READ-ONLY FILES

The files that you create are initially read–write, which means that you can open them and read the contents, and also edit them by adding or deleting data. If you are sharing files online you might want to change the status from read–write to read-only so people can see the contents but not change anything.

To make a file read-only:
1 *Display the Computer window.*
2 *Right-click on the file you want to make read only.*
3 *Choose* **Properties.**
4 *On the* **General** *tab select the* **Read-only** *checkbox.*

To make a file read-write again, simply deselect the **Read only** checkbox on the **General** tab.

Recently-used files

If you are looking for a file that you have used recently, you may be able to find it from the Start menu.

1 *Click the* **Start** *button to open the Start menu.*
2 *Point to the application you want to open – a list of recently used files with be displayed.*
3 *Click on a filename to open the application and the file.*

COMPRESSION

Some files, particularly those that contain graphics and lots of formatting, can become quite large. If you have plenty of room on your disk this poses no problem, but if you are short of disk space you could compress the file to make it smaller.

If you want to send a large file to someone – either by e-mail or by copying it onto a floppy disk, you might need to compress it to make it smaller.

You can compress a file from the File Properties dialog box.

1 *Open your Documents library (or the folder that contains the file you want to compress).*
2 *Right-click on the file and choose* **Properties**.
3 *Note the* **Size** *and* **Size on disk** *fields – they will be similar.*
4 *Click* **Advanced** *in the* **Attributes** *options.*
5 *Select the* **Compress contents to save disk space** *checkbox.*
6 *Click* **OK** *to return to the* **Properties** *dialog box.*
7 *Click* **Apply** *to compress the file.*
8 *Note the difference between the* **Size** *and* **Size on disk** *fields. The* **Size on disk** *field will be smaller than the* **Size** *field.*
9 *Click* **OK** *to close the dialog box.*
10 *Repeat steps 1–7, deselecting the checkbox at step 4, to uncompress a file.*

Winzip

This is a popular compression software package from WinZip Computing. The package is probably the most widely used compression software on Windows PCs. WinZip files have a zip file extension.

2.13 Using WordPad

The most commonly used application is word processing, using Word or WordPad, or some other text editing application.

In this section we will take a very brief look at WordPad. This is part of Windows and can be found in Accessories. (Microsoft Word is discussed in Chapter 5, and many of the formatting options discussed there are very similar in WordPad.) WordPad may be a pretty basic word processing package by today's standards, but it has all the features that you need to create, edit and print letters, reports and essays – and it is free!

To open WordPad:
1 *Click the* **Start** *button and then* **All Programs**.
2 *Select* **Accessories**.
3 *Click* **WordPad**.

A new file is created automatically, and all you need to do to produce your letter or report is start typing.

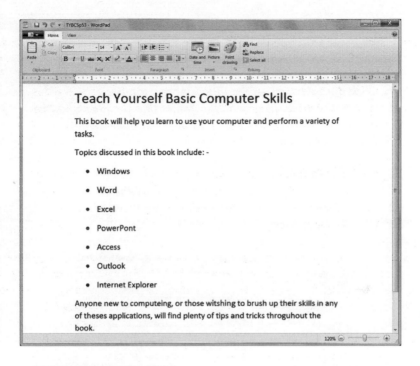

TEXT ENTRY AND EDIT

Your text will appear at the insertion point – the flashing black vertical bar in the document area.

▶ *When entering your text, keep typing when you reach the end of the line on the screen – the text will wrap onto the next line automatically.*

▶ *Press* **[Enter]** *between paragraphs (press it twice to leave a blank line between the paragraphs).*

▶ *To delete a mistake, move the insertion point until it is next to the error (use the arrow keys on the keyboard or the mouse). If the insertion point is to the left of the error, press* **[Delete]** *to remove it. If the insertion point is to the right of the error, press* **[Backspace]** *to remove it.*

▶ *To insert something that you have missed out, move the insertion point until it is where the text is missing – and just type – existing text will be pushed along to make room for whatever you type in.*

To save your file:
1 *Click the* **Save** *tool on the Quick Access toolbar.*
2 *Specify the drive, library and/or folder that the file should be stored in – your Documents Library will be the default.*
3 *Give the file a name and click* **Save***.*

To preview your document
1 *Open the* **WordPad** *menu – click the* **WordPad** *button.*
2 *Move the mouse pointer over* **Print** *in the menu.*
3 *Click* **Print Preview** *in the submenu.*

To print your document
1 *Open the* **WordPad** *menu.*
2 *Move the mouse over* **Print***.*
3 *Click* **Print***.*

4 *Complete the dialog box as required.*

5 *Click* **Print**.

Or

6 *Choose* **Quick print** *at step 3 to send the document straight to the printer.*

To create a new document

1 *Open the* WordPad *menu.*

2 *Click* **New**.

To open an existing document

1 *Open the* WordPad *menu.*

2 *Click* **Open**.

3 *Locate and select the file required.*

4 *Click* **Open**.

Or

5 *Open the* WordPad *menu.*

6 *Select the file required in the Recent Documents list.*

To close WordPad:

1 *Click the* **Close** *button at the right of the Title bar.*

Print Screen

If you want to print exactly what is displayed on the screen, press [Print Screen]. This takes a snapshot of what is on the screen. You can then paste the snapshot into a document, e.g. in WordPad, and print it out.

[Alt]-[Print Screen] will take a snapshot of the active window.

1 *Press* **[Print Screen]** *(usually to the right of the Function keys on your keyboard).*

2 *Go to a document (in* WordPad *or* Word*).*

3 *Open the* **Edit** *menu and click* **Paste**.

4 *Print the document in the normal way.*

TEST

1 *Why would you lock your computer? How do you lock the computer?*

2 *What operating system does your computer use – and what version is it? How much RAM does it have?*

3 *Explain how you would print what is on the screen.*

4 *What do the following icons represent:*

Win7text

Contents

5 *Give two examples of removable storage devices.*

6 *Suggest two potential benefits of using on-line storage devices.*

7 *Identify the file types from their extension.*
.png .docx .pdf .accdb .htm

8 *What is file compression?*

9 *Identify the following areas – A, B and C.*

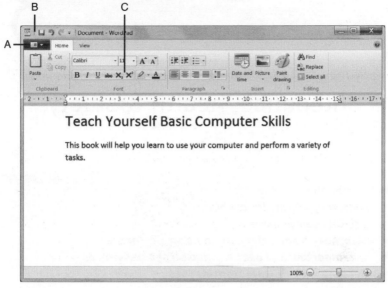

10 *Suggest two ways of deleting characters in your document.*

Maintenance, health & safety, and legal issues

In this chapter you will learn about
- *resolving routine PC problems*
- *printer maintenance*
- *your health and safety when using a computer*
- *the importance of user IDs and strong passwords*
- *keeping your PC safe from viruses*

3.1 Maintaining systems

MAINTENANCE

We will now take a quick tour of some of the routine maintenance that you should be doing to help make sure that your computer is kept in good order – and suggest how you can deal with some of the problems that will inevitably arise.

You don't need to be a techie to perform a lot of the regular maintenance. And just as making sure that your car has water, oil, petrol and the tyres are at the right pressure, helps it to function properly – you should make sure that certain things are routinely checked and maintained when using your computer. Then, just like your car, you can take it to a professional to get it serviced once in a while or when something a bit more serious goes wrong, but day to day you can pretty much cope on your own.

Maintenance schedules

Many of the routine system maintenance tasks can be set up to run automatically at a scheduled time. It is worth scheduling these tasks so that you don't forget to do them.

Things that can be set to run automatically:

- ▶ *Check for Windows updates*
- ▶ *Update Anti-virus software*
- ▶ *Update the computer date when the clocks change.*

Things to do yourself:

- ▶ *Back up files that you have been working on*
- ▶ *Organize your files/pictures/videos into folders*
- ▶ *Delete files/shortcuts that you don't need*
- ▶ *Empty the Recycle Bin*
- ▶ *Clean your screen with wipes and dust your keyboard and mouse.*

Things that you might need to do occasionally:

- ▶ *Defrag your disk – if your computer seems to be running slower than when you first bought it*
- ▶ *Take your computer to good local computer shop for a dust and clean – annual check up!*

PROBLEMS

As computers are such an integral part of our lives, you should be able to do at least a *little* basic system maintenance. Even if you are not confident trying to fix things for yourself, knowing what to check and what to look for can be useful when discussing any problems you encounter.

Components not working

If your computer doesn't seem to be working, the first things to check are:

- ▶ **Power** – *make sure that the plugs are in the sockets and that they are switched on. If that looks OK, check that the sockets are working properly – test something else in them, e.g. plug in your hairdryer or a lamp to check that it works. If the sockets are working, it might be that the plug has fused.*
- ▶ **Connections** – *make sure that all the cables are connected properly. The mouse, keyboard, screen and printer should be attached to the computer (the box containing the electronics and the disk drives).*
- ▶ **Hardware switched on** – *many computers have switches on the actual monitor and printer – so if they don't seem to be working, check that they are actually switched on.*

Error indicators

Your computer will give you clues when something is wrong. These include:

- ▶ *Flashing lights – perhaps on your printer to indicate that there is a paper jam.*
- ▶ *Nothing appearing on the monitor – indicating that it is switched off, or the screen saver has kicked in, or there is some other problem.*
- ▶ *Bleeps – when you ask your PC to perform some task that it can't do.*
- ▶ *No printer output – if there is no paper in the printer, or the printer is switched off.*
- ▶ *No mouse pointer – if the mouse is disconnected or missing, or faulty.*
- ▶ *A message on the screen – giving you a clue as to what the problem is.*

Resolving problems

Sometimes when things go wrong, you will be able to sort it out yourself. You can check your system and connect and cables that are disconnected, change the fuse in a plug, switch the computer on if necessary or put paper in the printer tray.

Other times you may need help.

If you are at work you need to know who to contact when you have a problem. It may be someone in your office, or you may have an IT Helpdesk that you can phone or e-mail. You might need to fill in a form, or give specific details about your computer – e.g. the type of computer or its serial number. Before reporting a problem, try to make sure that you have the information required so you can give as much information as necessary. Make a note of the problem, including any messages or error indicators that the system is giving, and be able to explain what you were doing when the problem occurred. All these things will help in diagnosing the problem.

If you are at home, you might need to contact your supplier or your local computer shop for help. Again, you will need to be able to explain the problem to them as fully as possible.

It is worth making a note of the type of computer you have, the operating system you are using, the applications that you are running, and the type of printer that you have, etc. so that you have this information to hand should you need to call someone. This information will be on the invoices that you have for your computer, or it can be found in the Properties for My Computer.

Printer maintenance

All printers are different – but whatever printer you have it will require routine maintenance. So find the printer instructions or manual and make sure you know how to:

- ▶ *Replace the paper*
- ▶ *Change the toner cartridge*
- ▶ *Print a test page and align the cartridges*
- ▶ *Clear a paper jam*
- ▶ *Install and update printer driver files.*

3.2 Print management

Default printer

Your computer system may be set up so that you can print your files to one of several different printers – a laser, an inkjet, etc. When you print a file from an application it uses the *default* printer – the printer that's been set up as the one that you normally print to. You can change the default printer if you wish.

The printer that you want to become the default must be installed before you do this procedure.

1 *Open the* **Control Panel.**
2 *Choose* **View Devices and Printers** *in the* **Hardware and Sound** *category.*
3 *Right-click on the printer that you want to be the default one.*
4 *Left-click on* **Set as default printer.**

Installing a printer

1 *Connect the printer to your PC following the manufacturer's instructions.*
2 *Open the* **Control Panel.**
3 *Click* **View Devices and Printers** *in the* **Hardware and Sound** *category.*
4 *Click* **Add a Printer.**
5 *Follow the instructions on the screen.*

The default printer will have a tick beside it.

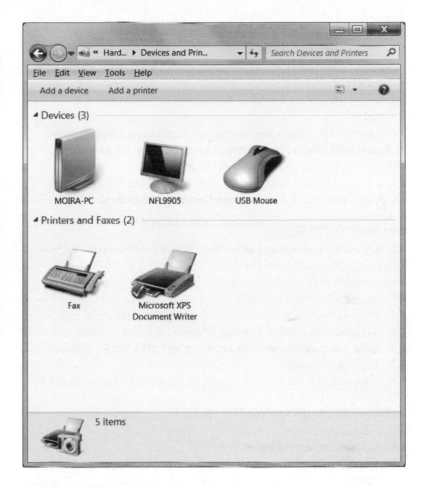

PRINT QUEUE

Printing a document was discussed in 2.13 *Using WordPad*.
Files that you send to print are sent to the print queue – and from
there they will print when they get to the top of the queue.

If you have sent several files to print, you may want to check on
their progress.

To display a list of files that are in the print queue:
1 *Open the* **Control Panel.**
2 *Click* **View Devices and Printers** *in the* **Hardware and Sound** *category.*
3 *Double click on a printer to display its print queue.*

You can use the menus in the printer window to **Pause Printing** or **Cancel All Documents** (empty the queue) for all documents. Choose the option required from the **File** menu.

To pause, resume, restart or cancel printing an individual document:
1 *Select the document.*
2 *Open the* **Document** *menu and click the option required.*

You can also manage the files in the queue by right-clicking on them.

▶ *To pause or resume printing of an individual document,* **right-click** *on the document and select the option required from the menu.*
▶ *To remove a file from the queue, select it and press* [**Delete**].

PRINTER MAINTENANCE

Get to know your printer!

Printer consumables – like paper and toner cartridges – will need replaced from time to time.

If you normally print out on standard A4 paper, but sometimes onto labels or photographic paper, you will need to know how to load the paper you require. All printers are different – but refilling the paper will involve finding the paper tray, probably removing it (or at least gaining easy access to it) and then placing the paper on the tray. Make sure that the paper is straight – there may be a guide to align it with. And the right way up – not always as easy as it sounds! You may need to refer to the user instructions.

Before loading paper into your printer tray 'fan' it to ensure that the pages are not sticking together. If you don't fan the paper it could result in several sheets being fed through at a time – increasing the risk of a paper jam.

You will often get a warning on your computer to let you know that your toner or ink is getting low – but you will be able to tell when it needs replaced when the print quality deteriorates. Again, you may need to refer to the printer manual to find out how to get to the cartridge, remove it and replace it. When buying a replacement cartridge, make sure that you buy the correct one. Check the printer documentation, or check what is already in the printer to find out what you need.

Once you have replaced the cartridge, you may need to print a test page to make sure that everything is aligned properly. Refer to the user manual/online Help and carry out this procedure each time you replace your cartridges. If the alignment is out the characters will appear blurred or out of alignment on the page.

If you do get a paper jam, locate the problem area and remove the paper carefully. Refer to the manufacturer's instructions – if you just try to pull the paper out you could end up tearing the paper (making it more difficult to remove it) or damage the paper feeders.

3.3 Health and safety

HEALTH

It is important that the area you work in is comfortable and suitable for the type of work you are doing. Your working environment must conform to the relevant Health and Safety at Work (HASAW) legislation.

Ergonomics is all about ensuring that your work area is safe and comfortable for you to work in. It is about making sure that the layout of your work area does not adversely affect your well being. An ergonomically well-designed workspace will ensure that the computer operator is comfortable when working.

Light is one area that must be considered when assessing whether or not the working environment is suitable for computer use.

Important areas to consider are:

▶ *The brightness of the area behind the screen*
▶ *The brightness of the screen*
▶ *The amount of light falling on the screen – from the window or artificial lights*
▶ *Reflection on the screen – from windows, overhead lights or bright objects.*

Things that can help:

1 *The positioning of the screen in relation to the light source.*
2 *Adjusting the brightness of the screen.*
3 *Using uplighters rather than overhead lights.*
4 *Blinds for the windows.*
5 *Anti-glare filters for the screen.*

Being able to adjust the brightness of the VDU is a legal requirement.

Useful online resources include:
http://www.hse.gov.uk/pubns/indg36.pdf
Working Safely with a VDU – a short online course:

http://www.rossiterandco.com/VDU-Health-and-Safety/
VDU01_03.htm for a useful on-line course.

OPERATOR COMFORT

Good posture plays an important role in operator comfort – especially if you are working at a computer for long periods.

Good posture means:

- *Sit up straight – your arms and thighs should both be at a 90° angle to your spine*
- *Keep your wrists straight when keying in*
- *Your screen should be square with your line of vision*
- *The screen should be about an arm's length away from you*
- *The screen should be about 15° – 30° below your line of sight*
- *Your feet should be on the floor – or on a footrest – rather than swinging under your seat*
- *Use a well-padded, adjustable chair that supports your back and arms.*

To help ensure operator comfort:

1 *There should be sufficient desk room and leg room to allow for posture changes.*
2 *The chair should be adjustable – it's worth spending some time getting it at the right height/position.*
3 *Movable keyboards should be provided – position and tilt the keyboard to ensure that you are comfortable with it.*
4 *There should be enough desktop space for all of your documents as well as your computer.*
5 *You can use a document holder at a suitable height if it makes reading a document that you are working from easier.*
6 *There should be space in front of your keyboard to rest your wrists when you aren't typing.*
7 *Wrist rests should be used if it makes things more comfortable but be very careful of your wrist position and don't rest on them when typing for extended periods.*
8 *Minimized printer noise (noise used to be a particular problem with dot-matrix printers).*

Wrist rests should be used with caution

Improper use of wrist rests may cause more RSI damage than not using one. The important thing to remember is that your wrists should not be lower than the keyboard, while you are typing. The traditional cupped hand, with the finger tips dropping down to the keys, is the correct position.

Resting your wrists on a wrist rest, often resulting in your wrists being lower than the keyboard will increase the pressure on the carpal tunnel and cause damage to your wrists.

The same applies to mouse rests.

There is no one solution that is suitable for all users – it is a case of finding what works well for you.

To help relax your muscles during work the operator should also take regular stretches and have breaks from their computer.

EYE RELAXATION TECHNIQUES

Some operators may also find that eye relaxation techniques help. There are several easy ones you could try, e.g.

▶ *Palming – place the palms of your hands over the area surrounding your eye sockets with your fingers lightly crossing on the center of your forehead. Keep your eyes closed, and gently and lightly rotate your palms over the area – changing direction from time to time. Do this for two or three minutes. This exercise increases the blood flow to the eye muscles and that will help relax your eyes.*

▶ *Sit or stand with your back and neck straight and body relaxed. Let your eyes roam and then focus on different objects at varying distances in your field of vision. Continue for two to three minutes. This scanning lets the focus of your eyes regain flexibility after the close work on the computer screen.*

▶ *Hold a pencil, finger or thumb in front of your nose and within comfortable near focus range, then find an object ten to fifteen feet away and focus on that. With each deep breath alternate your focus between your pencil/finger and the distant object repeating 15 times.*

Free eye tests

You have the right to a free eyesight test if you use, or are about to use, a VDU a lot during work hours. You can also get more free tests if recommended by your optician.

If you are prescribed glasses to help you work with a VDU, your employer must pay for a basic pair of glasses, provided they are needed especially for your work.

The types of discomfort that computer operators may suffer from include:

- *Backache and pains in general associated with bad posture and sitting in the same position for too long.*
- *Repetitive Strain Injury (RSI) – the result of poor ergonomics combined with repeat movements of the same joints over a long period of time.*
- *Eye strain – caused by flickering VDUs and not taking regular breaks from the PC screen (10 minutes every hour is recommended).*

Maximum operator comfort it is usually achieved through a combination of:

- *An ergonomically designed workspace*
- *Suitable lighting*
- *Good posture*
- *Regular breaks*
- *Eye relaxation techniques.*

SAFETY

You should also be aware of *safety risks* when working in an environment where a lot of technology is used. Safety risks could include:

- *Trailing cables or power leads*
- *Worn out or frayed power leads*
- *Overloaded power points*
- *Liquid near electrical components*
- *Moving heavy boxes of paper and/or computers.*

Cables should be carefully routed along walls, or through cable channels build into desks, so that they are not trailing between computers and across corridors and walk ways. Trailing cables are just waiting for someone to trip over them!

- *Worn out or frayed power leads should be replaced to reduce the risk of fire and electric shocks.*
- *Overloaded power points are also a fire risk – and all the cables running into them are often a trip hazard.*
- *Liquid near electrical components could easily be spilt resulting in electric shocks.*

Heavy objects should only be moved by staff trained to do so, and they should use trolleys whenever possible.

Problems that may be experienced by IT workers include:

- *Injuries resulting from tripping over trailing cables or other obstructions*
- *Electric shocks due to dangerous wiring or incorrect working practice*
- *Back injuries due to lifting heavy objects e.g. boxes of printer paper.*

It is the **employer's** responsibility to ensure that appropriate provision is made available to provide a safe and comfortable working environment. It is the **employee's** responsibility to make sure that he or she follows procedures and guidelines for keeping safe and goes about their job in a responsible manner.

Health and safety resources

The Internet is a useful resource when it comes to keeping up to date with health and safety laws and guidelines that affect the use of IT.

You will find lots of information at http://www.hse.gov.uk. The main pieces of legislation affecting the use of IT in the workplace are the:

- *Health and Safety at Work Act (1974)*
- *Health and Safety (Display Screen Equipment) Regulations 1992*
- *Workplace (Health, Safety and Welfare) Regulations 1992*
- *Control of Substances Hazardous to Health (COSHH).*

DISPOSAL OF EQUIPMENT

You should also be aware of issues affecting the safe disposal of IT equipment.

In most business PCs and ICT equipment will be replaced every three years or so. Many organizations have a rolling programme to help ensure that their hardware is kept up to date. This helps reduce maintenance, ensures the hardware specification can benefit from new computer programs and controls the expense of replacing equipment. It also means that there is a lot of old (sometimes not very old) equipment to get rid of.

When disposing of ICT equipment there are a number of options available – re-sale; employee purchase programmes; charitable donations; refurbishment; recycling; and landfill. The disposal method selected will depend on the age and condition of the equipment. Landfill would usually only be considered as a last result.

The WEEE directive

The UK Waste Electrical and Electronic Equipment Directive came into force on 2 January 2007. It aims to minimize the impact of getting rid of electrical and electronic goods on the environment.

The directive aims to increase the re-use and recycling of old equipment and reduce the amount of WEEE going to landfill. Any business or organization that uses or produces electrical and electronic equipment (EEE) is required by law to take responsibility of the recycling and disposal of their equipment.

As well as disposing of the hardware, there is often a requirement for the hard disks to be cleaned, in line with the requirements of the Data Protection Act.

It may also be necessary to remove software from PCs to ensure that licensing agreements are not breached.

Equipment that is going to be reused – perhaps donated to a local school or sold on to employees – should be safe and fit for purpose. It may be necessary to get an ICT technician to check that the equipment meets safety standards.

Useful internet link http://www.bbc.co.uk/schools/gcsebitesize/ict/implications/3healthandsafetyrev1.shtml

GUIDELINES AND POLICY

Most organisations will issue guidelines, policies and procedures for the safe and secure use of IT.

The guidelines will give details of what is *acceptable* use of ICT equipment at work, e.g. it may be used to help you do your job (not to chat with friends, or play your favourite online game). The guidelines will list many of the topics discussed above and they may also give a health and safety representative contact details, ICT service desk contact details, etc. so that you know who to contact to discuss any concerns that you have.

This information is often handed out at induction sessions, and then made available on the staff intranet, notice boards or at reception.

KEEP IT CLEAN!

Computer users should clean their computer equipment regularly to ensure that it maintains its functionality and looks good. There are various wipes, sprays, brushes and other supplies for this purpose. You should always follow the manufacturer's instructions when using, storing and disposing of the cleaning materials.

Smudges on the screen, dust on the keyboard, printer and monitor, and sticky mice are all the result of poor housekeeping.

3.4 Security

IDENTITY/AUTHENTICATION

This topic was also discussed briefly in Chapter 1 – see 1.2 for additional information.

Logins
Computer logins identify a user to the system.

If you have several people using one PC at home each could have a separate user account set up. The system administrator would do this (that could be you). Each user will have their own storage area and they will be able to customize their workspace to their own preferences. The users can set a password to restrict access to their area.

When working in a networked environment you will use a UserID and a password to access the system. These identify you so that appropriate rights are made available to you while you work and give you access to the drives that you need to use.

There are various levels of password protection available to help ensure that only authorized users can access the system and open and edit the files held on it.

Passwords
You should not share your password or PIN (Personal Identification Number) with anyone. If you do they may use it to access your data. Some organizations will take disciplinary action if they discover employees are not keeping their passwords secure.

Passwords can either be generated randomly, by computer, or they can be made up by users. Randomly generated passwords are more secure because of the very fact that they are random and cannot be easily associated with a user. They are usually very difficult to guess – but they can also be very difficult to remember!

Alternatively, people can be asked to make up the password. This is sometimes done by asking a series of questions when you set up an account. These are often easier for the user to remember, but they could be easily guessed by someone who knows you.

Or you might just be asked to choose a password – which is often where the weakest ones come in. It is worth thinking about your password carefully in this situation so that you can choose something that you will be able to remember but it will be tricky for someone to guess.

As a general rule you should follow these guidelines when choosing a password:

▶ *Include numbers, symbols, and both upper and lower case letters*
▶ *Make it at least 8 characters long – better still 12–14 characters*
▶ *Avoid dictionary words, letter or number sequences, usernames, pet names, dates of birth, etc.*

Try to avoid the obvious weak passwords e.g.

▶ *Default passwords – password, admin, default, guest, etc.*
▶ *Dictionary words*
▶ *Words with number substitutions, e.g. 1nd3x, blowf1sh, 3d1nburgh*
▶ *Common sequences – 12345678, qwerty, abcdefgh.*

Mnemonics

Some users use mnemonics to help them come up with a strong password that they can remember but others will not be able to guess easily. This means that they use a phrase that they can remember to help remind them what their password is.

At primary school you might have used one to help you remember the names of the planets – Mother very easily makes jam she uses no preserve – Mercury, Venus, Earth, Mars, Jupiter, Saturn, Uranus, Neptune, Pluto.

You could try things like:

- *Slash plays guitar well and so do I – Spgw&sd1*
- *Are you ready to work out a strong one? – Ru%r2%wo%as1?*
- *Some silly person used a weak password – SsP@51wP*

But make up your own – don't use these ones!

And remember to change your password regularly – just in case someone has picked it up somehow.

STAY SAFE

When using your IT-based communication be mindful of your personal data and protect it. More of us are putting information onto the web – in social networking sites like Facebook and Bebo or in Blogs or on our own websites.

Things to bear in mind:

- *If your information is available on line, anyone with the know-how can access it – so don't be fooled into thinking that your data is only available to those that you choose to share it with.*
- *Don't post personal information about yourself – your address, phone number, e-mail, etc.*

- *Don't arrange to meet people that you meet online because they seem really friendly – anyone can claim to be anybody that they want to be when online – you have no way of checking who they really are. It just isn't worth the risk.*
- *Watch what you say – mind your language – don't be rude, abusive, or say things that could get you into trouble.*
- *Images on web pages aren't just there for the taking – if you find an image on a website that you would like to use – ask – it may be protected by copyright. If you can't get hold of whoever owns it, identify your source if you use it (say where it comes from).*
- *Respect confidentiality – don't post information on others without their permission.*
- *If you are e-mailing several people, consider their privacy and whether or not it is appropriate to circulate their e-mail addresses publicly in your copy list. Use the Bcc field in e-mails if in doubt – this way you can send a message to several people at once, without letting everyone on the list know everyone else's e-mail address.*

DATA SECURITY

Data security was discussed in some detail in Chapter 1. You should revisit that chapter and remind yourself of some other important aspects of data security, in particular, Off-site backups, firewalls and data theft. Remember that viruses and spam are also security risks – see 1.1.

3.5 Law

COPYRIGHT

When someone has copyright of something they own it. Copyright is used to establish the owner of published works, e.g. written work, pictures, graphics, music, videos and software.

Software copyright legislation is in place to give the authors and developers of software the same rights as authors of published written or musical works.

When you buy software, you don't actually purchase the package, but you purchase a licence that allows you to **use** the software.

End User Licence Agreement
The terms of the licence are known as the **End User Licence Agreement**.

Each licence that you purchase has an identification code – you can usually check the product ID in the product information screen.

With some licences you are permitted to install a copy of the software on one computer, and take a backup copy of the software for security purposes. With other licences you may be able to install two copies of the software, e.g. one on your office machine and one on your laptop or home PC. This option recognizes the fact that people often use the software in two locations. Instead of having to buy two copies of the software you can install it on two computers – but you should only be using one copy at a time (you can't be in two places at once). You will need to check the software licence agreement to check what is and isn't allowed.

In a business situation, where you perhaps have 50 users on a network, you can buy a software licence that allows you to run the number of copies you require at any one time. This usually works out much cheaper than buying the same number of individual licences. The licence should cover the maximum number of users you expect to be using the software at any one time.

You can recognize licensed software by:

- ▶ *Checking the Product ID*
- ▶ *Check the product registration*
- ▶ *View the software licence.*

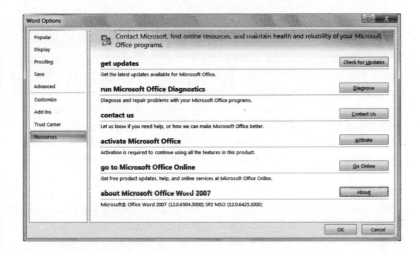

> In Office 2007 *this information is found in the* Options *dialog box, under* Resources – *click* about Microsoft Office Word 2007, *etc.*

Copyright

Items that are copyright should not be copied, used or distributed without the express consent of the copyright holder. The copyright holder might not give permission for their work to be used – or they might want to charge you for using it. Printed text, music and videos/DVDs are usually copyrighted.

Copyright also applies to text, pictures, videos and music that you find on the Internet. If you download any of these items from the Internet with the intention of using them in your own work you should get permission from the copyright holder if at all possible. At the very least you should acknowledge your source.

OTHER AGREEMENTS

Shareware

Shareware software is obtained on a kind of sale-or-return basis. You can obtain the software free, use it for a limited period, e.g. 30 days, then, if you decide that you want to continue to use the software you should forward that appropriate fee (typically £10–30) and become a registered user. At the end of the evaluation period the software may have been programmed to stop working or it may flash up messages telling you to pay up!

Sometimes the evaluation copy of a shareware package will be a scaled down version of the whole package. If you decide to pay up and register then the full package will be sent to you.

Freeware

Freeware is similar to shareware, but it doesn't cost anything. Freeware authors and developers often produce the software to solve a particular problem they have had, or just as a personal project/challenge. Once the software is written, they make it freely available to anyone else who thinks that they'll find it useful.

If you use shareware or freeware software, try to ensure that it comes from a reputable source or is recommended in PC magazines, etc. The software may not have been tested as thoroughly as commercial software and it may contain bugs or viruses. There is however some very good, useful and safe shareware and freeware software available – just be careful!

Open source

Open-source software is computer software for which the human-readable source code is made available under a copyright licence. Users are permitted to use, change, and improve the software, and to redistribute it in modified or unmodified form. It is often developed in a public, collaborative manner. OpenOffice.org from Sun MicroSystems is an example of a suite of office software (very similar to Microsoft Office – but much cheaper) based on open-source software.

DATA PROTECTION

The Data Protection Act appeared in 1984 in the UK, and it was updated in 1998.

The Act covers data that is collected and stored on paper or electronically.

It states that users of personal data relating to living, identifiable individuals should be registered with the **Data Protection Registrar** (the person responsible for overseeing the implementation of the Act in the UK).

The purpose of the Act is to:

▶ *Protect the rights of the* **data subject** *(the person that the information is about). The data subject has a right to know what data is being held about them and why. They can ask to see the information (there is often an administration fee charged for this) – and ask for it to be updated, amended or deleted if it is not accurate.*
▶ *Set out the responsibilities of the* **data controller** *(the person or persons who decide why the data is required and how it will be processed). The data controller is responsible for justifying why the information is being held, ensuring that it is held securely and kept confidential, is accurate and is used only for that purposes stated to the data subject.*

See 1.5 for a summary of the Data Protection Principles.

TEST

1   Give three examples of routine maintenance that you might carry out on your PC.

2   What is meant by the default printer.

3   Suggest three things that you can do to help prevent glare on your computer screen.

4   Give three examples of other things that contribute to operator comfort when working at a computer.

5   Identify ways in which you can help ensure the safe disposal of old ICT equipment.

6   What is the purpose of UserIDs and passwords.

7   Which of the following are examples of weak passwords
    ▷ Admin, password, courageous
    ▷ Qwerty, tuvwxyz, 13243546
    ▷ 1wCu@4@tCs, tbP12d4m2r!, £awaz3noy$

8   When sending e-mails to a distribution list, how can you protect the privacy of the individuals that you are sending to?

9   Give two examples of how you can help protect your PC from a virus.

10 Give three examples of types of software that you can use to help protect your PC from harm.

11 What is meant by the term copyright? Give three examples of things that could be protected by copyright.

12 Explain how shareware and freeware are different.

4

Common skills

In this chapter you will learn:
- *how to open and close applications*
- *how to use the online Help*
- *about file handling*
- *how to cut, copy and paste*
- *about font and paragraph formatting*
- *how to add shapes and graphics*
- *some time-saving keyboard shortcuts*

Word, Excel, PowerPoint and Access are all part of the Microsoft Office suite, and many commands and routines, e.g. save, copy and spell check, are the same (or very similar) in each. Your browser and e-mail applications will probably also be Microsoft products, and will have many similarities. This chapter covers the features that are standard, or nearly standard, across the applications. If you are familiar with these, you will have a head start on the applications. Read this before going onto the chapters discussing the individual applications, and refer back to it as necessary.

4.1 Opening and closing applications

To open an application:
1 *Click the* **Start** *button on the Taskbar.*
2 *Point to* **All Programs.**

3 *Select* **Microsoft Office.**
4 *Click the application name, e.g.* **Microsoft Office Word** 2007
   or **Microsoft Office Excel** 2007.

If the application is one that has been used recently, it may be on the
first level of the Start menu – so you just need to click on its name!

The Microsoft Office button

This is located at the top left of the screen. When clicked, it
displays a menu that gives you access to all the things you
can do with your file, e.g. print, save, open, send.

To close an application

When you have finished working in an application you must close it down – don't just switch off your computer.

▶ *Click the* **Microsoft Office** *button then* **Exit...** *at the bottom right of the menu.*

Microsoft Office button

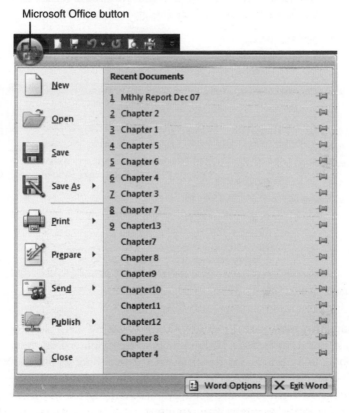

Or

▶ *Click the* **Close** *button in the top right-hand of the application title bar.*

4.2 Application window

Word, Excel and PowerPoint all display a new blank file, ready for you to start work. (Though Access is a bit different – see Chapter 6.) Once you are into an application, the window has a standard format, and you should be able to see these areas:

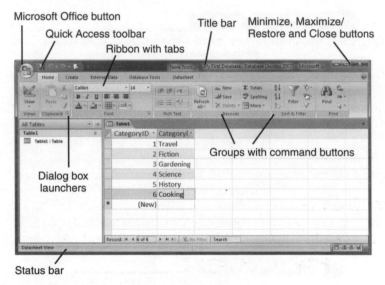

Ribbon and tabs
The application features and commands are displayed on the Ribbon along the top of the work area. The Ribbon is divided into task-orientated tabs, where the commands and features required to perform different tasks are grouped together, e.g. the Insert tab has all the objects you might want to insert.

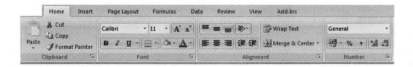

Show/hide the Ribbon

▶ *To toggle the display of the Ribbon, press* [Ctrl]-[F1].
▶ *If the Ribbon is hidden, to display it again temporarily, just click on any tab.*

Program tabs replace the standard tabs when you perform certain tasks, e.g. Print Preview.

The command buttons on each tab are arranged in groups, e.g. the Alignment group has all the buttons for aligning text.

Quick Access Toolbar
The Quick Access Toolbar has commands that are regularly used, and are independent from the tab being displayed. The toolbar can be displayed:

▶ *Above the Ribbon, (the default position).*
▶ *Below the Ribbon.*

To move it from one position to the other:
1 *Click the arrow at the right of the Quick Access Toolbar.*
2 *Click* **Show Below the Ribbon** *or* **Show Above the Ribbon.**

To customize the Quick Access Toolbar:

1 *Display the application* **Options** *dialog box.*

Either

　2 *Click the arrow at the end of the toolbar to display the* *Customize Quick Access Toolbar menu.*

　3 *Select one of the options to toggle its display on the toolbar.*

Or

　2 *Click the* **Microsoft Office** *button, and* *then the application* **Options** *button.*

　3 *Select the* **Customize** *category.*

　4 *Add or remove tools as required.*

　5 *Click* **OK**.

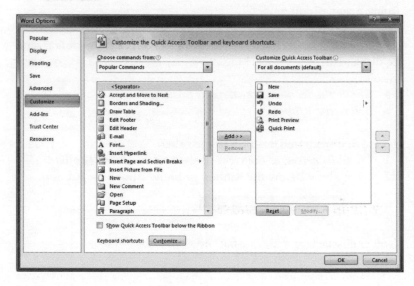

You can add a command to the Quick Access toolbar directly from the Ribbon. You might add your favourite tools, e.g. Quick Print, Open, Print, etc.

1 *Right-click on the command you wish to add.*
2 *Click on* **Add to Quick Access Toolbar.**

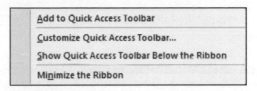

Dialog box launcher
Dialog box launchers are small buttons that appear at the bottom right of some groups. Clicking the launcher opens a dialog box that displays more options.

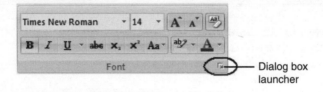
Dialog box launcher

RIBBON KEYBOARD SHORTCUTS

You can issue commands using the keyboard.

1 *Hold* **[Alt]** *down, and keep it down throughout the procedure. A ghost letter appears next to each tab on the Ribbon – these are called Key Tips.*
2 *Press the letter on your keyboard to activate the tab you want to use e.g.* **[H]** *for Home. Ghost letters/numbers will appear next to each command on the Tab.*
3 *Press the letter/number to select the command.*
4 *Release* **[Alt].**

Key tip

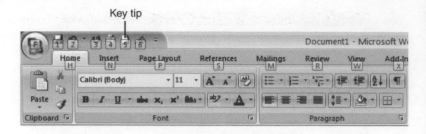

STATUS BAR

The Status bar displays indicators to show whether options like word count, track changes and macros are turned on or off.

It also displays information about the position of the insertion point within your file and the language setting used in spell and grammar checking.

To customize the Status bar:
1 *Right-click on it.*
2 *Select or deselect the options as required.*

4.3 MS Office Help

As you work with your applications you will most probably find that you come a bit unstuck from time to time and need help. To access the Help system:

▶ *Click the* **Help** *button to the right of the Ribbon tabs.*
▶ *Or press* **[F1]**.

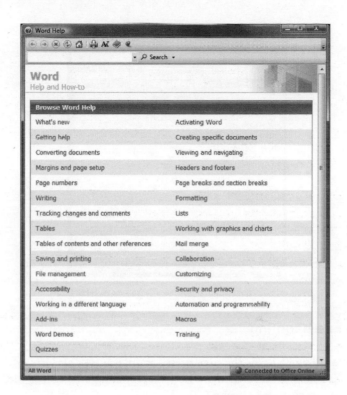

Use the Help toolbar as you work in the Help pages.

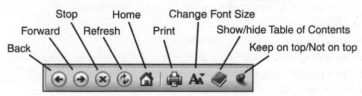

Back
Forward
Stop
Refresh
Home
Print
Change Font Size
Show/hide Table of Contents
Keep on top/Not on top

To search for Help on a topic:
  1 *Enter details of what you are looking for in the* **Search** *field.*
  2 *Click* **Search.**
Or
  3 *Click the* **Search** *drop-down arrow and select a search area.*

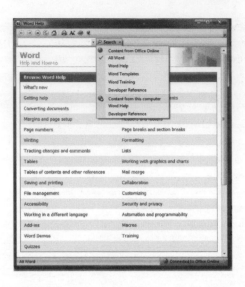

4.4 File handling

File handling routines that are pretty similar across all Office
applications include creating a new file, opening an existing file,
printing, saving and closing files.

Files are called different things in different applications.

- ▶ *In Word, a file is a document;*
- ▶ *In Excel, it is called a workbook;*
- ▶ *In PowerPoint, the file is called a presentation;*
- ▶ *In Access, it is a database.*

Each new file is automatically given a temporary filename,
e.g. Document1, Document 2 in Word; Book1 in Excel;
Presentation1 in PowerPoint. The name appears on the Title bar.

To create a new file:
1 *Click the* **Microsoft Office** *button, and then click* **New...** *At the* **New** *dialog box the* **Templates** *categories are listed down the left.*
2 *Select the category from the* **Templates,** *e.g.* **Blank and recent,** *and then the file type from the options displayed on the right – usually* **Blank Document** *or* **Blank Workbook.**
3 *Click* **Create.**

To open an existing file:
1 *Click the* **Microsoft Office** *button, then click* **Open...**
2 *Locate and select the file.*
3 *Click* **Open.**

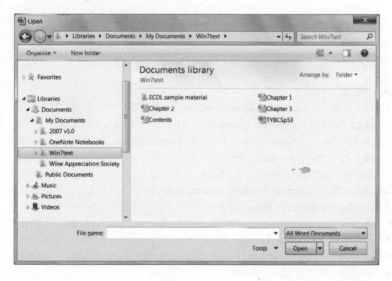

Recently-used files are listed to the right of the Microsoft Office button menu – to open one simply click on its filename.

Recently-used files list

This is displayed to the right of the Microsoft Office menu.

The default number of files to display is 17. This can be adjusted in the **Options** dialog box. Select the **Advanced** category, and scroll down to the **Display options**.

You may have files that you don't want to disappear off the recent file list. You can pin them into place – just click the pin icon beside the filename. It's a toggle – just click it again to unpin it!

SAVE A FILE

You must save your file (if you don't you may lose it when you exit the application). When you save it, you should give it a filename that reflects its contents rather than use the temporary name.

Save As...
1 *Click the* **Microsoft Office** *button, and then click* **Save As...** *in the menu.*
2 *At the* **Save As** *dialog box, locate the folder in which to save your file (usually your Documents or a subfolder).*
3 *Enter the name in the* **File name:** *field.*
4 *Leave the* **Save as type:** *at the default, e.g. Word Document or Excel Workbook.*
5 *Click* **Save.**

You are returned to your file. The name of the file appears on the Title bar.

You can save your file at any time – you don't need to wait until you've entered all your text and data. I suggest you save your file regularly – and remember to resave it when you make changes to it. If you haven't saved your file, and your computer crashes or you have a power failure, you may lose any unsaved data.

Save
Once the file has been saved you can save your changes to it whenever you wish.

▶ *Click* **Save** *on the Quick Access toolbar.*

Save

Or
▶ *Click the* **Microsoft Office** *button, then click* **Save**.

The Save As dialog box does not reappear, but the up-to-date version of your file replaces the old one saved to disk.

Save vs Save As
The first time you save a file, it doesn't matter if you choose Save or Save As... – both take you to the Save As dialog box. Once a file has been saved, use Save As... if you need to access the Save As dialog box again. There may be times that you save a file, edit it, then decide that you want to save the edited version of the file and keep the original version too. If you don't want to overwrite the original with the updated version, click the Microsoft Office button and choose Save As... so you can select a different folder and/or filename for the new version of the file. Otherwise, just use Save to save your changes.

SAVE IN A DIFFERENT FILE FORMAT

If the file is going to be opened in a different version of your
software or in a different application, it may be necessary to save
it in a different format. For example, if you have created a file in
Word 2007 and you are going to send it to someone who uses
Word 2000, you should save the file as a Word 97–2003 file, or a
Text file, so that they can open it successfully. In some file formats,
some (or all) of the text formatting may be lost.

To save in a different file format:
1 *Display the* **Save As** *dialog box.*
2 *Select the drive and/or folder and name the file as usual.*
3 *Select the appropriate format from the* **Save as type** *options.*
4 *Click* **Save.**

PASSWORD PROTECTION

If you wish to password-protect your file (so that no one can open
or edit it unless they know the password) you can do so from the
Save As dialog box.

1 *Click* **Tools** *at the bottom right of the* **Save As** *dialog box.*
2 *Choose* **General Options...**

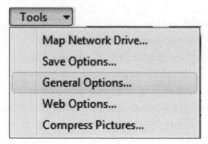

3 *Enter the password.*
4 *Click* **OK.**
5 *Re-enter the password at the prompt.*
6 *Click* **OK.**

CLOSE FILE

▶ *Click the* **Microsoft Office** *button, and then click* **Close.**
Or
▶ *Click the* **Close** *button on the file Title bar.*

If you try to close a file that has been edited since it was last saved, you will be prompted to save the file before you close it.

PRINT PREVIEW

It is a good idea to preview any file before you print it. You can decide whether or not the text and pictures are positioned correctly on the page before you waste paper and ink printing out something that isn't really what you intended.

To preview a file:

▶ *Click the* **Office** *button then click the arrow next to* **Print,** *then* **Print Preview.**

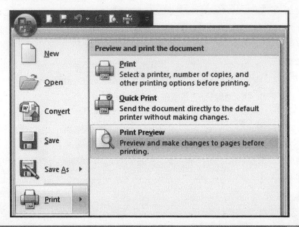

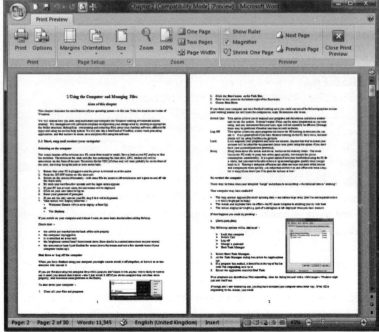

The previews vary between applications, but you can usually:

- *Move between the pages* – **Next Page/Previous Page.**
- *Zoom in and out* – *set a percentage using* **Zoom,** *or choose* 100%, **One Page, Two Page, Page Width,** *etc.*
- *Change the* **Page Setup** – *margins, orientation and paper size.*
- **Print.**

Print Preview is an option that you will use a lot – so if it isn't on your Quick Launch toolbar, I suggest you add it to it.

Moving through your document in Print Preview

If you have more than one page in your document, you can move through your document in several ways in Print Preview.

- *Use the* **Next Page/Previous Page** *buttons on the Print Preview Ribbon or those at the bottom of the vertical scroll bar.*

Or

- *Drag the elevator or click the arrows at the top or bottom of the vertical scroll bar.*

To close the preview window:

- *Click* **Close Print Preview** *on the Ribbon.*

Or

- *Press [Esc].*

PRINT

To print one copy of a file using the default setting:

- *Click the* **Microsoft Office** *button, then the arrow next to* **Print,** *then* **Quick Print.**

Or

- *Click the* **Quick Print** *command button on the Quick Access toolbar if it is displayed there.*

Quick print

To select print options:

You can specify how many copies you want printed, or select the range of pages to print from the Print dialog box.

1 *Click the* **Microsoft Office** *button and then* **Print.**
2 *Specify the options required in the* **Print** *dialog box.*
3 *Click* **OK.**

Which printer

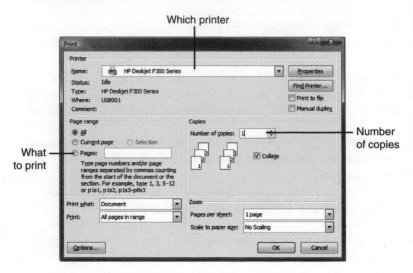

What to print

Number of copies

To print part of your file

If you want to print out part of your file, but not full pages, you should select the area you want to print first. This feature is often particularly useful in Word or Excel files.

1 *Select the text/data that you want to print.*
2 *Display the* **Print** *dialog box.*
3 *Select* **Selection** *in the* **Print What** *options.*
4 *Click* **OK.**

To print to another installed printer
When you print a file as above, it will print out to the default printer – the one specified to be used most of the time. In some situations, particularly in an office, there may be several printers on the network that you can print to. Only one can be your default, but you can easily print to any other installed printer.

1 *Display the* **Print** *dialog box.*
2 *Select the printer required in the* **Name** *field.*
3 *Set other options as required.*
4 *Click* **OK.**

To print to file
If you don't have a printer attached to your computer, or if you want to print your file out on a printer that doesn't have the application that you are using on it, you can print to a file. The file can then be printed out on any PC.

1 *Display the* **Print** *dialog box.*
2 *In the* **Name** *field select the printer that will be used to print the file out.*
3 *Select the* **Print to file** *checkbox.*
4 *Click* **OK.**
5 *In the Print to file dialog box, select the drive and or folder if necessary and give your file a name.*
6 *Click* **OK.**

Keyboard shortcuts

Many file handling commands can be activated using keyboard shortcuts. These ones are particularly useful:

[Ctrl]-[N]	New File	[Ctrl]-[F2]	Print Preview
[Ctrl]-[S]	Save File	[Ctrl]-[O]	Open File
[Esc]	Close Print Preview	[F12]	Save As...
[Ctrl]-[W]	Close File	[Ctrl]-[P]	Print File

4.5 Delete, Cut, Copy and Paste

DELETE

If you have a large piece of text or data to delete, it will usually be quicker to select it and then press [**Delete**], rather than press [**Backspace**] or [**Delete**] repetitively.

To delete a chunk of text or data:
1 *Select it.*
2 *Press* [**Delete**].

CUT, COPY AND PASTE

There will be times when you enter the correct information into a file but it is in the wrong place. When this happens you can move or copy the object, e.g. text in Word, data in cells in Excel, a picture or graph in any application, to the correct location.

▶ *Cut removes the object, but keeps a copy.*
▶ *Copy takes a copy of an object, but leaves the original in place.*
▶ *Paste places a copy of the object into a new position.*

You can move or copy an object within or between files.

Cut (move) and copy text:
1 *Select the object that you want to move.*
2 *Click* **Cut** *(to move) or* **Copy** *in the Clipboard group on the Home tab.*
3 *Position the insertion point where you want the object to reappear.*
4 *Click* **Paste** *in the Clipboard group. The object will appear at the insertion point.*

▶ *To specify the format of the pasted item, click the Paste*
Options smart tag (it appears below the pasted item) and
pick an option (see next page).

◉	**Keep Source Formatting**
○	**Match Destination Formatting**
○	**Keep Text Only**
•	**Set Default Paste...**

Keyboard shortcuts

Cut, copy, paste
[Ctrl]-[X] – Cut
[Ctrl]-[C] – Copy
[Ctrl]-[V] – Paste

OFFICE CLIPBOARD

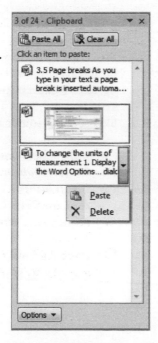

If you cut or copy an object in an Office
application it is stored in the Office Clipboard.
You can store up to 24 items in the Office
Clipboard.

To display the Office Clipboard task pane, click
the dialog box launcher in the Clipboard group.

▶ *To paste an individual item from the*
clipboard, click on it in the task pane.
▶ *To paste all items, click* **Paste All** *at the*
top of the pane.
▶ *To remove an individual item, click the*
drop-down arrow to the right of the item
and then click **Delete**.
▶ *To empty the clipboard, click* **Clear All** *at*
the top of the pane.

To specify how you want the Office Clipboard task pane to work, click Options at the bottom of the pane and select or deselect the options as required.

A Clipboard icon appears on the Taskbar when the task pane is displayed.

To Cut or Copy to a different file:

1 *Open the file you want to move or copy the object from (the source).*
2 *Open the file you want to move or copy the object to (the destination).*
3 *Display the file you want to move or copy from.*
4 *Select the object to move or copy.*
5 *Click* **Cut** *or* **Copy** *in the Clipboard group.*
6 *Display the file you want to move or copy the object to.*
7 *Position the insertion point where you want the object to go.*
8 *Click* **Paste** *in the Clipboard group.*

PASTE OPTIONS

When you paste text or data into your file, the Paste Options button will appear beside the pasted object. Click it to see the options, e.g. keep source formatting, match destination formatting, keep text only, etc. Text and data will usually be pasted into your file using the source text formatting.

▶ *If the object has pasted as you want it, ignore the* **Paste Options** *button.*
▶ *If you want to change the formatting of your pasted object, click the* **Paste Options** *button and select the option from those available (these vary between applications).*

If you usually have to change the Paste option when you copy or move an object, you could set a new default.

To change the default options:
  1 *Choose* **Set Default Paste...** *from the Paste Options list.*
Or
  2 *Display the Options dialog box and select the* **Advanced** *category.*
  3 *Set the options as required.*
  4 *Click* **OK.**

DRAG AND DROP

As an alternative to using Cut or Copy and Paste techniques to move and copy objects, you may find drag and drop useful.

Drag and drop is especially useful when moving or copying an object a short distance, i.e. to somewhere else on the screen. If you try to drag and drop over a longer distance, you will probably find that your file scrolls very quickly on the screen and that it is very difficult to control.

To move or copy:
  1 *Select the object that you want to move or copy.*
  2 *Position the mouse pointer anywhere over the selected object.*

To move the text:
  3 *Click and hold down the left mouse button (notice the 'ghost' insertion point that appears within the selected area).*
  4 *Drag the object and release the mouse button to drop it into its new position.*

To copy the text:
  3 *Hold down* [Ctrl].
  4 *Click and hold down the left mouse button.*
  5 *Drag the object and drop it into its new position.*
  6 *Release* [Ctrl].

4.6 Page Layout

The **margin** is the area between the edge of the paper and the text/data area on your page. There is a margin at the top, bottom, left and right of each page.

Page orientation describes whether your page is portrait (tall) or landscape (wide).

You will most likely be using A4 paper size for the bulk of your work – but you can easily select an alternative size.

These and other page formatting options (varying between applications), can usually be found on the Page Layout tab or the Print Preview tab (or both).

To change orientation:
1 *Display the* **Page Layout** *tab.*
2 *Click* **Orientation** *in the* **Page Setup** *group.*
3 *Select* **Portrait** *or* **Landscape**.

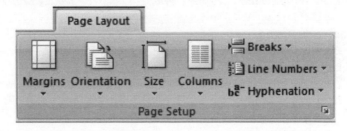

Or
1 *Click the dialog box launcher in the* **Page Setup** *group.*
2 *On the* **Margins** *tab, select the* **Orientation** *required.*
3 *Select the* **Apply to** *options.*
4 *Click* **OK**.

In Print Preview
▶ *Layout options are on the Page Setup group.*

To change the margin settings:
1 *Display the* **Page Layout** *tab.*
2 *Click the* **Margins** *button in the* **Page Setup** *group.*
3 *Select an option from the list.*
Or
4 *Click* **Custom Margins...**
5 *Set the* **Top, Bottom, Left** *and/or* **Right** *margins.*
6 *Click* **OK.**

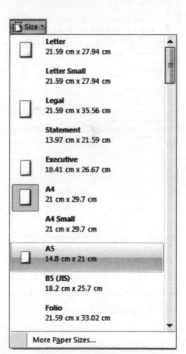

PAGE SIZE

If you are not printing onto A4 size paper, you may need to change the page size setting so that the application will insert page breaks in the correct place.

To change the page size:
1 *Display the* **Page Layout** *tab.*
2 *Click the* **Size** *button in the* **Page Setup** *group.*
3 *Select the paper size from the list displayed.*
Or
4 *Click* **More Paper Sizes...**
5 *Specify the paper size.*
6 *Click* **OK.**

4.7 Spelling and grammar

To help you produce accurate work, you should use the proofing tools to check spelling and grammar. Check that you are using the correct dictionary for your proofing. In the UK, you would normally use the English (United Kingdom) dictionary rather than English (United States). Your default language will have been set when you installed Microsoft Office.

LANGUAGE OPTIONS

To check/change your language options for Office:
1 *Click the* **Microsoft Office** *button.*
2 *Open the* **Options** *dialog box.*
3 *Select the* **Popular** *category.*

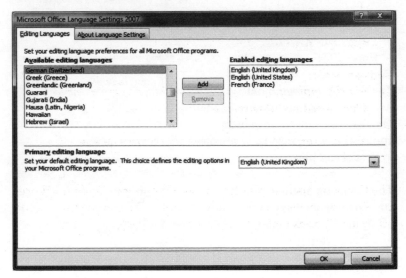

4 *Click* **Language Settings...**
5 **Add** *or* **Remove** *the languages from the list on the right until you have the languages you require.*
6 *Click* **OK.**

Word and PowerPoint

The language used for spelling and grammar checking may be displayed on the Status bar, e.g. English (United Kingdom). You can also check the language option on the Review tab.

▶ *Click* **Set Language** *in the* **Proofing** *group to display details of the language that is set.*

To change the default language from here, select the language you wish to use and click **Default...**

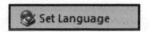

Excel and Access

▶ *You will find the current language option in the Options dialog box, in the Proofing groups.*

SPELLING AND GRAMMAR CHECKING

You can either:

▶ *Let the application check your spelling and grammar as you type (Word and PowerPoint only).*

Or

▶ *You can run a spellcheck at any time that suits you (all applications).*

The Checking Spelling and Grammar as you type option (in Word and PowerPoint) is operational by default. You can switch it on or off in the Options dialog box (Proofing category).

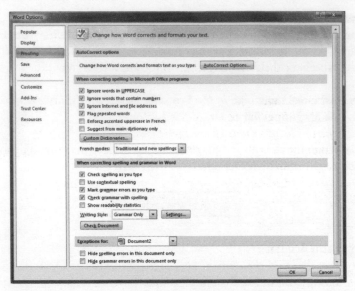

► *Words that aren't recognized will be underlined with a red, wavy line.*

► *Any words, phrases or sentences that have unusual capitalization or aren't grammatically correct will have a grey wavy underline.*

Spelling errors

Right-click on the error to open a list of suggested alternatives.

► *To change the word to a suggested one, click on it.*

► *To leave the word as it is, and stop it being picked up as an error in other areas of the file, choose* **Ignore All**.

► *To add the word to the dictionary, choose* **Add**.

Grammatical errors

These can be dealt with in a similar way. When you right-click on the error, the application will display the problem, and suggest a remedy if it can. You can choose whether you wish to change your text to that suggested or ignore it.

Checking Spelling and Grammar when you are ready

You can check your work at any time using the Spelling and Grammar command in the Proofing group on the Review tab (Word, Excel and PowerPoint) or the Records group on the Home tab (Access).

To start checking:
1 *Click the* **Spelling & Grammar** *button.*
   The application will check the spelling and grammar.

2 *Respond to the prompts as you see fit.*
3 *When the checking is complete, a prompt will appear.*
4 *Click* **OK** *to return to your file.*

4.8 Font formatting

One way of enhancing your text is to apply font formatting to it. These effects can be applied to individual characters.

The most commonly used font formatting options are usually located in the Font group on the Home tab – other options can be found in the Formatting dialog box (click the launcher button in the Font group to display it). The Font group varies a little from application to application – displaying formatting options that are particular to each. The options discussed here are available in most Office applications.

To format text or data as you type it in:
1 *Switch on the formatting option(s) required.*
2 *Type in text or data.*
3 *Switch off or change the formatting option.*

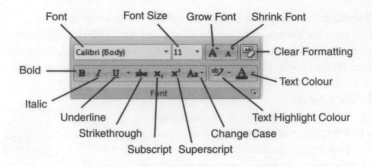

Font · Font Size · Grow Font · Shrink Font · Clear Formatting · Bold · Italic · Underline · Strikethrough · Subscript · Superscript · Change Case · Text Highlight Colour · Text Colour

To set or change formatting of existing text or data:

1 *Select the text or data.*
2 *Switch the formatting option required on or off, or apply an additional format.*

To set bold, italic and underline:

▶ *To switch bold or italic on or off, click the button.*
▶ *To switch underline on or off, click the button, or click the drop-down arrow and select an underline style.*

To change font:

1 *Click the drop-down arrow to the right of the* **Font** *command button in the* **Formatting** *group.*
2 *Scroll through the list of available fonts until you see the font you want to use.*
3 *Click on it.*

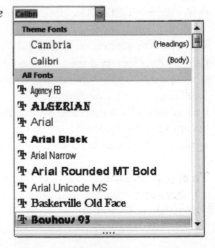

To change the font size:
1 *Click the drop-down arrow to the right of the* **Font Size** *command button in the* **Formatting** *group.*
2 *Scroll through the list of sizes until you see the one you want to use.*
3 *Click on it.*

To change the colour of a font:
1 *Click the drop-down arrow to the right of the* **Font Color** *command button to display the options.*
2 *Select the colour you want to use.*

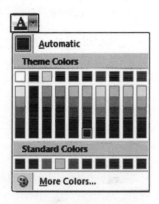

Other font formatting options in the group work in the same way – they either switch the option on and off, or display a list of options from which you can choose.

4.9 Paragraph/cell formatting

The default paragraph (Word/PowerPoint) or cell (Excel/Access) formatting options gives you a left-aligned text, with single line spacing. If this is not what you require you can change it.

Paragraph/cell formatting options are usually found in the Paragraph or Alignment group on the Home tab (depending on the application). Some are also in other groups, e.g. Font.

To apply formatting to a paragraph or cell as you type:
1 *Set the formatting option required.*
2 *Enter your text.*

To apply formatting to existing text:
1 *Select the text or cell(s).*
2 *Apply the formatting required.*

ALIGNMENT

To set the alignment of a paragraph, or data within a cell:

▶ *Click the Align Left, Centre, Justify or Align Right button.*

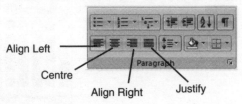

BORDERS AND SHADING

Borders and shading are paragraph or cell formatting options that can be very useful for emphasizing areas in your file.

To place a border around or between your paragraph(s) or cell(s), or through a cell:
1 *Select the paragraph(s) or cell(s).*
2 *Click the arrow to the right of the* **Borders** *button to display the options.*
3 *Select the border required.*

To remove a border:

1 *Select the paragraph(s) or cell(s) you want to remove borders from.*
2 *Display the* **Borders** *options.*
3 *Click the* **No Border** *button.*

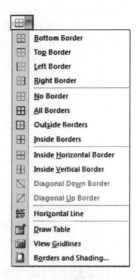

There are more options in the Borders and Shading dialog box. You can apply a border to all four sides (an outside border) using the Box, Shadow or 3-D setting.

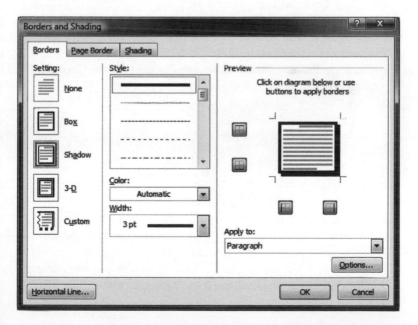

To display the dialog box:
1 *Display the* **Border** *options.*
2 *Choose* **Borders and Shading...** *(Word) or* **More Borders...** *(Excel) from the list of border options.*

Experiment with the options in the dialog box:

To switch individual borders on and off:
▶ *Click the border tools in the Preview window, or the lines around the edges of the example in the Preview window.*

To add a shading effect:
1 *Select the paragraph(s).*
2 *Click the down arrow by the* **Fill** *button in the* **Paragraph** *group and select a shading option.*

FORMAT PAINTER

If you need to apply the same formatting to different pieces of text or cells throughout your file, you could use the Format Painter to 'paint' the formatting onto your text.

1 *Select some text or data that has been formatted using the options you want to apply to other text.*
2 *Click the* **Format Painter** *command button (in the* **Clipboard** *group on the* **Home** *tab).*

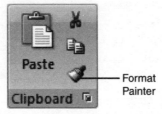

3 *Click and drag over the text/cells you want to 'paint' the formatting onto.*
4 *If you want to paint the formats onto several separate pieces of text, lock the Format Painter on by double-clicking on it. When you have finished, click the tool again to unlock it.*

Know your Ctrl alphabet

Some keyboard shortcuts are common to most applications, and it can therefore save you quite a bit of time in the long run if you learn and use them. Try the Ctrl alphabet!

Ctrl+	Effect
A	Select All
B	Bold
C	Copy
D	Font dialog box (Word)
D	Fill Down (Excel)
D	Duplicate (PowerPoint)
E	Centre
F	Find
G	Go To
H	Replace
I	Italics
J	Justify
K	Insert Hyperlink
L	Left Align
M	Left Indent (Word)
N	New file
O	Open file
P	Print file
Q	Remove paragraph formatting (Word)
R	Replace
S	Save file
T	Hanging indent (Word)
U	Underline
V	Paste
W	Close Active Window
X	Cut
Y	Repeat the last action
Z	Undo

4.10 Undo, Redo

To undo an action:
▶ *Click* **Undo** *on the Quick Access toolbar.*
Or
▶ *Press* [Ctrl]-[Z].

To redo something you undid by mistake:
▶ *Click* **Redo** *on the Quick Access toolbar.*
Or
▶ *Press* [Ctrl]-[Y].

4.11 Find and Replace

The Find and Replace commands can be useful when working with longer files. Find allows you to locate specific text or data quickly. Replace enables you to find the specified text and replace it with other text – selectively or globally.

To find specified text
1 *Display the* **Home** *tab and click* **Find** *(or press* [Ctrl]-[F]) *to display the* **Find and Replace** *dialog box.*
2 *On the* **Find** *tab, enter the text that you are looking for.*
3 *Click* **Find Next** *and repeat, if necessary, until you have located the instance required.*

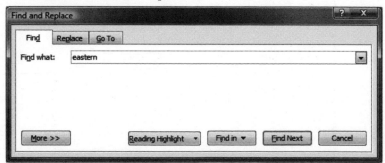

4 *Click* **Cancel** *to return to your document.*

SEARCH OPTIONS

If you are looking for text and you want to be more specific than just entering the text itself, you may find some of the Search Options useful.

To display the Search options click **More >>** in the **Find and Replace** dialog box in Word or **Options >>** in Excel.

Options that could be useful at this stage include:

- ▶ **Match case** – *the application will look for an exact match in upper and lower case letters if you choose this option.*
- ▶ **Find whole words only** – *the application will ignore matching characters that form part of another word.*

FIND AND REPLACE

Find and replace can be a very useful tool – especially if you've spelt a name wrong throughout a file!

1 *Open the* **Find and Replace** *dialog box at the* **Replace** *tab or press* [Ctrl]-[H].

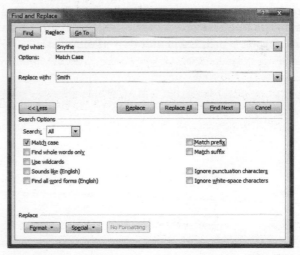

2 *Enter the text you want to find in the* **Find what:** *field.*

3 *Specify any options and formatting as necessary.*

4 *Enter the text to replace it with in the* **Replace with:** *field, and specify any options and formatting.*

5 *Click* **Find Next**. *The first occurrence of the text will be highlighted.*

6 *Click* **Replace** *to replace this occurrence, then click* **Find Next** *again.*

Or

7 *Click* **Replace All** *to get all occurrences replaced automatically.*

Experiment with the options and use the dialog box **Help** button as necessary to explore this feature fully.

Beware!

Be careful when using Replace All – it may replace something that you didn't anticipate. Particular danger spots are numbers, which may be tucked into a date, address, etc.

4.12 Illustrations

Illustrations include shapes, pictures, clip art, SmartArt and charts. The commands for these objects are on the Insert tab, and you can add them to your Word, Excel and PowerPoint files.

SHAPES

Shapes include basic shapes and lines, block arrows, flow chart symbols, callouts and stars and banners.

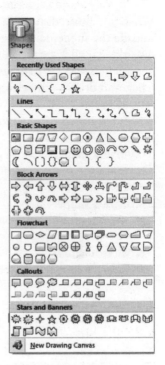

To add a shape:
1 *Display the* **Insert** *tab.*
2 *Click the* **Shapes** *button.*
3 *Select a shape.*
4 *Click and drag on your page to draw your shape.*

To draw a perfect square or circle:
1 *Select the* **Rectangle** *or* **Oval** *shape.*
2 *Hold down* [Shift] *and drag on the page to draw the shape.*

The line tools, e.g. curve, freeform or scribble, work slightly differently.

1 *Select a line shape, e.g. freeform or curve.*
2 *Click where you want the shape to start, and then click at each point you want the shape outline to change direction.*
3 *Double-click at the point you want to stop drawing.*
4 *With the scribble shape, click and hold down the left mouse button and move your mouse to, well, scribble! When you release the mouse button, the shape is complete.*

SELECTING AND DESELECTING SHAPES

When you finish drawing a shape it will be selected. If you click outside the shape, anywhere on your file, the shape will become deselected – click on it again and it will be selected. When selected, a shape has various handles along its edges and in its corners. Click and drag on these to manipulate the shape.

A selected object can be moved, resized or deleted.

To move a shape:
▶ *Place the pointer within the shape and click and drag.*

To resize a shape:
▶ *Click and drag on a blue square or circle handle.*

To delete a shape:
▶ *Select it and press* [Delete].

To rotate a shape:
▶ *Click and drag on the green circle handle.*

To change the aspect or tilt of a shape:
▶ *Click and drag on the yellow diamond handle.*

DRAWING TOOLS

When a shape is selected, the Drawing tools are displayed in the Ribbon. If no shape is selected, the tools disappear again. These tools can be used to format your shape in a variety of ways.

Shape Styles
Use the Shape Styles command buttons to select a different formatting style for your shape.

▶ **Shape Fill** *gives access to all the fill options available for an object, e.g. colour, picture, gradient or texture.*

- ▶ **Shape Outline** *gives access to all the line formatting options for the shape outline e.g. colour, weight, dashes and arrows.*
- ▶ **Shape Effects** *gives access to a range of preset and fully customizable 3-D and shadow effects for your shape.*

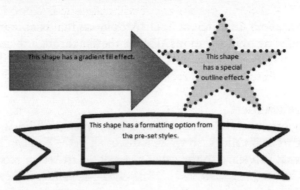

Adding text

To add text to a shape:

1 *Right-click on the shape.*
2 *Select* **Add Text**.
3 *Enter the text (or edit existing text).*

TEXT BOX

If you wish to add free text to your page, worksheet, slide or chart (not within a shape or other object), you can use a Text box. A Text box can be positioned anywhere in your file.

The Text Box button is on the Insert tab, in the Text group and in the Insert Shapes group on the Format tab of the Drawing Tools.

To insert a Text box:

1 *Click the* **Text Box** *button.*
2 *Drag to draw a rectangle where you want your text box.*
3 *Type in your text.*
4 *Click outside your text box.*

The text box can be resized, moved, formatted or deleted like any other shape.

SMARTART

There are about 80 different SmartArt objects that enable you to create all sorts of illustrations. Take a browse through them to see what is on offer. You may find that not all options are available for all objects, but most will be.

Organization chart

The Organization chart is one that is most often used, in Word documents or on slides, so we will discuss it here. You can then apply what you learn to the other types of SmartArt objects.

The Hierarchy category is the one to use for these charts (or other relationships that can be illustrated in a hierarchical way).

To create an organization chart:
1 *Click the* **SmartArt** *button in the* **Illustrations** *group on the* **Insert** *tab.*
2 *Select* **Hierarchy** *in the left panel.*
3 *Select the* **Organization Chart** *layout (or other hierarchy chart).*
4 *Click* **OK.**

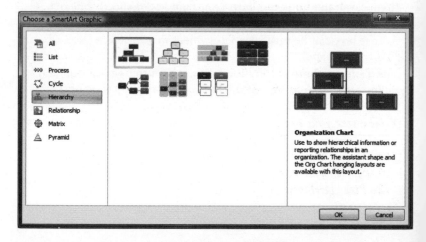

The **SmartArt** tools, with a **Design and Format** tab, are displayed when the organization chart is selected.

Entering text

1 *Click within a box.*
2 *Type in your text.*
3 *If you have more than one line of text to add in the box, press [Enter] to create a new line.*

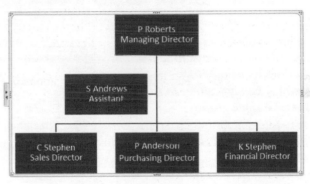

Adding, deleting and moving shapes

You can build up your chart by adding shapes. Each new shape must be related to an existing one.

To add a shape:

1 *Select the shape to relate a new shape to.*
2 *Click the **Add Shape** tool in the **Create Graphic** group.*
3 *Select the option required from the list.*
4 *Enter your text.*

To delete a shape:

1 *Select the shape.*
2 *Press [Delete].*

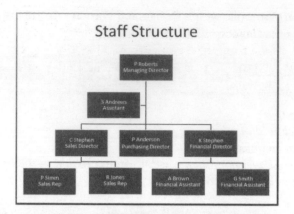

To reposition a shape:

  1 *Select the parent shape (one that has other shapes below it).*

  2 *Choose a* **Layout** *option in the* **Create Graphic** *group.*

Or

  ▶ *Drag and drop the shapes as required.*

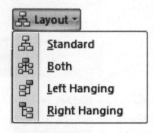

To reverse a graphic:

  ▶ *You can reverse the whole graphic, left to right, by clicking the command in the* **Create Graphic** *group.*

Promote and Demote

There may be times when you have your chart set up, then someone moves to a new job so their position within the hierarchy changes. You can promote or demote any shape using the Promote and Demote command buttons in the Create Graphic group.

This feature works best if you show the Text pane.

  1 *Select the point you wish to promote/demote – click anywhere within it.*

  2 *Click the* **Promote or Demote** *command button.*

Layout

To change the layout used in your chart, select an option from the Layout group on the Design tab.

Style and colours

The options on the SmartArt Styles group provide a variety of styles and colours to choose from.

There are simple styles and 3-D styles, as well as eight different colour themes, with several combinations within each theme.

Reset graphic

If you have been experimenting with the many options, you might decide that you want to get back to the original formatting.

▶ *To discard all your changes, click the* **Reset Graphic** *command button in the* **Reset** *group.*

Format tab

The Format tab offers more options. Experiment with them to see how they work.

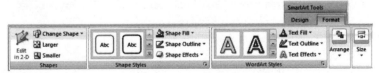

The Shapes group can be used to:

▶ *Change the shape of individual boxes in your diagram.*

Or

▶ *Make the shape larger or smaller.*

The Shape Styles group allow you to:

▶ *Choose a standard style for your shape.*

Or

▶ *Specify the fill, outline and effects options for shapes individually.*

4.13 Clip art

If you've installed Microsoft Office you'll find you've access to lots of clip art. If you've Internet access, you'll also find many more clips online.

To insert clip art:

1 *Click the* **Clip Art** *button in the* **Illustrations** *group.*

2 *Leave the* **Search for:** *text box empty in the task pane to display all clips.*

Or

3 *Enter a keyword in the text box if you are looking for something specific.*

4 *Set the* **Search in:** *options, e.g. specify the collections and media file types that you want (for clip art, search* **All collections** *in the b box, and choose* **Clip Art** *from the* **Results should be** *options).*

5 *Click* **Go.**

6 *Scroll through the list of clips.*

7 *Click on the one that you want to use.*

8 *Close the task pane.*

The Picture tools will be displayed when a clip art object is selected. Experiment with them.

Adjust tools for brightness, contrast and recolour options.

Picture Styles – just experiment with these! The Picture Shape, Picture Border and Picture Effects options display a wide range of options to choose from.

Arrange – the Text Wrapping option is particularly useful for controlling how text wraps around your clip art.

Size – set the height and width, or crop off any unwanted edges.

4.14 WordArt

WordArt lets you create special text effects that may be particularly useful for title pages, slide titles, posters – you can produce stunning titles and text effects wherever they are needed!

1 *Click the* **WordArt** *button in the* **Text** *group on the* **Insert** *tab.*

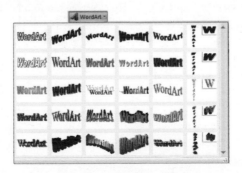

2 *Choose a style from the gallery.*
3 *Type in your text.*

4 *Click anywhere outside the WordArt object.*

To change the formatting of the text in the WordArt object:
1 *Select it – click on it.*
2 *Choose a* **Style** *from the gallery.*
Or
3 *Specify the* **Shape Fill, Shape Outline** *and* **Text Colour**
individually.

Experiment with the Shadow Effects and the 3-D Effects.

To edit the text:
1 *Select the object.*
2 *Click* **Edit Text** *in the* **Text** *group.*
3 *Edit as required and click* **OK.**

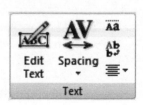

4.15 Zoom

Most files are displayed on screen at 100% zoom, full size. You can zoom in to get a closer look at something, or zoom out so that more of the file is displayed at any one time.

To adjust the zoom:

1 *Display the* View *tab.*
2 *Experiment with the commands in the* Zoom *group.*

View options on the Status bar

In Word, Excel and PowerPoint you can display View shortcuts, zoom and the zoom slider on the Status bar.

If you display them here they are available for use regardless of what tab is displayed on the Ribbon.

TEST

1   *How can you show/hide the Ribbon?*

2   *Every command on the Ribbon has a keyboard shortcut –*
    True or False?

3   *Suggest two ways of customizing the Quick Access toolbar.*

4   *Which keyboard shortcut opens the online Help?*

   [F10]   [F7]   [F1]   [Shift]-[F1]

5   *When might you use Save As?*

6   *Where can you set a password for a file?*

7   *You've made a mistake! How can you undo it so that things*
    are back how they were?

8   *Give two examples of proofing tools.*

9   *Give three examples of illustrations that can be added to a file.*

10   *Where can you display zoom shortcuts?*

5

Word processing

In this chapter you will learn:
- *about view options*
- *about indents and tabs*
- *how to add headers, footers and page numbers*
- *about numbered and bulleted lists*
- *about templates and styles*
- *how to use tables*
- *how to run a mail merge*
- *about importing data*

Do it!
Experiment with the topics covered in this chapter – you have to do it to learn it. Remember Undo (see section 4.10) if you try something out and it doesn't go as expected!

5.1 Starting Word

When you start Word, a new blank document is displayed on the screen.

Take a look at the Word screen. You should be able to recognize the areas and items labelled here.

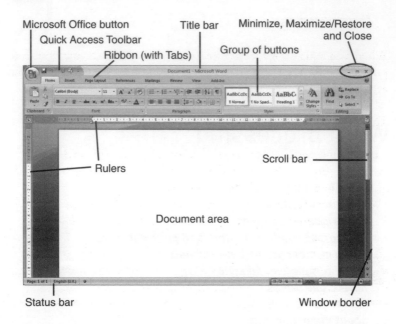

Microsoft Office button
Quick Access Toolbar
Ribbon (with Tabs)
Title bar
Group of buttons
Minimize, Maximize/Restore and Close

Rulers
Scroll bar

Document area

Status bar
Window border

The document name, Document1, is displayed on the Title Bar. Each document that you create during a session in Word is given a temporary name following the Document1 format. Your second document will be called Document2, the next one Document3 and so on. These names should be considered temporary – when you save your document, give it a meaningful name instead of the temporary name assigned by Word.

Starting with a recent file

If you want to start a session by working on a recently used file, you can open this from the Start menu. Click Start, pause over Microsoft Office Word 2007 – and the recently-used files will appear in the submenu. Click the one you want. Word will start and the file will be opened!

FILE HANDLING

The basic file handling features (Create New, Open, Save, Print and Close) are virtually the same in Word, Excel and PowerPoint – see Chapter 4 for information how these features work.

When you start Word, or create a new document, the insertion point – the flashing black vertical bar – is in the top left of the text area on the first page. You're ready to start, so just type!

Things to remember when entering text into your document:

- ▶ **Do not** *press* [Enter] *at the end of each line. If a sentence is going to run onto a new line, let it – the ext will be 'wrapped' automatically at the end of the line.*
- ▶ **Do** *press* [Enter] *at the end of short lines of text, e.g. after lines in an address at the top of a letter or after the last line in a paragraph.*
- ▶ *To leave one or more clear lines between paragraphs or headings, or in the signature block at the end of a letter, press* [Enter] *as often as is necessary to get the effect you want.*

5.2 Moving the insertion point

When you need to fix a mistake, the first thing you have to do is place the insertion point next to the error. If necessary, use the scroll bars to bring the text you want to edit into view.

There are several different ways of moving the insertion point. Experiment with the various options as you work.

Using the mouse

1 *Position the I-beam (the name given to the pointer when it is over text) where you want to move the insertion point to.*
2 *Click the left mouse button.*

If your mouse has a wheel between the buttons, you will be able to scroll through your document by rotating the wheel.

Using the keyboard

To move a character or line at a time	[Left], [Right], [Up], [Down] arrow keys
To move right or left by a word	[Ctrl]+[Left] or [Right]
To move up or down a paragraph	[Ctrl]+[Up] or [Down]
To go to the end of the line	[End]
To go to the start of the line	[Home]
To go to the start of the document	[Ctrl]+[Home]
To go to the end of the document	[Ctrl]+[End]

5.3 Editing

To insert new text:
1 *Position the insertion point where you want the new text.*
2 *Type in your text.*

To delete existing text:
1 *Position the insertion point next to the character that you want to delete.*
2 *To delete characters to the left, press the* [Backspace] *key once for each character.*

Or

3 *To delete characters to the right, press* [Delete] *once for each character.*

Both [Backspace] and [Delete] repeat – if you hold them down they will zoom through your text removing it much quicker than you could type it in, so be careful with them!

OVERTYPE

You can type over existing text, replacing the old text with the new in one operation, instead of deleting the old then entering the new.

Display the Overtype button on the Status bar so you know what mode you are in. Then, to toggle between Insert and Overtype, click the button on the Status bar.

To display the Overtype button on the Status bar, right-click on the Status bar and select Overtype.

You can also use the Insert button to toggle overtype – but you must switch this option on if you want to use it. Once switched on you can toggle between Insert and Overtype modes by pressing [Insert] on your keyboard.

To use the Insert key to toggle Overtype:
1 *Click the* **Microsoft Office** *button, then click* **Word Options.**
2 *Select* **Advanced** *from the list of* **Categories.**
3 *In the* **Editing** *options, select the* **Use the Insert key to control Overtype mode** *checkbox.*
4 *Click* **OK.**

Try it out!

1 *Press* [Insert] *to switch on Overtype mode (or click the Overtype button on the Status bar).*
2 *Position the insertion point within some existing text and type. Watch carefully to see what happens. The existing text will be replaced with the new text you enter.*
3 *Press* [Insert] *(or click the button on the Status bar) to switch Overtype mode off again.*

The Overtype/Insert indicator on the Status bar will show which mode you are in.

To insert a new paragraph:
▶ *Position the insertion point where the paragraph break should be and press* [Enter] *– twice if you want to leave a blank line.*

To join two paragraphs:
- ▶ *Delete the* [**Enter**]*s between the paragraphs (you can see these if you turn on the non-printing characters – see section 5.7).*

Experiment! You could type:

- ▶ *A letter to a friend*
- ▶ *Some notes on a hobby you pursue*
- ▶ *A future best-selling novel!*

Switching between documents

If you have more than one document open, you can easily move from one document to another. Place the mouse pointer over the application icon on the Taskbar – a miniature of each open document will appear. Click on the one you want to go to.

5.4 Word options

When Word is initially set up on your computer, the default file location for documents is your Documents library (unless someone has changed this option). Other preferences and options, e.g. unit of measure for page layout, and user information, e.g. name, initials, are also set, but you can easily change any of these from the Word Options dialog box.

To change the options:
1. *Click the* **Microsoft Office** *button, then click* **Word Options**.
2. *Select the* **Category** *required from the list on the left.*
3. *Set the options as required.*
4. *Click* **OK** *to close the* **Word Options** *dialog box.*

The options most commonly changed include the default file location, the units of measurement used on the rulers and for margins and tabs, and user information. Full instructions for each of these options follow – but browse through the others to see if there is anything else you might want to customize.

To change the default folder (for Save and Open operations):
1 *Display the* **Word Options** *dialog box.*
2 *Select the* **Save** *category.*
3 *Click the* **Browse...** *button to the right of the* **Default File Location** *field in the* **Save** *options.*
4 *Locate and select the folder that you want to become the default folder for save/open operations.*
5 *Click* **OK** *to return to the* **Word Options** *dialog box.*
6 *Click* **OK** *to close the dialog box.*

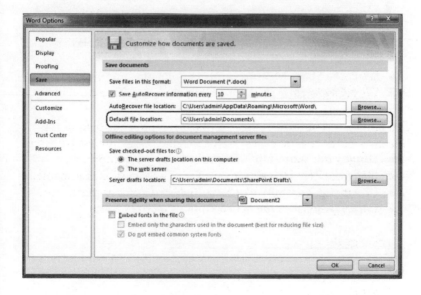

To change the units of measurement:
1 *Display the* **Word Options** *dialog box.*
2 *Select the* **Advanced** *category.*

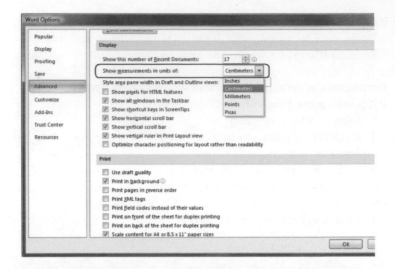

3 *Scroll through the options until you can see the* **Display** *options.*
4 *Select the* **Show Measurements in units of:** *option required.*
5 *Click* **OK** *to close the* **Word Options** *dialog box.*

To update user information:

1 *Display the* **Word Options** *dialog box.*
2 *Select the* **Popular** *category.*
3 *Update the user information as required.*
4 *Click* **OK** *to close the* **Word Options** *dialog box.*

5.5 Page breaks

As you type in your text a page break is inserted automatically when you reach the end of your page.

However, if you want a page break to occur at a specific point, e.g. at the end of a chapter or topic, you can easily insert a manual, or forced, page break. The quickest way to do this is by using the keyboard shortcut!

To insert a page break:

1 *Position the insertion point where the break is wanted.*

2 *Press* [Ctrl]-[Enter].

If you can't remember the keyboard shortcut, you can use the Ribbon to enter a page break.

1 *Position the insertion point where the break should go.*

2 *Select the* **Insert** *tab.*

3 *Click* **Page Break** *in the* **Pages** *group.*

Or

1 *Position the insertion point where the page break should go.*

2 *Select the* **Page Layout** *tab on the Ribbon.*

3 *Click* **Breaks** *in the* **Page Setup** *group.*

4 *Select* **Page** *from the* **Page Breaks** *option.*

5.6 Special characters and symbols

Most of the characters that you will want to type into your document are available through the keyboard. However, there may be times when you want a character that is not on the keyboard. You may find the character required in the Symbols dialog box.

To insert a symbol:

1 *Position the insertion point where you want the character.*

2 *Select the* **Insert** *tab.*

3 *Click* **Symbol** *in the* **Symbols** *group.*

4 *Select the symbol from the list, or click* **More Symbols...** *if the one you want is not displayed.*

5 *At the* **Symbols** *dialog box (if open), select the font to pick a character from (spend some time exploring your fonts to see what characters are available).*

6 *Select a character – click on it.*

7 *Click* **Insert**.

8 *Click* **Close** *to close the* **Symbol** *dialog box.*

5.7 View options

When working in a document, there are several view options. These control how your document looks on the screen – not how it will print out. You will usually work in Print Layout view or Draft view when entering and editing text. Full Screen Reading view is useful when reading online documents.

In Print Layout view your objects will be positioned on the page as they would appear when printed. Your margins are displayed (with any headers or footers), and pictures, drawings, multiple columns, etc. are all displayed in their true position. Print Layout view is useful if you are working with headers and footers, altering your margins, working in columns, or are combining text and graphics on a page and wish to see how they will be placed relative to each other.

Draft view displays the text, graphics and page breaks, but not margins or multiple columns.

To change the document view:
1 *Display the* **View** *tab on the Ribbon.*
2 *Select the view from the options in the* **Document** Views *group.*

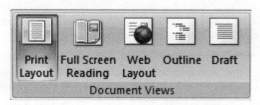

Or
3 *Click one of the* **View** *tools* 🔲 on the Status bar.

ZOOM

You can also change the zoom (magnification) options when viewing your document. Zoom is discussed in section 4.15.

Show/hide white space

The top and bottom margins are usually displayed as white space in Print Layout view. You can opt to show or hide this space.

1 *Go into Print Layout view (if necessary).*
2 *Move the mouse pointer to the top or bottom edge of a page.*

▶ *The mouse pointer becomes* ⊞ *when the option is Hide White Space or* ⊞ *when it is to Show White Space.*

3 *Double-click – the display of the white space is toggled.*

Full Screen Reading, Web Layout View and Outline View are not discussed in this book.

NON-PRINTING CHARACTERS

Non-printing characters are those which affect the layout of your text, but don't print. For example, those inserted when you press the spacebar, [Enter], tab or non-breaking space character. You can toggle their display – you can opt to have them on your screen or hidden. Either way they will not be printed.

1 *Display the* **Home** *tab.*
2 *Click the* **Show/Hide** *button* ¶ *in the* **Paragraph** *group.*

5.8 Selection techniques

Selection techniques are very important in Word. You need to use them if you want to:

▶ *Copy or move text within a document, or from one document to another;*
▶ *Change the formatting of existing text;*
▶ *Quickly delete large chunks of text.*

There are several ways to select text in Word – try some out and use whatever seems easiest for you.

Using the mouse, to select:

Any amount	Click and drag over it
Any amount	Click at the start, hold down [**Shift**], click at the end of text
A word	Double-click on it
A sentence	Hold down [**Ctrl**] and click anywhere within it
A paragraph	Double-click in the selection bar to the left of the paragraph or triple-click anywhere within it
The document	Triple-click in the selection bar.

The selection bar is the area to the left of the left margin. Your mouse pointer changes to the white pointer arrow when it is in this area.

To deselect any unit of text:

▶ *Click anywhere within your text, or press one of the arrow keys on your keyboard.*

Selecting with keys

Using the keyboard, to select:

A character or line	[Shift]+ [Left], [Right], [Up] or [Down]
A word	[Shift]+[Ctrl]+ [Left] or [Right] depending on the direction you want to select in
A paragraph	[Shift]+[Ctrl]+ [Up] or [Down] depending on the direction you want to select in
To the end of the line	[Shift]-[End]
To the start of the line	[Shift]-[Home]
To the start of the file	[Shift]-[Ctrl]-[Home]
To the end of the file	[Shift]-[Ctrl]-[End]
The whole document	[Ctrl]-[A].

Experiment with the different selection techniques. Many of the keyboard methods are much more efficient than click and drag.

5.9 Font formatting

Standard formatting routines are used when formatting characters in Word (see section 4.8).

Explore the Font group on the Home tab and experiment with the font formatting options.

To display additional Font formatting:
1 *Click the* **Font** *dialog box launcher at the bottom right of the* **Font** *group.*
2 *Explore the* **Font** *tab.*
3 *Choose the effects you want – a preview of your selection is displayed in the Preview window.*

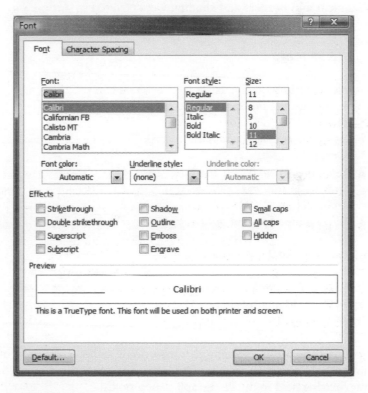

4 *Click* **OK** *to apply the effects to your text, or* **Cancel** *to return to your document without making any changes.*

Clearing formatting

You can quickly remove all formatting from selected text by holding down [Ctrl] and pressing the spacebar.

5.10 Paragraph formatting

Some formatting options are applied to complete paragraphs, regardless of whether the paragraph consists of a few words or several lines. A paragraph is created each time you press [**Enter**].

Alignment and Borders and shading were covered in section 4.9. Word has additional paragraph formatting options.

LINE SPACING

Initially, your line spacing is set to 1.15. You can set different spacing using the Line Spacing button.

1 *Select the text that you want to format.*
2 *Click the arrow beside the* **Line Spacing** *button in the* **Paragraph** *group (***Home** *tab).*
3 *Select a* **Line Spacing** *option.*

You can also use the shortcuts.

[**Ctrl**]-[**2**]   Double-line spacing
[**Ctrl**]-[**5**]   1½ line spacing
[**Ctrl**]-[**1**]   Single-line spacing

If you wish to set line spacing to a measurement other than one of those listed, click **Line Spacing Options...** and enter the value in the **Line Spacing** field in the **Paragraph** dialog box.

SPACING BEFORE AND AFTER PARAGRAPHS

You can control the amount of spacing that appears before and after a paragraph using the Spacing options. It is good practice to use these, rather than pressing [**Enter**] a couple of times, as you can be more precise about the amount of space.

1 *Select the text.*
2 *Click the down arrow by the* **Line Spacing** *button.*
3 *Click* **Add Space Before Paragraph** *or* **Add Space After Paragraph.**
Or
4 *Choose* **Line Spacing Options...**
5 *At the dialog box, set the* **Spacing Before** *or* **After** *values.*
6 *Click* **OK.**

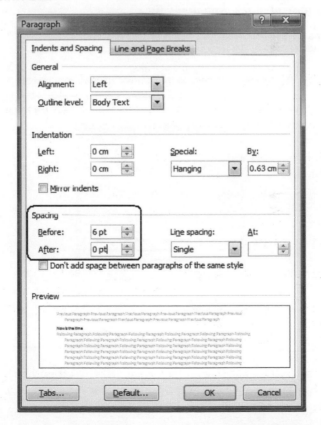

BULLETED AND NUMBERED LISTS

You can add bullets or numbers automatically to paragraphs.

▶ *Click the* **Bullets** *button in the* **Paragraph** *group to switch bullets on or off.*
▶ *Click the* **Numbering** *button to switch numbers on or off.*

To change the bullet or number style:
1 *Select the paragraphs you want bulleted.*
2 *Click the down arrow beside the* **Bullets** or **Numbering** *button.*
3 *Select the* **Bullet** *or* **Number** *option required.*

Or

4 *Choose* **Define New Bullet...** *or* **Define New Number Format...** *at the end of the drop-down list.*

Opens the Symbol dialog box – select a character from any font for your bullet.

Opens the Picture Bullet dialog box – select from a range of picture characters (perhaps best suited to Web pages).

Opens the Font dialog box to specify the size/colour, etc. of the bullet.

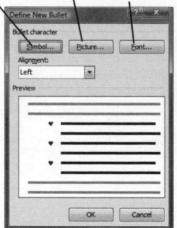

Define New Bullet dialog box

5 *Complete the dialog box as required.*
6 *Click* **OK.**

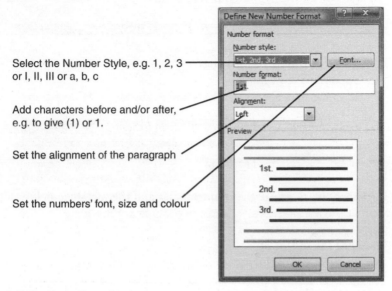

Select the Number Style, e.g. 1, 2, 3 or I, II, III or a, b, c

Add characters before and/or after, e.g. to give (1) or 1.

Set the alignment of the paragraph

Set the numbers' font, size and colour

Define New Number Format dialog box

INDENTS

Paragraphs normally run the full width of your typing line – from the left margin to the right margin. As you enter your text, it extends along the line until it reaches the right margin, then it automatically wraps to the next line (unless you press [**Enter**]).

To increase the indent of all lines in a paragraph from the left:

▶ *Click the Increase Indent button* in the Paragraph group.

To decrease the indent of all lines in a paragraph:

▶ *Click the* **Decrease Indent** *button* in the **Paragraph** *group.*

When using the Increase Indent/Decrease Indent buttons the paragraph indents to the next tab position.

Changing the indents using the ruler

You can also use the ruler to set your indents. The ruler must be displayed along the top of your text area.

To toggle the display of the ruler:
1 *Open the* **View** *tab.*
2 *Select/deselect the* **Ruler** *checkbox in the* **Show/Hide** *group.*

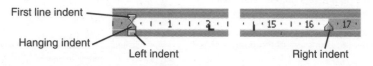

First line indent

Hanging indent

Left indent

Right indent

The indent markers are the two triangles and the rectangle below them at the left of the ruler, and the triangle at the right.

To adjust the indent of:
▶ *The first line in the paragraph from the left margin – drag the First Line Indent marker at the left edge of the ruler.*
▶ *All other lines (except the first) from the left – drag the Hanging Indent marker.*
▶ *All lines in the paragraph from the left – drag the Left Indent marker (the rectangle).*
▶ *All lines from the right – drag the Right Indent marker.*

To help improve accuracy when setting indents using the ruler, hold down [Alt] while you click and drag – the exact position of the indent will be displayed on the ruler.

The final option using the ruler is to use the Tab/Indent style button to select the type of indent required, and then specify the position of the indent by clicking on the ruler.

1 *Click the* **Tab/Indent** *style button until you display the indent type required – First line or Hanging.*

2 *Click on the ruler at the place you want the indent set.*

Or

1 *Click the* **Paragraph** *dialog box launcher (bottom right of* **Paragraph** *group on the* **Home** *tab).*

2 *Set the indents required in the Indentation fields.*

3 *Click* **OK** *to close the* **Paragraph** *dialog box.*

Keyboard shortcuts

[Ctrl]-[M]	Increase left indent
[Shift]-[Ctrl]-[M]	Decrease left indent
[Ctrl]-[T]	Increase hanging indent
[Shift]-[Ctrl]-[T]	Decrease hanging indent

TABS

Tabs are used to align your text horizontally on the typing line. If you want to type up a list of names and telephone numbers you could use tabs to align each column.

The default tabs are set every 1.27 cm (half inch) – the small dark marks along the bottom edge of the ruler indicate their positions.

Each time you press [**Tab**], the insertion point jumps forward to the next tab position that is set. The default tabs have left alignment – when you enter your text or numbers the left edge of the text or data entered is at the tab position.

Tabs can be aligned to the left, right, centre or decimal point.

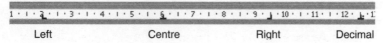

| Left | Centre | Right | Decimal |

Alignment:	**Possible use:**
Left	Any text or numbers
Right	Text, or numbers you want to line up on the unit
Centre	Anything – often used for headings
Decimal	Figures you want to line up on the decimal point.

If you need to use tabs and the pre-set ones are not what you require, you must set tabs at the positions you need them.

Display the ruler if necessary – View tab, Show/Hide group.

To set a tab using the ruler:
1 *Select the type of tab – click the* **Tab/Indent** *button to the left of the ruler until you've got the alignment option required.*

 Left   Centre   Right   Decimal

2 *Point to the lower half of the ruler and click – your tab is set.*

To move a tab:
▶ *Drag it along the ruler to its correct position.*

To delete a tab:
▶ *Drag it down off the ruler, and drop it.*

To set tabs in the Tabs dialog box:
1 *Click the* **Paragraph** *dialog box launcher.*
2 *Click* **Tabs...** *to open the* **Tab** *dialog box.*
3 *Enter the Tab stop position.*
4 *Select the alignment.*
5 *Click* **Set**.
6 *Repeat steps 3–5 until all your tabs are set.*
7 *Click* **OK**.

NEVER use the spacebar and [**Enter**] to give indent and tab effects to your document. Although you may get the layout to look OK, it will become a nightmare if you need to edit it!

Document Properties

You can view and edit document properties e.g. Author, title in the Properties panel. Open the Microsoft Office Menu, click Prepare and then Properties. Edit the properties as necessary and then close the panel (click the Close button at the top right of it).

HYPHENATION

Hyphenation gives a document a more professional look by limiting the amount of white space at the end of each line, and between words when text is justified.

The easiest way to ensure that your text is hyphenated appropriately is to have the Automatic hyphenation option turned on.

To check or edit the hyphenation option:
1 *Display the* **Page Layout** *tab.*
2 *Click* **Hyphenation** *in the* **Page Setup** *group.*
3 *Select the option required – None, Automatic or Manual.*

To set the Hyphenation options:
1 *Click* **Hyphenation Options** *in the Hyphenation list.*
2 *Select the options required, e.g. Hyphenation zone size.*
3 *Click* **OK.**

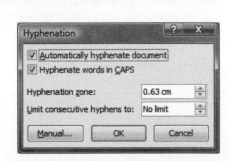

Optional hyphens

An optional hyphen controls where a word is hyphenated if it falls within the hyphenation zone in your document.

To insert an optional hyphen:
1 *Click where you want the hyphen to appear.*
2 *Press* [Ctrl]-[Hyphen].

The word will only be hyphenated if it falls within the hyphenation zone.

Optional hyphens are displayed when you show non-printing characters (click the **Show/Hide** button in the **Paragraph** group on the **Home** tab).

MANUAL LINE BREAK

A manual line break ends the current line of text and continues your text on the next line. A manual line break does not start a new paragraph, it simply forces a new line within the current paragraph.

To insert a manual line break:
1 *Hold down* [Shift].
2 *Press* [Enter].

Manual line breaks are useful at the end of lines that have used tabs to align columns of text or figures. If you separate the lines in your tabbed layout with manual line breaks, then try moving the tabs when the insertion point is within your tabbed layout, the whole column moves, not just the line that the insertion point is on (as would be the case if you pressed [Enter] at the end of each line to create a new paragraph).

5.11 Print preview and print

See Section 4.4 for standard preview and print information.

When you preview your file a full page is displayed at a time. You can zoom in and out and you can edit your text if you wish.

ZOOM

If you move your pointer over a page in print preview, you will notice it looks like a magnifying glass with a + on it.

▶ *Position the pointer over your page and click the left button and you will be zoomed in and out of your document.*

EDITING TEXT IN PRINT PREVIEW

1 *Deselect the* **Magnifier** *checkbox in the* **Preview** *group.*
2 *The insertion point will appear in your document. Edit your document and then select the* **Magnifier** *checkbox again so that you can zoom in and out.*

PRINT

If you are happy with the appearance of your document, and want to print it from the preview window, click the Print button in the Print group on the Print Preview tab. One copy of the document will be printed.

PRINT PREVIEW TAB

The Print Preview window has its own tab on the Ribbon, which can be used to control the display of your document on the screen. Experiment with the buttons to see what effect they have.

Print group

- ▶ *Print displays the* **Print** *dialog box.*
- ▶ **Print Options** *opens* **Word Options** *at the* **Display** *group.*

Page Setup group

- ▶ *With buttons that allow you to set your margins, page orientation, and paper size.*

Zoom group

- ▶ *With a variety of zoom options to choose from.*

Preview group

- ▶ *Show ruler toggles the display of the rulers.*
- ▶ **Magnifier** *toggles the zoom in/zoom out feature.*
- ▶ **Shrink One Page** – *If a small amount of text appears on the last page of your document you may be able to reduce the number of pages by clicking this tool. Word decreases the size of each font used in the document to get the text to fit on to one page less.*
- ▶ **Next Page/Previous Page** *for moving from page to page in a multi-page document.*
- ▶ **Close Print Preview** *returns your document to Print Layout View (or the last view you were in before previewing).*

5.12 Word templates

A template is a pattern on which a document is based.

To create a document using the Blank Document template, just click the New tool on the Quick Access toolbar. The document has an A4 paper size, portrait orientation, 2.54 cm (1 inch) margins and 1.15 line spacing.

Word comes with other templates. Look through these as you may find some of them useful. There are several letter, report, fax and résumé (CV) templates to choose from, as well as a blog. If you find a template that you would like to use, you can customize it with your own company details, etc., and save it for future use.

To create a document using a Word template:
1 *Display the* **New Document** *dialog box.*
2 *Select* **Installed Templates** *in the* **Templates** *list.*

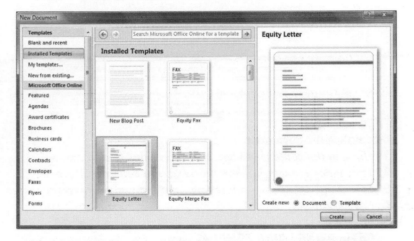

3 *Scroll through the templates and select the one you want.*
4 *Check the* **Create new:** *option under the preview window –*
   it should be set to **Document.**
5 *Click* **Create.**

Explore the document. Check out the layout – notice that some include areas for a company name, address, telephone, etc.

Many of the documents created from a template include details on how to use and complete it. In the main, you just follow the instructions on the screen.

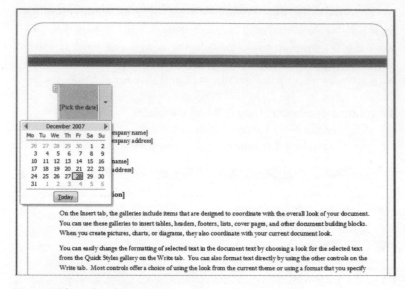

On the Insert tab, the galleries include items that are designed to coordinate with the overall look of your document. You can use these galleries to insert tables, headers, footers, lists, cover pages, and other document building blocks. When you create pictures, charts, or diagrams, they also coordinate with your current document look.

You can easily change the formatting of selected text in the document text by choosing a look for the selected text from the Quick Styles gallery on the Write tab. You can also format text directly by using the other controls on the Write tab. Most controls offer a choice of using the look from the current theme or using a format that you specify

To complete the document:

1 *Click in the content holders and enter your text.*
2 *Delete any content holders that you don't require.*
3 *Select and delete the sample text, and type in your own.*
4 *Save and print.*

CUSTOMIZING WORD TEMPLATES

If you find a template that you like, but it isn't exactly what you want, you can customize it, perhaps by adding your company details, and save it as a template, so that it will be just as you really want it each time you base a new document on it.

You can customize any part of a template – page layout, headers, footers, styles, etc.

To customize your template:

1 *Display the* **New Document** *dialog box.*
2 *Choose the template you wish to customize.*

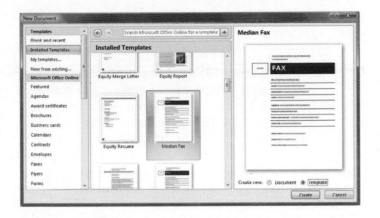

3 *Select the* **Template** *option in the* **Create new:** *options.*
4 *Click* **Create.**
5 *Edit your template as required.*
6 *Save your file – it should go into the Templates folder.*
7 *Close your file.*

To create a new template from scratch:
1 *Create a new blank document (or template) and specify the layout, enter standard text, etc. as required. Page setup, headers and footers (section 5.14), styles (section 5.13), etc. can all be set up to suit your requirements.*
2 *Click the* **Microsoft Office** *button to display the* **Office** *menu and choose* **Save As...**
3 *Select* **Word Template** *from the submenu.*
4 *Select the folder in which you wish to store your template.*
5 *Give your template a name and click* **Save.**

Try out some of the templates on your system – they could help you produce a very professional looking document easily.

Note: other file types are discussed in Section 2.11.

5.13 Styles

Instead of formatting text manually (using the Font or Paragraph group) you could format it using a set of options that have been saved in a style. Each document you create in Word will have several styles already set up. The Quick Styles are in the Styles group on the Home tab.

The default Normal style is a paragraph style that is left aligned and in single line spacing. The characters are formatted using the Calibri font, size 11 (unless you have changed it).

Click the **More** button to display the Quick Styles gallery.

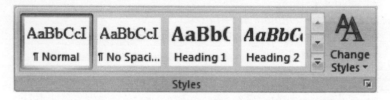

- ▶ *Paragraph styles are those with the paragraph mark* ¶ *beside the style name.*
- ▶ *Character/Font styles have no paragraph mark.*

You can apply styles in the same way as any other formatting:

To apply a style to new text:
1 *Select the style required.*
2 *Type in your text and press* [**Enter**].

To apply a style to existing text:
1 *Select the text.*
2 *Click the* **More** *button to display the* **Quick Styles** *gallery.*
3 *Choose the style from those available.*

If you have live preview enabled (Word Options), you will notice that when you move your mouse pointer over each style, you can see the effect that it will create within your document before you actually select it.

APPLY STYLES

If the style you want is not displayed in the Quick Style gallery, you can display the Apply Styles dialog box and select the style you want from the list.

To use the Apply Styles dialog box:
1 *Press* **[Ctrl]-[Shift]-[S]**.
Or
2 *Click* **Apply Styles...** *at the bottom of the Quick Style gallery.*

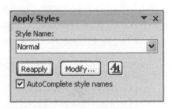

3 *Scroll through the list and select a style.*
Or
4 *Start to type the style name into the* **Style Name** *field.*
5 *Click* **Apply**.
6 *Close the* **Apply Styles** *dialog box.*

Styles are magic!
Styles will help you achieve a consistent look within and across your documents. You can also set up your own styles – check out the online Help.

PAGE SETUP

Page setup refers to the orientation of a page, the margins and the page size – see section 4.6.

5.14 Headers and footers

Headers and footers are displayed at the top and bottom of each page in your document. They usually contain things like page numbers, the name of the author of the document, the filename or the date that the document was produced.

You should be able to insert, edit and remove a header/footer from your file.

To insert a header or footer:

1 *Display the* **Insert** *tab and click the* **Header** *(or* **Footer***) button in the* **Header & Footer** *group.*

2 *Select the* **Header** *(or* **Footer***) style from the list –* **Blank (Three Columns)** *is a good one to start with. The insertion point moves to the header area and the* **Header** *and* **Footer** *tools are displayed. The document text is dimmed.*

3 *Click on the content holders and type in the detail required.*

4 *Close the* **Header & Footer** *area when you have finished – click* **Close Header and Footer** *in the* **Header & Footer** *tools.*

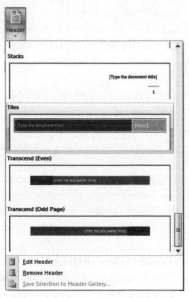

HEADER & FOOTER TAB

The Header & Footer tab is displayed when you are in the Header area, displaying options that are specific to working in these areas.

To edit the text:

1 *Click the* **Header** *or* **Footer** *command button.*
2 *Choose* **Edit Header** *or* **Edit Footer.**
3 *Make the amendments required.*
4 *Close the* **Header & Footer** *area.*

To remove a header or footer:

1 *Display the* **Insert** *tab and click the* **Header** *(or* **Footer***) button.*
2 *Click* **Remove Header** *or* **Remove Footer.**

To add a page number:

1 *Click in the area that you want to contain the page number.*
2 *Click* **Page Number** *in the* **Header & Footer** *group.*
3 *Select* **Current Position** *from the list.*
4 *Choose a style.*

Always use headers and footers for text or numbers that you want at the top or bottom of every page. Never type them into the main text area!

Lost the header?

The header and footer options are found on the Insert tab. Not a problem for new users – but may be a bit confusing for those that have used previous versions, when they have always been in the View menu. You'll soon get used to it!

5.15 Tables

Tables are used to help you arrange text and data in columns on your page. Tables are arranged in a grid, consisting of rows and columns. Where a row and column intersect, you get a rectangular area called a cell.

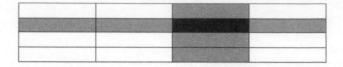

To create a table:
1 *Display the* **Insert** *tab.*
2 *Click* **Table** *in the* **Tables** *group.*
3 *Drag over the grid to set the size of the table.*
4 *Release the mouse button – an empty table will be displayed on your page.*

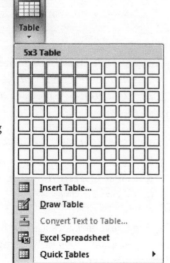

You can move around your table using the keyboard or the mouse.

▶ *Press* [**Tab**] *to move to the next cell.*
▶ *Hold down* [**Shift**] *and press* [**Tab**] *to move back to the previous cell.*

Or

▶ *Click in the cell you want to move to.*

TABLE TOOLS

The Table tools are displayed automatically when the insertion point is inside a table.

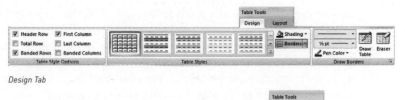

Design Tab

Layout Tab

SELECTION TECHNIQUES

To select the cell, column, row or table the insertion point is in:

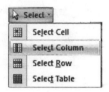

1 *Click the drop-down arrow to the right of* **Select** *in the* **Table** *group on the* **Layout** *tab of the* **Table** *tools.*
2 *Select the option required.*

Alternatively, use the cell, column or row selector areas – the mouse pointer will be a black arrow when it is over one:

- ▶ *To select a cell – click just within the left cell border.*
- ▶ *To select a column – click at the top of the column.*
- ▶ *To select a row – click to the left of the row.*
- ▶ *To select any group of adjacent cells – drag over them.*
- ▶ *Click and drag in the row or column selector areas to select multiple adjacent rows or columns.*

Other things to note:
When you create a table, each column is the same width, and the table stretches across the page.

To enter text or data, go to the cell then just type! Text will automatically wrap once it reaches the right edge of the cell, and the row will deepen to accommodate it.

Text and numbers automatically align to the left of a cell.

If you press [Tab] when the insertion point is in the last cell in the last row of your table, a new row is created.

You can format the text or data in the cells, using the normal formatting commands.

By default, the table has inside and outside borders around the cells.

Row heights and column widths

▶ *To adjust a row height – drag the lower border up or down.*
▶ *To adjust a column width – drag the left border right or left.*
Or
▶ *Set the* **Height** *and* **Width** *required in the* **Cell Size** *group on the* **Layout** *tab.*

Cafés and pubs – Scottish Borders		
Address	**Notes**	**Cost**
Old Mill Inn Old Mill Lane Melrose	Delightful retreat in the Scottish borders. Food available from 10 am through until 10 pm. Excellent lunches and evening meals. Accommodation available. Working waterwheel, herb garden and riverside walks.	Lunches from £5. Dinner from £12.50. Dinner, Bed and Breakfast: £38 per head.
Kathy's Kitchen 12 High Street Duns	Excellent family run coffee shop. Soup, baked potatoes, sandwiches, etc. available all day. Delicious home baking.	Various.

To make all rows the same height:
1 *Select the rows.*
2 *Click* **Distribute Rows** *in the* **Cell Size** *group.*

To make all columns the same width:
1 *Select the columns.*
2 *Click* **Distribute Columns** *in the* **Cell Size** *group.*

There are also AutoFit options in this group, so that you can automatically get your table to fit around the cell contents, or to the width of the window, or adopt a fixed width. Experiment with them to see how they affect your columns.

Inserting rows and columns
Adding rows to the end of a table is done automatically – just press [Tab] when the insertion point is in the last cell of the table to add a new row. If you need to add or delete rows or columns anywhere else in your table, use the command buttons.

To insert rows:
1 *Position the insertion point anywhere in the row above or below the one you want to insert.*
2 *Click* **Insert Above** *or* **Insert Below** *in the* **Rows & Columns** *group.*

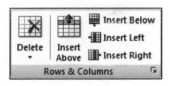

To insert columns:
1 *Position the insertion point anywhere in the column to the right or the left of the one you want to insert.*
2 *Click the* **Insert Left** *or* **Insert Right** *command button in the* **Rows & Columns** *group.*

Delete cells, columns, rows or table
1 *Position the insertion point anywhere in the cell, column, row or table you wish to delete.*
2 *Click the* **Delete** *button, then an option.*

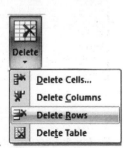

If you select some cells in your table then press [**Delete**], the contents of the table are deleted, but the table remains in place.

Cafés and pubs – Scottish Borders			
Contact	**Address**	**Notes**	**Cost**
Jill Syme	Old Mill Inn Old Mill Lane Melrose	Delightful retreat in the Scottish borders. Food available from 10 am through until 10 pm. Excellent lunches and evening meals. Accommodation available. Working waterwheel, herb garden and riverside walks.	Lunches from £5. Dinner from £12.50. Dinner, Bed and Breakfast: £38 per head.
Kathy or Anna	Kathy's Kitchen 12 High Street Duns	Excellent family run coffee shop. Soup, baked potatoes, sandwiches, etc. available all day. Delicious home baking.	Various.

TABLE STYLES

Instead of manually formatting your tables, you can create a professional look very quickly by using the table styles. These have pre-set shading and border effects.

To apply a style:
1 *Click anywhere within your table.*
2 *Scroll through the styles, or click the* **More** *button to display the* **Style** *gallery.*

3 *Select a style.*

Once a table style has been applied, you can customize it:

▶ *Modify the options using the* **Shading** *and* **Borders** *buttons.*
Or

- *Switch elements of the table style on and off, using the* **Table Style Options** *checkboxes to the left of the Table Styles.*

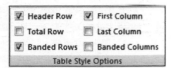

Tables are brilliant! They make presenting text and data in columns easy, and can also be used to produce some excellent forms!

Cafés and pubs – Scottish Borders			
Contact	**Address**	**Notes**	**Cost**
Jill Syme	Old Mill Inn Old Mill Lane Melrose	Delightful retreat in the Scottish borders. Food available from 10 am through until 10 pm. Excellent lunches and evening meals. Accommodation available. Working waterwheel, herb garden and riverside walks.	Lunches from £5. Dinner from £12.50. Dinner, Bed and Breakfast: £38 per head.
Kathy or Anna	Kathy's Kitchen 12 High Street Duns	Excellent family run coffee shop. Soup, baked potatoes, sandwiches, etc. available all day. Delicious home baking.	Various.

Cover Pages

Need an impressive front page for your document? Try the Cover Pages. You'll find them on the Insert tab in the Pages group.

5.16 Mail merge

Mail merge uses jargon and techniques that are similar to those found in database applications. You are actually performing basic database routines when you use mail merge.

▶ The **main document** *contains the layout, standard text and field names that point to the data source.*

▶ The **data source** *is the file containing the records for the mail merge, perhaps a name and address file. It is usually in a table layout, and could be a Word file or an Access or Excel table. Other sources can be used – see the online Help for details. We will create ours from Word.*

▶ A **record** *holds all the information on each item in your data source.*

▶ A **field** *is an item of data in a record. Title, username, first name, phone number, etc. would all be held in separate fields.*

▶ A **field name** *is used to identify a field.*

▶ The **result document** *is produced when you combine the records in the data source with the main document.*

There are three steps involved in mail merge:

1 *Creating the main document.*
2 *Creating and/or locating the data source.*
3 *Merging the two to produce the result document.*

It doesn't matter whether you create the main document or data source first, but you must have both to get a result document.

If you are going to produce a mail merge letter, I suggest that you type and save the standard letter before you begin. If you wish to use an existing file, open the one that will be your main document. Then work through the process described in the following pages.

This example creates a mail merge letter.

THE MAIN DOCUMENT

Main documents can be letters, email messages, envelopes, labels or directories (lists).

We will set our main document up as a letter. With these, when you run the merge, each record is merged into its own copy of the main document, and each result letter starts on a new page.

To set up your main document:
1 *Type up your letter and save it, or open an existing letter.*
2 *Display the* **Mailings** *tab.*
3 *Click the* **Start Mail Merge** *button and choose* **Letters.**

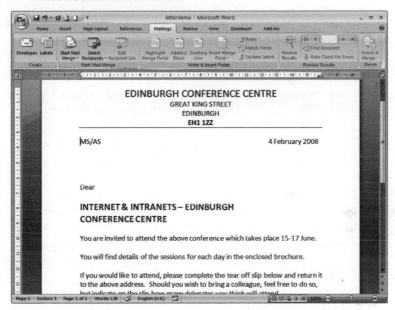

THE DATA SOURCE FILE

We will create a new data file. If you had a data file that you wanted to use, you would select Use Existing List... and open the file. If you use Outlook, you have the option Select from Outlook Contacts...

To create a new list:
1 *Click* **Select Recipients** *on the* **Mailing** *tab.*
2 *Select* **Type New List...** *to open the* **New Address List** *dialog box.*
3 *Click* **Customize Columns...**
4 *At the* **Customize Address List** *dialog box edit the field names – add, remove or rename the fields, or move them into the order you want.*
5 *Click* **OK** *to close the dialog box.*

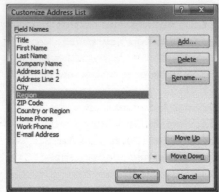

To enter your names and addresses:
1 *Type your data into the first column in the first row.*

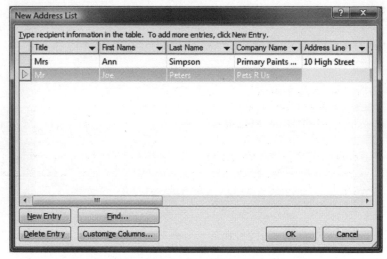

2 *Press* **[Tab]** *to move to the next column.*
3 *Repeat steps 1 and 2 for each column, until the row is complete – leave empty any fields you don't have data for.*

4 *At the end of the first record, press* [Tab] – *a new entry will be created.*

Or

5 *Click* **New Entry.**

6 *Repeat until all records have been entered.*

7 *Check your entries carefully, and amend any errors – just click in the field and insert/delete characters as necessary.*

8 *Click* **OK.**

To save the address list:
The Save Address List dialog box is displayed when you click OK in the New Address List dialog box.

1 *Select the folder that you want to store the address list in – the default is* **My Data Sources.**

2 *Give your address list a name.*

3 *Click* **Save.**

Editing the data source

You can edit the data source at any time, by adding new records, deleting ones you no longer require or amending the contents of existing records.

To edit the data source:

1 *Click* **Edit Recipient List** *in the Start Mail Merge group.*

2 *At the Mail Merge Recipients dialog box, select the Data Source file in the Data Source list.*

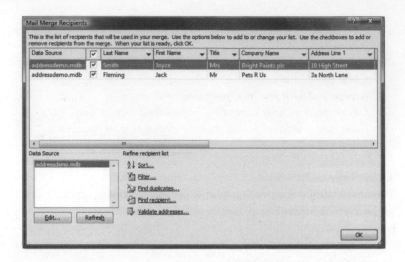

3 Click **Edit**.
4 At the Edit Data Source dialog box, amend the data source as necessary.

- ▶ To add a record, click **New Entry** and enter the record.
- ▶ To delete a record, click on the row and then click **Delete Entry**.
- ▶ To edit a record, click in the field you wish to edit (this selects the field contents) and then type to replace the current data, or press [Delete] to delete the contents of the field. Click again to deselect the field and then insert and delete characters within the field as required.

5 Click **OK** at the Edit Data Source dialog box once all changes have been made.
6 At the prompt, click **Yes** to update the list and save the changes.
7 Click **OK** at the Mail Merge Recipients dialog box.

SETTING UP THE MAIN DOCUMENT

On saving the address list, you will be returned to the main document – the letter in our example.

To insert merge fields:

1 *Put the insertion point where you want the first merge field to appear.*
2 *Click the down arrow on the* **Insert Merge Field** *on the* **Mailing** *tab.*
3 *Select the field you want to merge data from.*
4 *Repeat until all the fields required have been added to your letter.*

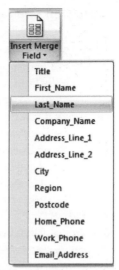

You can also use the Address Block button to add the inside address, or the Greeting Line button to add the salutation.

At the Insert Address Block dialog box, select or deselect options to get the layout you want.

At the Insert Greeting Line dialog box, customize the format and greeting line for invalid recipient names, if necessary.

PREVIEW RESULTS

Preview your result document before you commit it to print.

1 *Click* **Preview Results** *in the Preview Results group. The current record will be merged with the main document.*

2 *You can move through the records using the navigation buttons – the current record number is displayed.*
3 *Click* **Preview Results** *again to cancel the preview.*
4 *If you notice any problems in the preview, e.g. incorrect spacing or typing errors, fix the error on the main document, and then preview again to check it out.*

MERGING THE DOCUMENT WITH THE DATA

1 *Click the* **Finish & Merge** *button.*
2 *Select a merge option:*

   ▷ **Edit Individual Documents...**
      if you want a result document
      that can be edited and checked
      before printing.
   ▷ **Print Documents...** *if you are sure that everything is OK,*
      e.g. page breaks.
   ▷ **Send E-mail Messages...** *if you want to email the result*
      document to the recipients.

3 Choose **All, Current record** *or*
specify the range of records to
be merged in the **Merge to New**
Document *(or* **Merge to Printer**
or **Merge to E-Mail)** *dialog box.*
In the Merge to E-mail dialog
box, the To: field defaults to
Email_Address – those in the

data source file will be used. You should add a Subject in the
Subject line. The Mail format can be HTML (the default),
Attachment or Plain Text.
4 *Click* **OK.**

THE RESULT DOCUMENT

If you merge to a new document you can make adjustments to individual letters if you wish, and check that the document is satisfactory before you print.

Things to note:

▶ *The new file has a temporary filename, e.g. Letters1.*
▶ *There are many pages in it – to correspond with the number of merged records and the length of the letter.*
▶ *The file can be printed as normal.*
▶ *The result document would not usually be saved – you can recreate it again at any time from the main document and the data source.*

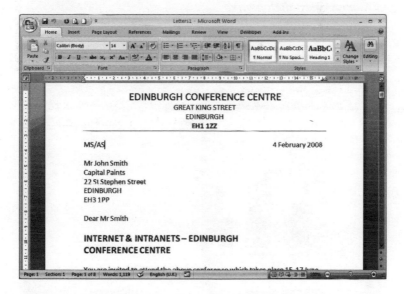

Lessons from the experts

There are lots of lessons that you can dip in and out of on the Microsoft site. Have a look at http://office.microsoft.com/en-us/training/HA102155661033.aspx

5.17 Charts

If you need to create a chart in your document, you may have access to the charting power of Excel, if it is installed on your PC. If you don't, you will have access to Microsoft Graph. When using this, a chart appears with its associated data in a table called a datasheet. You can then type your data into the datasheet, import it from a text file, or paste it in from another program.

The following instructions assume you have Excel 2007.

To create a chart:
1 *Click* **Chart** *in the* **Illustrations** *group.*
2 *Select the chart type you want to create in the left pane of the* **Create Chart** *dialog box.*
3 *Choose a subtype from the right pane in the dialog box.*

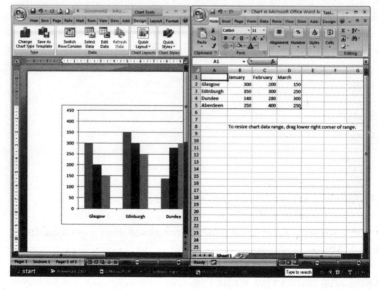

4 *Click* **OK**.
5 *Sample chart data is displayed in an Excel window, side-by-side with your document.Edit the contents on the Excel worksheet as required.*

6 *Close Excel when you have entered your data. Your chart will be displayed in your Word document.*

When you create a chart in this way, its data is embedded in the Word file, but you input and edit the data using Excel.

When you select your chart, the Charting tools will be displayed. These work in exactly the same way as they would in Excel. See section 6.23 for more information on working with charts.

5.18 Importing objects

You can insert data, e.g. figures from a spreadsheet, a chart or text from an existing file into your Word document. It may be that you are preparing a report and want to include some figures from an existing spreadsheet file, or insert the text contained in another Word document.

At its simplest, you could copy and paste the data, chart or text.

Copy and paste
1 *Launch Word and the application you want to copy from.*
2 *Select the object, text or data you want to copy.*
3 *Click the* **Copy** *button in the* **Clipboard** *group.*
4 *Switch to Word.*
5 *Place the insertion point where you want the object, text or data to appear.*
6 *Click the* **Paste** *command in the* **Clipboard** *group.*

If you copy and paste data from Excel, the data is displayed in a Word table.

If you wish to copy the entire contents of an existing Word file into your document, you could insert it.

1 *Position the insertion point where you want the text to appear.*
2 *Display the* **Insert** *tab.*

3 *Click the arrow beside the* **Object** *button in the* **Text** *group.*
4 *Select* **Text from File...**
5 *Locate and select the file required.*
6 *Click* **Insert** *at the dialog box.*

LINKING DATA

You can copy data into Word with a link to the original data in Excel. A representation of the data is displayed in Word, but the actual data is held and updated in Excel. This option is useful when the file size is a consideration, or when it is important that the data in Word is kept in line with the data in Excel.

If you wish to link the data that you paste from Excel to the source file, follow the Copy and Paste instructions above, then click the Paste Options button and choose the link option required.

○	Keep Source Formatting
○	Match Destination Table Style
○	Paste as Picture
○	Keep Text Only
○	Keep Source Formatting and Link to Excel
◉	Match Destination Table Style and Link to Excel

Linked objects

By default, the updating option for linked objects is set to Automatic. This means that the file in Word is updated automatically each time you open it, or each time the source data in Excel is updated when the destination file in Word is open.

View Side by Side

If you want to compare the contents of one document with another you can view them side by side. Open both documents and then display the View tab and click View Side by Side in the Window group. By default the windows will be synchronized – click Synchronous Scrolling in the Window group to toggle this option.

5.19 Keyboard shortcuts

Some useful keyboard shortcuts when working in Word – try them out and learn any that could be useful to you.

Keystrokes	Effect
[Ctrl]-[B]	Toggle bold
[Ctrl]-[U]	Toggle underline
[Ctrl]-[I]	Toggle italics
[Shift]-[Ctrl]-[+]	Superscript
[Ctrl]-[=]	Subscript
[Ctrl]-[D]	Display Font dialog box
[Shift]-[F3]	Change case
[Shift]-[Ctrl]-[C]	Copy formatting
[Shift]-[Ctrl]-[V]	Paste formatting
[Ctrl]-[Shift]-[Space]	Create a non-breaking space
[Ctrl]-[1]	Single line spacing
[Ctrl]-[5]	One and a half line spacing
[Ctrl]-[2]	Double line spacing
[F5] or [Ctrl]-[G]	Go to tab
[Ctrl]-[F]	Find
[Ctrl]-[H]	Replace
[Shift]-[Enter]	Manual line break
[Ctrl]-[Enter]	Manual page break
[Ctrl]-[M]	Increase left indent
[Shift]-[Ctrl]-[M]	Decrease left indent
[Ctrl]-[T]	Increase hanging indent
[Shift]-[Ctrl]-[T]	Decrease hanging indent
[Ctrl]-[Hyphen]	Insert optional hyphen

TEST

1 *Give two examples of non-printing characters.*

2 *How can you display these characters?*

3 *You can select text by dragging over it, or using [Click]-[Shift]-[Click]. What other method can be used to select a:*
   ▷ *Word*
   ▷ *Sentence*
   ▷ *Paragraph*
   ▷ *Whole document*

4 *How can you insert a manual page break?*

5 *What is a Word template?*

6 *Text can be formatted using the font format options. What feature allows you to apply a set of saved formatting options?*

7 *If you want something repeated at the top or bottom of each page in a document, where should you enter it?*

8 *How do you insert a new row at the end of a table in Word?*

9 *What two files do you need before you can perform a mail merge?*

10 *How can you keep data that has been copied and pasted from Excel into Word up-to-date with the Excel data.*

6

··

Spreadsheets

In this chapter you will learn:
- *the basic skills required in Excel*
- *how to enter and format text and data*
- *about formulas and functions*
- *how to sort data*
- *how to create and format charts*

6.1 The Excel screen

When you start Excel, you are presented with a new workbook displaying a blank worksheet. If the Workbook window is maximized, the workbook and the application share one Title bar containing the application and workbook names.

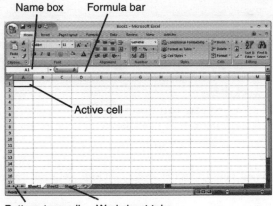

Name box   Formula bar

Active cell

Buttons to scroll   Worksheet tabs
through sheets

6.2 Workbooks and worksheets

When working in Excel, the files that you work with are called workbooks. Each consists of a number of worksheets (the default is three). You can add more worksheets if necessary, or remove any that you don't need. Related data is usually best kept on separate worksheets within the same workbook – this makes it easier to find and manage your data.

WORKSHEETS

The worksheet tabs appear at the bottom left of your screen, to the left of the horizontal scrollbar.

To move from one sheet to another:
▶ *Click the tab of the sheet you want to work on.*

If you can't see all the sheet tabs in the bar, you can use the navigation buttons to the left of the sheet tabs to scroll the sheet tabs into view.

To insert a new worksheet:
▶ *Click the* **Insert Worksheet** *tab (to the right of the existing sheet tabs).*

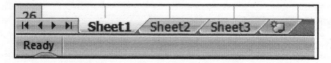

To delete a worksheet:
You can delete any sheets you don't need.
1 *Right-click on the tab of the sheet you wish to remove.*
2 *Click* **Delete** *in the pop-up menu.*

Be careful when deleting worksheets – Undo will not restore them for you!

You can also insert and delete sheets from the Home tab.

1 *Display the* **Home** *tab.*
2 *Click the drop-down arrow to the right of* **Insert** *or* **Delete** *in the* **Cells** *group.*
3 *Select* **Insert Sheet** *or* **Delete Sheet** *from the list of options.*

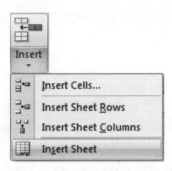

To rename a worksheet:
By default, worksheets are named Sheet1, Sheet2, etc. You can easily rename the worksheets to give them a name that actually means something.

1 *Double-click on the sheet tab you want to rename.*
2 *Type in the new name.*
3 *Press* [**Enter**] *or click anywhere on the sheet.*

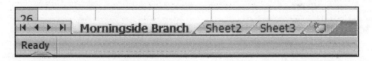

To move or copy a worksheet:
You can easily move or copy a worksheet within the workbook, or to another open workbook.

1 *Display the worksheet that you want to move or copy.*
2 *Right-click on its tab and choose* **Move or Copy...**

3 *Choose the book you want to move or copy the worksheet to in the* **To book:** *field.*

4 *Select a sheet – this doesn't apply if you choose new book in the* **To book:** *field.*

5 *Tick the* **Create a copy** *checkbox if you want to make a copy of the sheet rather than move it.*

6 *Click* **OK** *– the sheet will be inserted before the one you selected.*

If you move or copy your worksheet to a new book, remember to save the new workbook.

Moving by dragging

You can also move or copy worksheets within a workbook by dragging them to the position required.

To move the worksheet:

▶ *Click and drag the tab of the worksheet you want to move, along the sheet tabs until it is in the correct place.*

To copy the worksheet:

▶ *Click on the worksheet tab, hold down [Ctrl] and drag the worksheet tab to the required position.*

6.3 Spreadsheet jargon

Before going any further, spend a little time getting familiar with some of the jargon you will encounter. There's nothing difficult about it – once you know what it means!

ROWS, COLUMNS AND CELLS

The worksheet area consists of rows, columns and cells. Rows are identified by the numbers displayed down the left side of the worksheet area. There are lots of rows on a worksheet – 1,048,576 in fact!

Columns are identified by letters displayed along the top of the worksheet area. After Z, columns are labelled AA to AZ, then BA to BZ, and so on to XFD, giving 16,384 columns in all.

Where a row and column intersect you have a cell. These are identified using a cell address which consists of the letter of the column followed by the number of the row that intersect at it.

Cell A1, B9, C3, E7 and G4 have been highlighted in the screenshot.

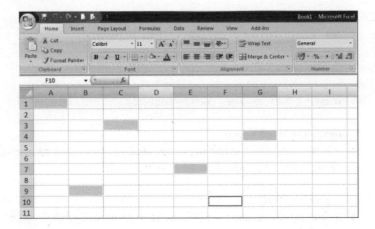

TEXT, DATA, FORMULAS AND FUNCTIONS

The cells can contain text, numeric data, formulas or functions.

Text is used for titles or narrative to describe the figures you are presenting – worksheet headings, column and row labels will usually be text entries.

Numeric data means the figures that appear in your worksheet. The data may be entered through the keyboard, or it may be generated as the result of a calculation.

Formulas are used to perform calculations on your data. They are used to add the value in one cell to that in another or multiply the values in different cells, etc. Some of your formulas will be very basic while others may be quite complex.

Functions are predefined formulas that perform simple or complex calculations. There are many different kinds – statistical, logical, financial, database, engineering and more. You're bound to find some useful ones, whatever type of data you work with.

6.4 Moving around your worksheet

Before you can enter anything into a cell, you must make it active. The active cell has a dark border and its address appears in the Name box to the left of the formula bar. You can move into a cell (thus making it active) using the keyboard or the mouse.

Navigation with the mouse
▶ *Scroll the cell into view if necessary and click.*

Navigation with the keyboard
To go to the next cell:
▶ *Use the [Up], [Down], [Left] and [Right] arrow keys.*

To move onto the cell below:
▶ *Press* [Enter].

To go to a specific cell address:
1 *Press* [F5].
2 *At the* Go To *dialog box, enter the address in the* Reference *field.*
3 *Click* OK.

To go to cell A1:
▶ *Press [Ctrl]-[Home].*

To move to the end of your work area:
▶ *Press [Ctrl]-[End].*

Check out the Excel shortcut and function keys in the online Help to see if there are any others that you would find useful.

6.5 Selection techniques

You will often work on more than one cell at a time. You may need to format a group of cells in a particular way or copy or move a group, or apply a function to a group of cells.

A group of cells is called a range. Ranges are identified by using the first cell address followed by the last cell address in the group of cells you wish to work on, e.g. A1:A7, C3:D12, F5:H6 are highlighted in the picture below.

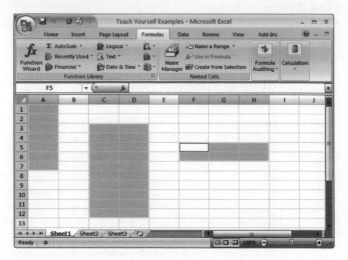

The simplest way to select ranges is to use the mouse.

To select a group of adjacent cells:
► *Click and drag.*

To select a group of adjacent cells:
1 *Click on a cell in one corner of the range.*
2 *Hold down* [Shift] *and click on the cell in the diagonally opposite corner of the range.*

To select a row:
► *Click the number to the left of the row you want to select.*

To select several adjacent rows:
► *Click and drag down over the numbers to the left of the rows.*

To select a column:
► *Click the letter at the top of the column.*

To select several adjacent columns:
▶ *Click and drag across the letters at the top of the columns.*

To select the whole worksheet:
▶ *Click the box at the top left of the row and column headers*

To select a range of non-adjacent cells:
1 *Click on one of the cells you want to select.*
2 *Hold down* [Ctrl] *and click on each of the other cells.*

To deselect a range of cells:
▶ *Click on any cell in your worksheet or press any arrow key.*

6.6 Entering text and numeric data

Entering text or data into your worksheet is easy.

1 *Select the cell you want to enter text or data into.*
2 *Type in the text or data – the text or data will appear in the Formula bar as well as in the active cell.*
3 *Press* [Enter] *or click the 'tick' button to the left of the Formula bar when you've completed the cell.*

Things to note when entering text:

▶ *Text automatically aligns to the left of a cell.*
▶ *Text that doesn't fit into a single cell will spill over into the cell to the right if it is empty.*
▶ *Excess text will not be displayed if the cell to the right is not empty.*

Things to note when entering numeric data:

▶ *Numeric data automatically aligns to the right of a cell.*

▶ *If a cell displays ########, you need to change the number format or make the column wider to display the figures.*

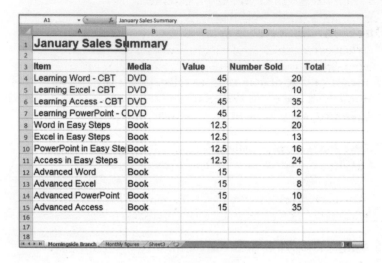

6.7 Editing text and numeric data

If you make an error when entering your work, you can fix things by deleting, replacing or editing the contents of the cell.

To delete the contents of a cell (or cells):
   1 *Select the cell (or cells) whose contents you want to erase.*
   2 *Press [Delete].*

To replace the contents of a cell:
   1 *Select the cell whose contents you want to replace.*
   2 *Type in the text or data that should be in the cell.*

To edit the contents of a cell:
   1 *Select the cell whose contents you want to edit.*
   2 *Click in the Formula bar to place the insertion point in it.*

Or

▶ *Double-click in the cell to place the insertion point in it.*

3 *Edit the cell contents and press* [**Enter**].

One item per cell

When entering text or data into a worksheet, each cell should contain one piece of data only. For example, if entering names, put the first name in one cell and the surname in another. When entering a product list, put the code in one cell, description in another, price in another, etc.

This will make sorting and searching the worksheet much easier.

When entering a list of data, don't leave blank rows/columns within the list. Format the cells as necessary to enhance its appearance, but try to avoid leaving blank rows/columns. Blank rows/columns can cause problems when sorting or charting the data.

6.8 Row height and column width

All the columns are the same width unless you change them.

To change the height of a row manually:

▶ *Click and drag the dividing line (in the row number area) under the row whose height you want to adjust e.g. to change the height of row 5 drag the line between rows 5 and 6.*

To adjust the row height automatically:

▶ *Double-click the dividing line below the row you want to adjust. Its height will adjust to fit its contents.*

To change the width of a column manually:

▶ *Drag the dividing line (in the heading area) to the right of the column whose width you want to change, e.g. to change the width of column B drag the line between columns B and C.*

To adjust the column width automatically:

▶ *Double-click the dividing line to the right of a column. Its width will change to accommodate the widest entry.*

You can also adjust the row height or column width from the Home tab.

1 *Click in the row or column.*

Or

▶ *Select the range of rows or columns.*
2 *Click the drop-down arrow on the* **Format** *command in the* **Cells** *group.*
3 *Select the* **Cell Size** *option, e.g.* **Row Height...** *or* **Column Width...**
4 *Specify the size required.*
5 *Click* **OK.**

6.9 Insert/delete rows and columns

If you have typed up your spreadsheet, but missed out a row(s) or column(s) in the middle of it, you can easily insert them. You can also delete unwanted rows or columns.

To insert a row:

1 *Select a cell in the row that will go below the new row.*
2 *Display the* **Home** *tab.*
3 *Click the down arrow to the right of the* **Insert** *command in the* **Cells** *group.*
4 *Select* **Insert Sheet Rows.**

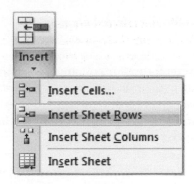

Or

5 *Select the row that will be below the inserted row.*

6 *Right-click within the selected area and choose* **Insert** *from the pop-up menu.*

To insert a column:

1 *Select a cell in the column that will go to the right of the new column.*

2 *On the* **Home** *tab, click the down arrow to the right of the* **Insert** *command in the* **Cells** *group.*

3 *Select* **Insert Sheet Columns.**

Or

4 *Select the column that will go to the right of the column you are inserting.*

5 *Right-click in the selected area and choose* **Insert.**

To delete a row or column:

1 *Select a cell in the row or column you wish to delete.*

2 *Display the* **Home** *tab.*

3 *Select the* **Delete Sheet Rows** *or* **Delete Sheet Columns** *from the* **Delete** *command options.*

Or

4 *Select the row or column you wish to delete.*

5 *Right-click within the selected area.*
6 *Choose* **Delete.**

To add or delete several rows or columns at a time:
1 *Click and drag in the row or column label area to indicate the number of rows or columns you want to insert or delete.*
2 *On the* **Home** *tab, select an option from the* **Insert** *or* **Delete** *command buttons in the* **Cells** *group.*
Or
3 *Right-click in the selected area and choose* **Insert** *or* **Delete.**

Switching between workbooks

If you have more than one workbook open, you can move between them by pointing to the application icon on the Taskbar, then click on the workbook you want to display.

6.10 Fitting text into cells

When entering text into cells you might want to try some other formatting options to help you display your work effectively. These options can be used on any cells, but may be particularly effective on column headings. They include merged cells, text wrapping, orientation and vertical alignment. They can all be found in the Alignment group on the Home tab.

To change the orientation:
1 *Select the cells you want to format.*
2 *Click the drop-down arrow beside the* **Orientation** *command button.*
3 *Select the orientation required.*

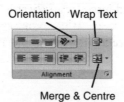

Orientation   Wrap Text

Merge & Centre

To turn on text wrapping:
1 *Select the cells you want to format.*
2 *Click the* **Wrap Text** *command button.*

To set Merge and Centre:
1 *Select the cells you want to merge.*
2 *Click the arrow beside the* **Merge and Centre** *button.*
3 *Select the option required.*

You may need to adjust the row height or column width manually if it doesn't adjust automatically to accommodate the alignment options you choose.

These options and others can also be set in the Format Cells dialog box. Click the Format Cells: Alignment dialog box launcher in the Alignment group to open the dialog box at the Alignment tab.

Cut and Paste

You can move and copy data – within a worksheet, between worksheets and from one workbook to another using normal copy/cut and paste techniques.

To move or copy data into an existing list and move the existing data left or down to make space:
1 *Copy or cut the data you want to move.*
2 *Right-click where you want to move it to.*
3 *Choose* **Insert Copied cells…** *or* **Insert Cut cells.**

6.11 Number formats

A lot of the data entered into a worksheet is currency. Most of the times that you enter currency values, you will want the appropriate currency symbol to precede the figure – usually, but not always, a £, $ or € symbol.

If you want the £ symbol in front of a figure you can either:

▶ *Format the cells to display the entry in a currency format.*
Or
▶ *Enter the £ symbol through the keyboard.*

If you enter your figures through the numeric keypad, it's probably easiest to format the cells to display the figures as currency.

You can format cells before or after you have entered your text or data.

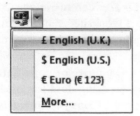

To display the figures in currency format (£):
1 *Select the cells you want to format.*
2 *Click the* **Accounting Number Format** *command button in the* **Number** *group on the* **Home** *tab.*

To display the figures with £ or $ signs:
1 *Select the cells you want to format.*
2 *Click the drop-down arrow beside the* **Accounting Number Format** *button in the* **Number** *group on the b tab.*
3 *Select the currency format required.*

On UK keyboards, the shortcut for the € is [Alt Gr]-[4]. If this doesn't work on your keyboard, check out 'How to type the Euro sign' in the online Help.

	A	B	C	D	E	F
1	**January Sales Summary**					
2						
3	**Item**	**Media**	**Value**	**Number Sold**	**Total**	
4	Learning Word - CBT	DVD	£45.00	20		
5	Learning Excel - CBT	DVD	£45.00	10		
6	Learning Access - CBT	DVD	£45.00	35		
7	Learning PowerPoint - CBT	DVD	£45.00	12		
8	Word in Easy Steps	Book	£12.50	20		
9	Excel in Easy Steps	Book	£12.50	13		
10	PowerPoint in Easy Steps	Book	£12.50	16		
11	Access in Easy Steps	Book	£12.50	24		
12	Advanced Word	Book	£15.00	6		
13	Advanced Excel	Book	£15.00	8		
14	Advanced PowerPoint	Book	£15.00	10		
15	Advanced Access	Book	£15.00	35		
16						

The Number group has other formatting options – Percent, Comma, Increase and Decrease Decimal. Others can be found in the Number Format list. You can access even more formatting options in the Format Cells dialog box.

To apply a format from the Format Cells dialog box:
1 *Select the cells you want to format.*

2 *Click the* **Format Cells: Number** *dialog box launcher in the*
   Number *group.*
3 *Choose a category from the list, e.g. Currency.*
4 *Complete the dialog box as required, e.g. you may want*
   to select a different symbol if the currency isn't the pound
   sterling.
5 *Click* **OK.**

Date formats

When you enter a date e.g. 10/2/10, the default date format
used is a short date e.g. 10/02/2010. You can change to a
long date format from the Number Format drop down list
(Home tab, Number group). Other date formats can be
found in the Format cells dialog box, Number tab, Date
category.

6.12 Freeze/unfreeze headings

Many of the worksheets you create will be too large to fit on to
your screen. You will need to scroll vertically and horizontally to
display the data you want to work with. When you scroll your
worksheet, the column headings or row labels will disappear
off-screen as other data appears. This can be inconvenient, as you
need to see the headings or labels to make sense of your data. In a
situation like this, you can freeze part of the worksheet window so
that it doesn't move, and scroll the 'unfrozen' part.

To freeze the top row of your worksheet:
1 *Display the* **View** *tab.*
2 *Click* **Freeze Panes** *in the* **Window** *group.*
3 *Select* **Freeze Top Row.**

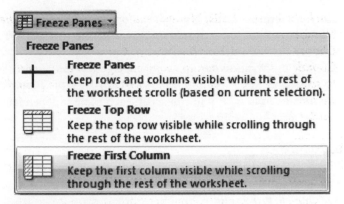

To freeze the first column:

1 *Display the* View *tab.*
2 *Click* Freeze Panes *in the* Window *group.*
3 *Select* Freeze First Column.

To freeze panes above/to the left of the current cell:

1 *Select the cell you want to freeze panes above/to the left.*
2 *Click* Freeze Panes *in the* Window *group.*
3 *Select* Freeze Panes *from the options.*

To unfreeze panes:

1 *Display the* View *tab.*
2 *Click* Freeze Panes *in the* Window *group.*
3 *Select* Unfreeze Panes *from the options.*

6.13 Split screen

There will also be times when you want to compare the data on one part of your worksheet with that on another – but the data ranges that you want to compare are in separate areas of the worksheet. When this happens, you should split your screen so that you can scroll each part independently, to bring the data you require into view.

To split your screen:
1 *Select the cell you want to split the screen above or to the left of.*
2 *Display the* **View** *tab.*
3 *Click in the* **Window** *group.*

When your screen is split, you can scroll each pane independently to view the data you want to see.

To remove a split:
▶ *Click* **Split** *in the* **Window** *group on the* **View** *tab.*
Or
▶ *Double-click the split.*

USING THE SPLIT BOXES

Alternatively, you can use the split boxes to split your screen.

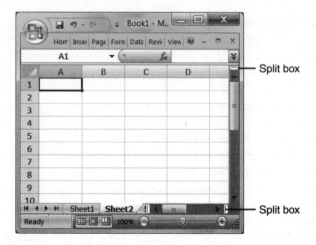

If you look carefully at the top of the vertical scroll bar (above the up arrow), or to the right of the horizontal scroll bar (outside the right arrow), you will notice the split box.

To split your screen horizontally:
▶ *Drag the split box at the top of the vertical scroll bar down to where you want your split to be (or double-click on the split box).*

To split your screen vertically:
▶ *Drag the split box at the right of the horizontal scroll bar along to where you want your split to be (or double-click on the split box).*

6.14 Formulas

Any cell in your worksheet which will contain a figure that has been calculated using other entries in your worksheet should have a formula or function in it (do not do your calculations on a calculator, and then type the answer into your worksheet).

Formulas allow you to add, subtract, multiply, divide and work out percentages of the values in cells.

OPERATORS USED IN FORMULAS

+ Add   – Subtract   / Divide

* Multiply   % Percentage

Formula examples – and note that formulas start with '=':

=A7/B6	Divide the figure in A7 by the figure in B6
=D22*12	Multiply the figure in D22 by 12
=C7*25%	Calculate 25% of the figure in C7

Order of precedence
If there is a mixture of operators, Excel will deal with multiplication and division before addition and subtraction, e.g.

=A4+C7*D7	Multiply the figure in C7 by the one in D7, and add the answer to the figure in A4

Parentheses (brackets)

Some formulas can become quite long and complicated. If you want to force the order in which a formula is worked, or make a long formula easier to read, you must use parentheses ( ). In this example, the problem within each set of parentheses is solved before working through the formula, from left to right.

$$=((A_1+B_2)*C_3) - (D_4/E_5)$$

Add A1 to B2	we'll call this XX
Multiply XX by C3	we'll call this YY
Divide D4 by E5	we'll call this ZZ
Subtract ZZ from YY	

Remember the BODMAS rule: Brackets before Division, Multiplication, Addition then Subtraction!

ENTERING FORMULAS

You can enter a formula either by typing it into the Formula bar, or by pointing with the mouse. Let's say that you wanted to enter the formula =C4*D4 into cell E4. You would:

1 *Select the cell that will contain the formula, E4.*
2 *Type =*
3 *Either type C4*D4*
Or
  ▶ *Click on C4, type '*', and then click on D4.*
4 *Press* [Enter].

	A	B	C	D	E
	SUM ▼ (X ✓ Ａ =C4*D4				
1	**January Sales Summary**				
2					
3	Item	Media	Value	Number Sold	Total
4	Learning Word - CBT	DVD	£ 45.00	20	=C4*D4
5	Learning Excel - CBT	DVD	£ 45.00	10	
6	Learning Access - CBT	DVD	£ 45.00	35	
7	Learning PowerPoint - CBT	DVD	£ 45.00	12	
8	Word in Easy Steps	Book	£ 12.50	20	
9	Excel in Easy Steps	Book	£ 12.50	13	
10	PowerPoint in Easy Steps	Book	£ 12.50	16	
11	Access in Easy Steps	Book	£ 12.50	24	
12	Advanced Word	Book	£ 15.00	6	
13	Advanced Excel	Book	£ 15.00	8	
14	Advanced PowerPoint	Book	£ 15.00	10	
15	Advanced Access	Book	£ 15.00	35	
16					

6.15 AutoFill

AutoFill can be used to copy formulas down columns or across rows. In the screenshot, the formula in cell E4 is =C4*D4. We need a similar formula in the other cells in the column. You could enter them following the instructions above, substituting the appropriate cell addresses as required. Or, you could use AutoFill.

To complete the cells using AutoFill:
1 *Select E4.*
2 *Position the mouse pointer over the bottom right corner of the cell. The Fill Handle – a small black cross – should appear.*
3 *Click and drag the cross down over the other Total cells.*

When you release the mouse button, the formula in cell E4 will be copied to the cells you dragged over.

If you click on each cell in the *Total* column and keep an eye on the Formula bar, you will notice that Excel has automatically changed the cell addresses in the formula relative to the position you have copied the formula to.

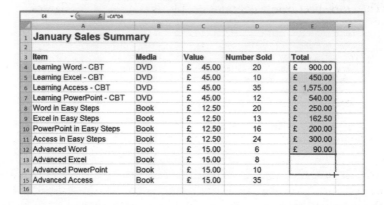

You can also use AutoFill to automatically generate days of the week, months of the year or dates.

Try the following:

1 *Enter January, Jan, Monday or Mon in any cell.*
2 *AutoFill it down or across.*

Dates

1 *Enter the first date in your series.*
2 *AutoFill using the right mouse button.*
3 *Select the Fill option (Days, Weekdays, Months or Years) required from the popup menu.*

AutoFill can be a real time saver when you are entering similar formula into adjacent cells, or are populating cell contents with data from a pre-defined series, e.g. days of the week, dates, etc.

6.16 AutoSum

The worksheet below contains details of monthly sales figures.

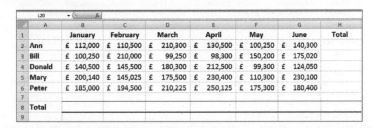

To calculate each sales rep's total for the period, and the total for each month, we could use formulas, e.g. =B2+B3+B4+B5+B6, but the easiest way to calculate a total is to use AutoSum.

To calculate the totals using AutoSum:
1 *Select a cell in which you want a total figure to appear, e.g. the one for the total of the first sales person or for January.*
2 *Click in the **Editing** group on the **Home** tab (or on the **Formulas** tab in the **Function Library** group). The range of cells that are going to be added together will be highlighted, and the function will appear in the Formula bar.*
3 *If the suggested range of cells is correct, press [**Enter**].*
Or
▶ *If the suggested range is not the range you want to total, drag over the correct range, and then press [**Enter**].*

	January	February	March	April	May	June	Total
Ann	£ 112,000	£ 110,500	£ 210,300	£ 130,500	£ 100,250	£ 140,300	=SUM(B2:G2)
Bill	£ 100,250	£ 210,000	£ 99,250	£ 98,300	£ 150,200	£ 175,020	SUM(number1, [number2], ...)
Donald	£ 140,500	£ 145,500	£ 180,300	£ 212,500	£ 99,300	£ 124,050	
Mary	£ 200,140	£ 145,025	£ 175,500	£ 230,400	£ 110,300	£ 230,100	
Peter	£ 185,000	£ 194,500	£ 210,225	£ 250,125	£ 175,300	£ 180,400	
Total							

Use AutoFill to copy the formula into the other total cells.

	A	B	C	D	E	F	G	H
		January	February	March	April	May	June	Total
1								
2	Ann	£ 112,000	£ 110,500	£ 210,300	£ 130,500	£ 100,250	£ 140,300	£ 803,850
3	Bill	£ 100,250	£ 210,000	£ 99,250	£ 98,300	£ 150,200	£ 175,020	£ 833,020
4	Donald	£ 140,500	£ 145,500	£ 180,300	£ 212,500	£ 99,300	£ 124,050	£ 902,150
5	Mary	£ 200,140	£ 145,025	£ 175,500	£ 230,400	£ 110,300	£ 230,100	£ 1,091,465
6	Peter	£ 185,000	£ 194,500	£ 210,225	£ 250,125	£ 175,300	£ 180,400	£ 1,195,550
7								
8	Total	£ 737,890	£ 805,525	£ 875,575	£ 921,825	£ 635,350	£ 849,870	£ 4,826,035
9								

You can also use AutoSum to total non-adjacent cells if you wish.

To total non-adjacent cells:
1 *Select the cell that will contain the result of the calculation.*
2 *Click the* **AutoSum** *tool in the* **Editing** *group.*
3 *Click on the first cell you want to include in the range.*
4 *Hold down* **[Ctrl]** *and click on each of the other cells to be included in the function.*
5 *Press* **[Enter]**.

To type the function into a cell, use '= SUM(cell range)'.
▶ *Start with an = (equals sign).*
▶ *AutoSum uses SUM(), a maths function. The data that the function is to work on is given in brackets after its name.*
▶ *A range of adjacent cells has the first address, followed by a colon, then the last address, e.g. =SUM(B2:G2).*
▶ *The addresses for non-adjacent cells must be separated by a comma, e.g. =SUM(B2,C6,D9).*

6.17 Statistical functions

Statistical functions include Minimum, Maximum, Average, Count, and many others. These can be used to display a value from a range of cells.

MIN returns the minimum value.

MAX returns the maximum value.

AVERAGE returns the average value.

COUNT returns the number of cells containing numbers.

You can use the drop-down list beside the AutoSum command to display the functions.

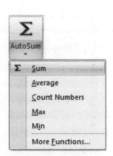

1 *Select the cell that the function will go in.*
2 *Click the arrow on the* **AutoSum** *command.*
3 *Select a function. If it is not listed, click* **More Functions...**, *and select it from the* **Insert Function** *dialog box.*
4 *Check/amend the cell range as necessary.*
5 *Click* **OK**.

You can also display the dialog box by clicking the Insert Function button to the left of the Formula bar.

INSERT FUNCTION DIALOG BOX

1 *Type a description of what you are trying to do and click* **Go**.
Or
▶ *Select a function* **Category**, *then select a* **Function**.
2 *Once you've selected the function, click* **OK** – *the* **Function Argument** *dialog box will be displayed, where you provide details of the range(s) you want the function to work on.*

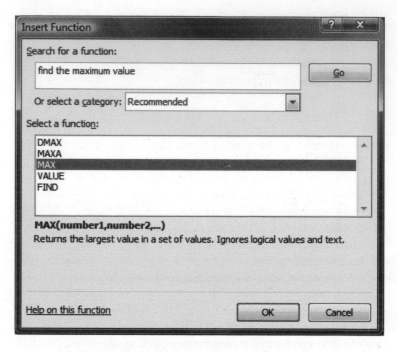

> ▷ If the function you want has been used recently, it will be listed in the **Most Recently Used** list.
> ▷ If you're not sure what category a function is in, select the **All** category (they are all listed here, in alphabetical order).
> ▷ Minimum, Maximum, Average and Count can be found in the Statistical category.

3 Enter the range you want the function to operate on – either drag over the range, or type the cell addresses.

▶ If necessary, minimize (click the **Collapse/Restore** button to the right of each argument field to collapse/restore the dialog box) or move the **Function Argument** dialog box so you can see your worksheet.

4 Click **OK**.

	A	B	C	D	E
1	END OF TERM EXAM RESULTS				
2					
3	Firstname	Surname	Mark awarded	Result	Grade
4	Gill	McLaren	45		
5	Pauline	Watson	65		
6	William	Smith	72		
7	Ann	Allan	48		
8	Andrew	Borthwick	52		
9	Peter	Jackson	91		
10	Alison	Smith	50		
11	Marion	Williamson	49		
12	Hector	Smith	68		
13	David	Watson	59		
14					
15	Highest mark	91			
16	Lowest mark	45			
17	Average mark	59.9			
18	Number of Students	10			

In this example, statistical functions were used to display:

▶ *The lowest result in each exam (Minimum)*
▶ *The highest result in each exam (Maximum)*
▶ *The average mark for each subject (Average)*
▶ *The number of students (Count).*

Other useful functions

CountA – Similar to Count, except that it is used to count cells containing text entries, whereas Count will count the number of cells containing numeric entries. The function will not count empty cells.

Round – Rounds a number to the number of digits specified. In the Formula bar the function would appear =Round(C3, 1) where C3 is the cell containing the figure that you want to round and 1 is how many digits that you want it to round to.

CountBlank – counts the number of empty/blank cells in a range. =CountBlank(range)

6.18 View formula

When setting up your worksheet, it is sometimes useful to display and print the formulas and functions that you have entered into the cells.

To toggle the display of the formulas:
1 *Display the* **Formulas** *tab.*
2 *Click in the* **Formula Auditing** *group, or use the keyboard shortcut* [**Ctrl**]-[¦].

You may need to adjust the column widths to display the whole formula or function in some columns.

▶ *You can print a copy of your worksheet with the formulas displayed – you may find it useful for reference purposes.*

The formulas used in the Exam Results sheet are displayed here.

15	Highest mark	=MAX(C4:C13)
16	Lowest mark	=MIN(C4:C13)
17	Average mark	=AVERAGE(C4:C13)
18	Number of Students	=COUNT(C4:C13)

6.19 Sort

The data in your worksheet can be sorted into ascending or descending order. A simple sort is where the data is sorted using the entries in one column only. You can also have more complex sorts, where you can sort on up to 64 columns at a time.

To perform a simple sort:
1 *Select any cell in the column you want to base your sort on.*
2 *Click* **Sort & Filter** *in the* **Editing** *group on the* **Home** *tab.*

3 *Choose* **Sort Smallest to Largest** *to sort in ascending order.*
Or
▶ **Sort Largest to Smallest** *to sort in descending order.*

If the selected cell contains text, the options are **Sort A to Z** and **Sort Z to A**.

The Sort commands can also be found on the Data tab, in the Sort & Filter group.

To perform a multi-level sort (on up to 64 columns):
1 *Select any cell within the area you want to sort.*
2 *Click the* **Sort & Filter** *command button.*
3 *Choose* **Custom Sort...** *to open the* **Sort** *dialog box.*

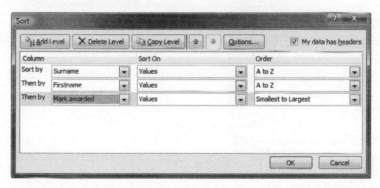

4 *Select the main sort column from the* **Sort by** *list.*
5 *Set the* **Sort On** *option – choose values if you are sorting by text, number or date or time – or cell colour, font colour or cell icon if you are sorting by format.*
6 *Choose the* **Order**.
7 *Click* **Add level** *to add the next column for the second level sort.*
8 *Repeat steps 4–7 as necessary.*
9 *Click* **OK**.

Note that Excel assumes that your list has a header row – the one that normally contains the column labels or field names. It your list doesn't have a header row, i.e. you want the first row included in the sort, deselect the My data has headers checkbox.

To delete a sort level:
1 *Open the* **Sort** *dialog box – click the* **Sort & Filter** *command button and then choose* **Custom Sort...**
2 *Select the sort row you wish to remove.*
3 *Click* **Delete Level** *and then* **OK**.

To change the sort level of an item:
1 *Open the* **Sort** *dialog box.*
2 *Select the sort row you wish to move.*
3 *Click the Up arrow or Down arrow to move the item.*
4 *Click* **OK**.

The list in the example above has been sorted into Surname order (ascending) then First name order (ascending).

6.20 IF function

IF is a logical function and is found in the *Logical* category. It is used to return one value if the condition you specify is True, and another value if the condition is False. The values returned can be text, numbers, or the result of a formula or function.

For example, we could use an IF function to indicate whether a student has passed or failed an exam. If a student has 50% or more in the exam, a pass will be awarded, if less than 50% is achieved, the result is a fail.

COMPARISON OPERATORS

This example uses a comparison operator to check if the Total Mark is greater than or equal to 50. The operators include:

=	equal to	<>	not equal to
>	greater than	>=	greater than or equal to
<	less than	<=	less than or equal to

To return a 'Pass' or 'Fail' message in the Result column, we need to enter the IF function.

To enter the IF function:
1 *Select the first cell in the result column.*
2 *Display the* **Formulas** *tab and select* **IF** *from the* **Logical Functions** *list. The* **Function Arguments** *dialog box is displayed.*

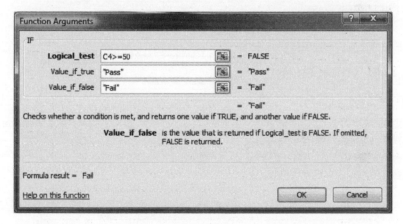

3 *Enter the condition in the* **Logical test** *field, e.g.* C4>=50.
4 *Specify the value if the condition is found to be true. You don't need to type in the quotes – Excel will add them automatically when you enter text.*
5 *Specify the value if the condition is found to be false.*
6 *Click* **OK**. *AutoFill the function down through the Result column. Pass will appear in the rows where the condition is true, Fail will appear in the rows where the condition is false.*

	A	B	C	D	E
1		END OF TERM EXAM RESULTS			
2					
3	Firstname	Surname	Mark awarded	Result	Grade
4	Gill	McLaren	45	Fail	
5	Pauline	Watson	65	Pass	
6	William	Smith	72	Pass	
7	Ann	Allan	48	Fail	
8	Andrew	Borthwick	52	Pass	
9	Peter	Jackson	91	Pass	
10	Alison	Smith	50	Pass	
11	Marion	Williamson	49	Fail	
12	Hector	Smith	68	Pass	
13	David	Watson	59	Pass	
14					

With the formulas displayed, the worksheet looks like the illustration below.

	A	B	C	D
1		END OF TERM EXAM RESULTS		
2				
3	Firstname	Surname	Mark awarded	Result
4	Gill	McLaren	45	=IF(C4>=50,"Pass","Fail")
5	Pauline	Watson	65	=IF(C5>=50,"Pass","Fail")
6	William	Smith	72	=IF(C6>=50,"Pass","Fail")
7	Ann	Allan	48	=IF(C7>=50,"Pass","Fail")
8	Andrew	Borthwick	52	=IF(C8>=50,"Pass","Fail")
9	Peter	Jackson	91	=IF(C9>=50,"Pass","Fail")
10	Alison	Smith	50	=IF(C10>=50,"Pass","Fail")
11	Marion	Williamson	49	=IF(C11>=50,"Pass","Fail")
12	Hector	Smith	68	=IF(C12>=50,"Pass","Fail")
13	David	Watson	59	=IF(C13>=50,"Pass","Fail")
14				

6.21 Relative and absolute addresses

You have noticed that when you AutoFill or copy a formula, the cell addresses used in the formula change automatically, relative to the position that you copy them to. By default, the addresses used in formulas are *relative addresses*.

There will be times when you use a cell address in a formula, and want to copy the formula down some rows or across some columns, but you don't want the cell address to change relative to its new position.

In this example, we are going to calculate the amount of pay due to our part-time staff, based on the hours they have worked plus their Christmas bonus.

The formula required in cell E6 is =D6+C3

The Christmas bonus cell, C3, must remain constant when we copy the formula down the column – we don't want it to change. To stop the cell address changing when we copy it, we must make it *absolute*. An absolute address will not change when the formula or function containing it is copied or moved.

To create an absolute cell address:
▶ *Enter a $ sign in front of each coordinate that you do not want to change. You can type the '$' sign, or press* [F4].

To create absolute addresses in a formula:
1 *Select the cell that contains the formula (E6 in this example) – the formula appears in the Formula bar.*
2 *Click in the Formula bar.*
3 *Place the insertion point to the right of the cell address (C3) you want to make absolute.*

	A	B	C	D	E	F
1	**December Pay Calculations**					
2						
3	**Christmas Bonus**		£ 20.00			
4						
5		Hourly Rate	Hours Worked	Basic Pay	Total Due	
6	Brian	£ 5.25	6	£ 31.50	=D6+$C$3	
7	Fiona	£ 6.00	3	£ 18.00		
8	Karen	£ 5.75	7	£ 40.25		
9	Robert	£ 6.20	2	£ 12.40		
10						

4 *Press* [F4] *until you have the cell addressed properly.*

▶ *Each time you press* [F4] *it moves through the four absolute addressing options.*

$C$1   neither coordinate will change
C$1   the column can change, but not the row
$C1   the row number can change, but not the column
C1   both coordinates will change

Your final worksheet should look similar to the one below. The first picture displays the formulas (you may have different cell addresses if you have used different rows and columns for your data), the second one shows the results.

	A	B	C	D	E
1	**December**				
2					
3	**Christmas B**		20		
4					
5		Hourly Rate	Hours Worked	Basic Pay	Total Due
6	Brian	5.25	6	=B6*C6	=D6+$C$3
7	Fiona	6	3	=B7*C7	=D7+$C$3
8	Karen	5.75	7	=B8*C8	=D8+$C$3
9	Robert	6.2	2	=B9*C9	=D9+$C$3

	A	B	C	D	E
1	**December Pay Calculations**				
2					
3	**Christmas Bonus**	**£ 20.00**			
4					
5		Hourly Rate	Hours Worked	Basic Pay	Total Due
6	Brian	£ 5.25	6	£ 31.50	£ 51.50
7	Fiona	£ 6.00	3	£ 18.00	£ 38.00
8	Karen	£ 5.75	7	£ 40.25	£ 60.25
9	Robert	£ 6.20	2	£ 12.40	£ 32.40

Common error messages

There will be times when error messages appear on your worksheet. Some of the common ones are described here.

Error:	Common reason:
#######	Column not wide enough
Value!	A value in a formula is of the wrong type, e.g. text
#DIV/o!	You are dividing by a cell that is empty or contains o
#REF!	The cell referenced has been deleted
#NAME?	Excel doesn't recognize the reference or cell name used in a formula.

Full details of error messages, possible causes and solutions, are available in the online Help.

6.22 Preview, Page Setup and Print

It is very important that the worksheet that you print and distribute is accurate and well presented. You must check the accuracy of the each spreadsheet carefully, e.g. spellcheck the file, check that the data and formulas are correct.

In addition to this, there are several options that you can use to ensure that your worksheet is displayed effectively.

PRINT PREVIEW

At some stage you will want to print your file. Before sending a worksheet to print, it's a good idea to preview it.

▶ *Click* **Print Preview** *on the Quick Access toolbar (see Section 4.2 for instructions on customizing the toolbar if necessary).*

Or

▶ *Press* [**Ctrl**]-[**F2**].

Or

▶ *Click the* **Microsoft Office** *button, select* **Print** *and then* **Print Preview.**

You cannot edit an Excel worksheet in Print Preview. If you want to change something when you see the preview, close the preview to return to your worksheet.

The Excel Print Preview tab has the following options.

Margins, orientation and page size are discussed in Section 4.6.

Scale to Fit

If a worksheet is more than a page in size, you can specify the number of pages you want it to be printed on using the Scale to Fit group on the Page Layout tab.

1 *Specify the number of pages wide in the* **Width** *field.*

Width:	Automatic ▾
Height:	Automatic ▾
Scale:	100% ↕
Scale to Fit	⤓

And/or

  2 *The number of pages high in the* **Height** *field.*

Or

  3 *Leave both the* **Width** *and* **Height** *field at automatic, and set the percentage scaling that you wish to use.*

Scaling can be very useful if the last page of your worksheet contains only a small amount of data. You can specify that the worksheet prints on one page less than it really needs – Excel will scale it down to fit onto that number of pages.

Headers and footers

To insert a header or footer:

▶ *Click the* **Header & Footer** *command in the* **Text** *group on the* **Insert** *tab.*

There are three sections to the header and footer area – at the left, in the middle and at the right.

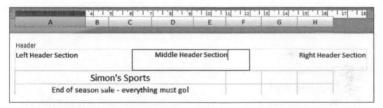

  1 *To move from one section to another, just click in it, or press* **[Tab]** *to cycle through the sections.*

  2 *Type your header and/or footer in through the keyboard.*

Or

To insert a standard header or footer, e.g. combinations of the sheet name, workbook name and other elements:

▶ *Display the options available in the* **AutoHeader** *and* **AutoFooter** *lists and select the options required.*

To remove a header or footer:

▶ *Choose* **None** *from the* **AutoHeader** *or* **AutoFooter** *list.*

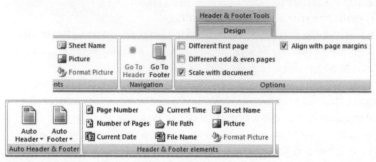

Header and Footer tab.

To insert individual standard elements:

▶ *Use the buttons in the* **Header & Footer elements** *group.*

To move between the Header and Footer areas:

▶ *Use the buttons in the* **Navigation** *group.*

To add a page number:

1 *Click in the area that you want to contain the page number.*

2 *Click* **Page Number** *in the* **Header & Footer elements** *group.*

Other options are available in the Options group.

When you choose the Header & Footer command, Excel takes your worksheet into Page Layout view. You can use the View buttons at the bottom right of the screen to return to Normal view, or display the View tab and choose Normal from the Workbook View group.

Gridlines, row and column headings

Another useful page layout feature in Excel is printing the gridlines and/or row and column headings on a worksheet. You might not want to print these areas out on a final copy of your worksheet, but there are times when this option is useful, e.g. when printing out the formulas and functions.

To print the gridlines:
▶ *Select the* **Print** *checkbox in the* **Gridlines** *section for the* **Sheet Options** *group.*

To print the row and column headings:
▶ *Select the* **Print** *option in the* **Headings** *section of the group.*

Page order
If your worksheet is going to print out on more than one sheet of paper, the pages can be printed down then across, or across then down. You can specify the order you prefer.

1 *Click the* **Page Setup** *dialog box launcher.*
2 *Select the* **Sheet** *tab.*
3 *In the* **Page order** *options, select the order required.*
4 *Click* **OK.**

Breaks
Page breaks are inserted automatically by Excel if your data will not fit onto one sheet of paper. If the automatic page breaks do not occur exactly where you would want them, you can insert manual page breaks.

To insert a horizontal page break:
▶ *Select the cell (or the whole row) below where you want to insert a page break.*

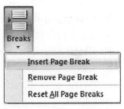

To insert a vertical page break:
▶ *Select the cell in row 1 (or select the column) to the right of where you want to insert a page break.*

To insert a horizontal and vertical page break at the same time:
1 *Select the cell immediately below and to the right of where you want to start a new page.*
2 *Click the* **Breaks** *button on the* **Page Setup** *group.*
3 *Select* **Insert Page Break.** *A page break will be inserted above the current row or to the left of the current column.*

To remove a page break:
 1 *Select any cell in the row below the page break you wish to remove.*
Or
 ▶ *Select any cell in the column to the right of the page break you wish to remove.*
 2 *Click the* **Breaks** *button on the* **Page Setup** *group.*
 3 *Select* **Remove Page Break.**

To remove all page breaks:
 1 *Select any cell in your worksheet.*
 2 *Click the* **Breaks** *button on the* **Page Setup** *group.*
 3 *Select* **Reset All Page Breaks.**

To repeat rows at top of page
If you have a big spreadsheet, with headings that you would like repeated at the top of each printed page, you can use the Repeat rows at top of page option.

 1 *Display the* **Page Setup** *dialog box.*
 2 *Select the* **Sheet** *tab.*
 3 *Click in the* **Print Titles** *area, in the* **Rows to repeat** *at top field.*
 4 *Enter the range required e.g. 1:3.*
Or
 ▶ *Drag over the range required.*
 5 *Click* **OK.**

Print Area
When you preview or print your worksheet, the print area is the area that Excel will select by default.

If you regularly print part of your worksheet, you can specify the range as a print area. A print area remains set until you clear it.

To set the print area:
1 *Select the range of cells.*
2 *Go to the* **Page Setup** *group on the* **Page Layout** *tab.*
3 *Click* **Print Area.**
4 *Select* **Set Print Area.**

If you have a print area set, and wish to print a different range of cells you can still select a range of cells and print (see below) using print selection.

If you have a print area set and wish to print the whole sheet:
1 *Click the Microsoft Office button.*
2 *Select* **Print,** *then* **Print...** *from the menu.*
3 *In the Print dialog box, select* **Active sheet** *in the* **Print what** *options.*
4 *Select the* **Ignore Print area** *checkbox.*
5 *Click* **OK.**

To remove a print area:
1 *Go to the* **Page Setup** *group on the* **Page Layout** *tab.*
2 *Click* **Print Area.**
3 *Select* **Clear Print Area.**
▶ *Once you have a print area set, you can add more cells to it. These will normally be adjacent to the original print area.*

6.23 Charts

Excel can create charts, bar and line graphs, pie charts, scatter diagrams, etc., from the data in your worksheet. The chart can be an object on the same worksheet as the data on which it is built, or on a separate chart sheet.

Data that you want to chart should ideally be in cells that are adjacent to each other. If the area has blank rows or columns within it, remove these before you try to chart the data.

▶ *When non-adjacent cells are selected, the selected areas must be able to combine to form a rectangle.*

To chart data that is not in adjacent cells:
1 *Select the first group of cells you want to chart.*
2 *Hold down [Ctrl] while you click and drag over the other groups you want to include in your chart.*

Depending on the type of data, it must be laid out correctly on the sheet to chart it successfully. See 'How to arrange data for specific chart types' in 'Create a Chart' in the online Help.

CREATING A CHART

To create a chart:
1 *Select the cells you want to create a chart from.*
2 *On the* **Insert** *tab, in the charts group, click the chart type button and then click on the subtype you want to use.*
Or
▶ *Click* **All Chart Types** *at the bottom of the drop-down list to display the* **Create Chart** *dialog box, where all chart types and subtypes are located and select the chart type you want to use from here and click* **OK**.

The resulting chart is embedded within the worksheet that contains the source data.

When the chart is selected the Chart Tools appear on the Ribbon. The tools have three tabs – Design, Layout and Format.

▶ *If you click outside the* **Chart** *area, the* **Chart Tools** *disappear. Click within the* **Chart** *area again and they reappear.*

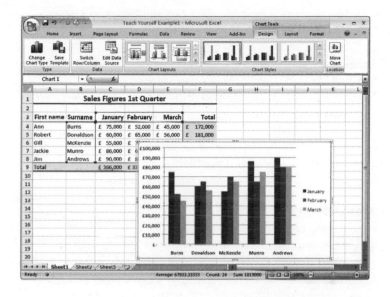

The Design tab in Chart tools.

Quick charts!

You can create a default chart quickly by selecting the data you with to chart, and then press [F11].

MOVE, RESIZE AND DELETE CHARTS

If you want to move, resize or delete a chart that is an object on a worksheet, you must select the chart first.

To move the chart:
1 *Select the chart.*
2 *Point to the edge of the chart – the mouse pointer changes to a 4-headed arrow when you are in the correct place.*
3 *Drag and drop the chart in its new location.*

To move a chart to a new location e.g. another sheet:

1 *Select the* **Design** *tab from the* **Chart Tools** *tabs.*
2 *Click* **Move Chart** *in the* **Location** *group.*
3 *Select the location.*
4 *Click* **OK**.

To resize the chart:

1 *Select the chart.*
2 *Point to a handle in a corner or on an edge – the pointer changes to a 2-headed arrow when in the correct place.*
3 *Click and drag to resize the chart.*

To delete the chart:

▶ *Select the chart and press* [**Delete**].

If your chart doesn't look the way you expected, and you think a different chart type would be better, you can change the type.

1 *Click* **Change Chart Type** *in the* **Type** *group on the* **Design** *tab.*
2 *Select the type and subtype required.*
3 *Click* **OK**.

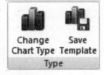

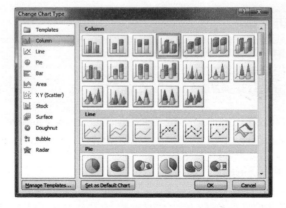

CHART OBJECTS

Each area of your chart is an object – you have a chart area object, plot area object, category axis object, legend object, etc. The chart must be selected (if it is an object in your workbook) before you can select the individual objects within it.

To select a chart object:
▶ *Choose the object from the* **Chart Objects** *list.*
Or
▶ *Click on the object you want to select.*

CHART STYLES AND LAYOUTS

Excel has a variety of chart layouts and styles that you can use to quickly adjust and format your chart.

Chart Style
The chart styles give you access to a wide range of carefully colour coordinated options that can be applied to your chart.

To change the chart style:
1 *Select your chart.*
2 *Scroll through the* **Chart Style** *options on the* **Design** *tab of the* **Chart** *tools.*
Or

▶ *Click the* **More** *button at the bottom right of the* **Chart Style** *group to display all the styles available.*
3 *Select the one you want to use.*

Chart Layout
The layout affects the inclusion and positioning of objects like the heading, legend, data table, axis labels, etc. The quickest way

to include or exclude objects from your chart is to use one of the predefined chart layouts.

1 *Select your chart.*
2 *Scroll through the* **Chart Layout** *options on the* **Design** *tab of the* **Chart** *tools.*

Or

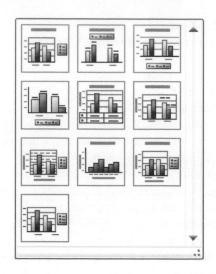

▶ *Click the* **More** *button at the bottom right of the* **Chart Layout** *group to display all the layout options.*
3 *Select the one you want to use.*

If you wish, you can customize any object within your chart.

To delete a chart object:
1 *Right-click on it.*
2 *Select* **Delete** *from the menu.*

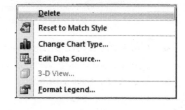

To format a chart object:
1 *Right-click on the object.*
2 *Click on the* **Format Chart Area...**, **Format Chart Title...**, **Format Data Series...** *option (depending on the object).*
3 *Explore the dialog box, selecting the options required.*
4 *Click* **OK**.

Chart titles and axis labels

These areas are text boxes, and initially contain default text – 'Chart Title' in the Title area and 'Axis Title' along each axis.

To replace the default text with your own:
1 *Click once on the label to select it.*
2 *Click a second time on the label to place the insertion point within in.*
3 *Delete the default text.*
4 *Type in your label.*
5 *Click outside the title or label area – anywhere on your chart.*

Chart Layout options

You can switch individual objects on and off using the command buttons in the Labels, Axes and Background groups of the Layout tab, or reposition objects that have been displayed by applying one of the standard layouts.

▶ *The Labels group includes the chart headings, axis titles, legend, data labels and data table.*
▶ *The* **Axes** *group includes the axes and the gridlines.*
▶ *The* **Background** *group includes the plot area (on a 2-D chart), chart wall, chart floor and 3D view (on a 3-D chart)*

To display an object or change its position:
1 *Click its command button on the Layout tab.*
2 *Select the position required.*

To remove an object:
1 *Click its command button.*
2 *Select None.*

To adjust the format of an object:
1 *Click its command button.*
2 *Select More Options... and explore the dialog box.*
3 *Select the options required and click OK.*

Some objects have many more options than others. Walls, floors and plot areas have fill colours and fill effects. Lines have styles, colours and widths. The best idea is to experiment – some will appeal to you, others will not. But don't overdo things! The purpose of your chart will be to clearly and effectively present your data – not demonstrate every chart formatting option!

PRINTING YOUR CHART

You can print your chart with or without the data on which it is based. If it is an object in a worksheet you have several print options. Check it through Print Preview before you print.

▶ *If you also want to print out the data on which the chart is based, choose a layout with a data table before you print.*

To print out all of the data on the worksheet and the chart:

▶ *Print the worksheet as normal (with the chart deselected).*

To get a printout of the chart only:
▶ *Select the chart on the worksheet, then print.*

To get the chart and its data, but no other data, from the sheet:
1 *Select the chart.*
2 *Choose a layout that displays the data table.*
3 *Print out with the chart selected.*

To print a chart that is on a separate chart sheet:
1 *Select the chart sheet.*
2 *Print as usual.*

Enhance your chart

You can use the Shapes command buttons to create different effects on your worksheet data and charts. If you create charts, try using an arrow and a text box to add emphasis to it!

Remember that there are also some other features, e.g. font formatting, cut/copy and paste, page setup and printing options that are covered in Chapter 4.

TEST

1 *How can you quickly return to cell A1 from anywhere in your worksheet?*

2 *Suggest three different number formatting options.*

3 *Identify two features that can be particularly useful when working with a large amount of data on a worksheet.*

4 *You want to add the value in cell A7, to that in B24 and then divide the answer by the value in D10. What formula would you use?*

   =A7+B24/D10
   =A7/D10+B24
   =(A7+B24)/D10
   =D10/(A7+B24)

5 *Identify two statistical functions and explain what they do*

6 *How can you display the formula in your worksheet?*

7 *A discount of 10% is given if the value of an order is over £500. The value of the order is in cell C8. Create a function/formula that would check to see what the order value was, and then calculate the discount if it was due*

8 *What is a multi-level sort?*

9 *What effect will absolute addressing have on a cell address in a formula when you copy the formula?*

10 *Identify three different chart objects.*

7

......

Databases

In this chapter you will learn:
- *how to create tables within a database*
- *how to input and edit data*
- *how to extract records using specific criteria*
- *how to produce reports*

7.1 Planning and design

A simple database could be used to record name and address details (e.g. a Christmas card list). You could also use a database to store and manage details of your CD collection, or to organize the data you need to run your company.

In a simple database, it may be feasible to store all the information together in one table, perhaps with a Christmas card name and address list. Other databases are more complex with several tables, e.g. a company database with details of customers, staff and suppliers. In business you will find large databases used for things like airline booking systems, government records, bank account records, hospital patient information, student records, customer details and personnel/staff files.

DATABASE JARGON

Some database terminology may be unfamiliar to you. Below you will find brief definitions of the terms you are likely to encounter in the near future.

Table: In a simple database, you might have only one table. In a relational database, there will be several tables, but each will contain the data on one topic.

Record: A record contains information about a single item in your table. All the detail relating to one book will be held in that book's record in the Book table.

Field: A field is a piece of data within a record. In your book's record, things like book code, title, classification, and price are each held in a field.

Relationship: This determines how the detail in one table is related to the detail in another, e.g. through the publisher code.

Join: The process of linking tables or queries.

Data definition: The process of defining what data will be stored in your database, specifying the data field's type (number, text, currency, etc.), the data field's size and indicating how it is related to data in other tables.

Data manipulation: Once your data is in place, you can work with it in many ways. This may involve sorting it into a specific order, extracting specific records from tables, or presenting data from a number of different tables into one report.

EXAMPLE DATABASE

In this chapter we will set up a database that could be used to record details of the books in your personal (or public) library. This will give you something to practise on, but set up your own practice database if you prefer.

The database will hold details of the:

▶ *Book title, author, price, year published;*
▶ *Publisher name, address and other contact details;*

▶ *Book category e.g. Science, Travel, Children's Fiction.*

The diagram below illustrates our database.

Library database

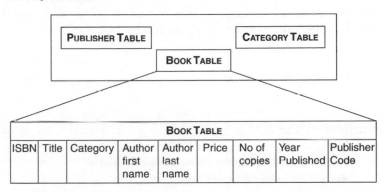

▶ *Each record in a table is presented in a row.*
▶ *Each field in a record is in a column.*
▶ *Each field has a field name at the top of the column.*

ACCESS OBJECTS

An Access database consists of objects that can be used to input, display, interrogate, print and automate your work. They are listed in the navigation pane. The objects that you will use are summarized below:

Tables
Tables are the most important objects in your database. Tables hold your data and are used for data entry and editing. They display data in a datasheet (it looks like an Excel worksheet).

Queries
You use queries to locate specific records within tables, using various criteria, e.g. publishers who have no phone number, or all Travel books.

Forms

You can use Forms to provide an alternative front end to your tables for entering and editing records. They are usually more user-friendly than the datasheet.

Reports

Reports can be used to produce various printed outputs from the data in your database.

PREPARING YOUR DATA

Before you set up a database you should work out the answers to a couple of questions:

▶ *What data do you want to store in the database? (Publisher names/addresses, book titles, etc.)*
▶ *What information do you want to get out of it? (A list of all books from a publisher, or all books in a particular category.)*

If you work out the answers to these questions, you will be in a position to start working out what fields you need.

From data to information

The tables in your database contain raw data. The product number and description of an item you sell. The names and addresses of suppliers. The ISBN, author and title of a book. The names and contact details of library members.

This raw data is then processed in some way, and perhaps combined with other data, to produce useful information. For example, a report showing a list of items that you purchase from each of your suppliers. Or a list of who has borrowed what books from the library.

The raw data becomes useful once it has been processed to give information to the user.

If you are setting up names, you would probably break the name into three fields – Title, First name (or Initials) and Last name. This way you can sort the file into Last name order, or search for someone using the First name and Last name.

If you are storing addresses, you would probably want separate fields for Road/Street, Town/City, Region and/or Country. You can then sort your records into order on any of these fields, or locate records by specifying appropriate search criteria. For example, using Road/Street and Town/City fields, you could search for details of people who live in St John's Street (Road/Street), Stirling (Town/City) rather than St John's Street, Dundee.

When planning your database, take a small sample of the data you wish to store and examine it carefully. This will help you confirm what fields will be required.

How big are the fields?
You must also decide how much space is required for each field. The space you allocate must be long enough to accommodate the longest item that might go there. How long is the longest last name you want to store? If in doubt, take a sample of some typical names (Anderson, Johnston, Mackenzie, Harvey-Jones?) and add a few more characters to the longest one to be sure.

Primary Key
Most records will have a unique identifier – a field that holds different information in every record in your table. In our database, each book would have a 13-character ISBN number and this would be different (unique) for each book title. The field that must be unique in each record is set as the Primary Key. You cannot enter duplicate information into a Primary Key field – Access will not allow it.

Minimize duplication
Try to group your fields into tables with a view to minimizing the duplication of data in your database.

There are several benefits to this approach:

> ▶ *Each set of details is stored (and therefore typed in) only once.*
> ▶ *The tables end up smaller than they would be otherwise.*
> ▶ *As you don't have much duplication of data, the database is easier to maintain and keep up to date.*

It is very important that you spend time organizing and structuring your data before you start to computerize it – it'll save you a lot of time and frustration in the long run!

> Each table in your database should contain data on one subject e.g. customer, student, course, enrolment, book, booking, order, product. The tables can then be related to give information on that means something e.g. a list of students enrolled on a particular course, a list showing what customer ordered what and when.

7.2 Starting Access

When you start Access, the Getting Started window is displayed.

This window is divided into four main areas:

> ▶ *Template categories on the left;*
> ▶ *New database options in the upper part of the middle section;*
> ▶ *Links to Office Online in the lower part of the middle section;*
> ▶ *A list of recently-used databases on the right, with the* **More...** *option so that you can locate and open other databases that you have.*

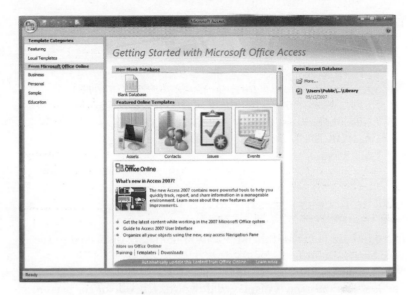

To create a new blank database in the default location:

1. *Click* **Blank Database** *under the New Blank Database heading.*
2. *To store your database in the suggested location, give it a name, e.g. Library, and Click* **Create**.

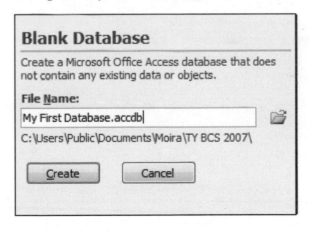

Blank Database

Create a Microsoft Office Access database that does not contain any existing data or objects.

File Name:

My First Database.accdb

C:\Users\Public\Documents\Moira\TY BCS 2007\

[**Create**]   [**Cancel**]

To create a database in a different location:

1 *Click* **Blank Database** *under the* **New Blank Database** *heading.*
2 *Click* **Browse.**
3 *Specify a drive/folder for your file in the* **Save in** *field.*
4 *Enter a name for the database in the* **File Name** *field.*
5 *Leave the* **Save as Type** *at* Access 2007 Databases.
6 *Click* **OK** *to close the* **File New Database** *dialog box.*
7 *Click* **Create.**

7.3 The Access screen

The database name and the application name are displayed in the Title bar.

The Navigation pane is displayed down the left side of the screen, and a new table is presented in Datasheet view.

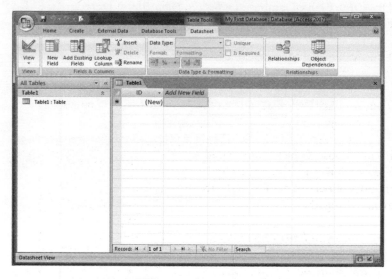

NAVIGATION PANE

The Navigation pane will display a list of the tables, queries, forms and reports in your database.

You can hide and display the Navigation pane by clicking the Shutter button at its top right.

When collapsed, the pane becomes a narrow column at the left of the screen. Click the Shutter button at the top of the column to restore the pane.

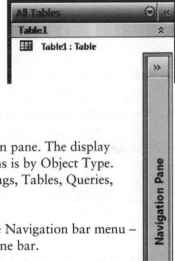

The Navigation pane display
You can change the way that objects are grouped in the Navigation pane. The display that most resembles previous versions is by Object Type. This groups objects under the headings, Tables, Queries, Forms and Reports.

You can change the display from the Navigation bar menu – to open this, click the Navigation pane bar.

You can filter the objects using the Navigation pane menu, e.g. by Object type.

If you choose Tables and Related Views, all the queries, forms and reports associated with a table are grouped together.

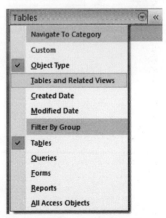

► *Once you have some tables, forms, queries and reports set up, come back to this and experiment with the different options.*

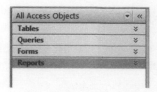

7.4 Field data types and properties

DATA TYPES

There are several data types to choose from when setting up table
structures. Brief details on each are given in the table below. Most
of your fields will probably be Text.

Data type	Usage	Size	Notes
Text	Alphanumeric data	up to 255 bytes	Default data type
Memo	Alphanumeric data	up to 64 Kbytes	
Number	Numeric data	1, 2, 4 or 8 bytes	Can be used in calculations
Date/Time	Dates and times	8 bytes	Values for the years 100 through to 9999

Data type	Usage	Size	Notes
Currency	Monetary data	8 bytes	Accurate to 4 decimal places and 15 digits to the left of the decimal separator
AutoNumber	Unique long integer created by Access for each new record	4 bytes	Cannot be updated. Useful for Primary Key fields
Yes/No	Boolean data	1 bit	Yes and No values, and fields that contain 1 of 2 values On/Off, True/False
OLE Object	Pictures, graphs or data objects from other Windows applications	Up to 1 gigabyte	Cannot be indexed
Hyperlink	Inserts a 'hot spot' to jump to another location on your computer, intranet or on the Internet	The address can contain up to 3 parts (each part can be up to 2048 characters)	The three parts are: Address, Subaddress*, Screentip** optional

(Contd)

Data type	Usage	Size	Notes
Attachment	Any supported type of file		Images, spreadsheets, documents, charts, etc.
Lookup Wizard	Lets you look up values in another table or from a list	The same as the Primary Key used to perform the lookup	Choosing this option starts the Lookup Wizard to define the data type

PROPERTIES

You can customize each field by specifying different properties. The properties vary depending on the data type. The properties that are most often used are summarized here:

Property	Data Type	Notes
Field size	Text and Number	Text from 1 to 255 characters
	Number field sizes are:	Values:
	Byte (single byte)	0 to 255
	Integer (2-byte)	−32,768 to +32,767
	Long Integer (4-byte)	−2,147,483,648 to 2,147,483,648
	Single (4-byte)	-3.4×10^{38} to 3.4×10^{38}
	Double (8-byte)	-1.797×10^{308} to $+1.797 \times 10^{308}$
Format	Controls how data looks	Options depend on the data type
Decimal places	Number and Currency	Auto (displays 2 d.p. for most formats except General Number, where decimal places depend on the precision of the number) or Fixed from 0 to 15 d.p.

Property	Data Type	Notes
Default value	All data types except Memo, OLE Object and AutoNumber	
Validation rule		You specify conditions to check that only the right sort of data is entered
Validation text		You can specify the message to appear on the screen when a validation rule is not met
Required		Set to Yes if data must be entered
Indexed	Text, Number, Currency, Date/Time and AutoNumber types	Indexing speeds up access to its data – fields that will be sorted or queried on should be indexed. You can insist that data is unique, e.g. ref numbers, or allow duplicates, e.g. names.

One item per field

Each field in a table should contain one piece of information only – firstname, lastname, city, postcode, item number etc. This makes it easier to sort and query the data as required.

7.5 Tables in the Library database

The tables that will be in the Library database are:

Category table

Field Name	Data Type	Properties
ID	AutoNumber	Primary Key
Category Name	Text	

Publisher table

Field Name	Data Type	Properties
PublisherID	Text	Field Size = 6, Primary Key
Company Name	Text	Field Size = 35
Address	Text	Field Size = 30
Town	Text	Field Size = 20 Indexed (Duplicates OK) Default Value = London
Postcode	Text	Field Size = 10
Telephone No	Text	Field Size = 20
Email	Text	Field Size = 40

Book table

Field Name	Data Type	Properties
ISBN	Text	Primary Key, Field Size = 25
Title	Text	Field Size = 35, Indexed (Duplicates OK)
Category	LookUp	Field Size = 25, Indexed (Duplicates OK)
No of Copies	Number	Integer
Year published	Text	Field Size = 4
PublisherID	Number	Field Size = Long Integer
Author Firstname	Text	Field Size = 15
Author Lastname	Text	Field Size = 15
Price	Currency	Validation Rule <100 (No book is over £100)

Primary Key and Foreign Key

Each table that you create will have one field in it identified as the Primary Key. Most, but not necessarily all, tables will have a Primary Key field. The Primary Key field is the one that is the unique identifier in each table.

In the tables above, the Primary Key in the Category table is the CategoryID, in the Books table it is the ISBN, and in the Publisher table it is the PublisherID.

In the Books table, the PublisherID and CategoryID fields also appear. Neither of these fields is the Primary Key in the Books table, but they are Primary Keys in other tables in the database.

When these fields appear in the Books table, they are called a Foreign Key.

7.6 Defining the table structures

The table structure can be defined in Datasheet view or Design view. We will try both. My personal preference is Design view – but you can use whichever you prefer.

THE CATEGORY TABLE

To create a new table in Datasheet view:

1 *Display the* **Create** *tab.*
2 *Click* **Table** *in the* **Tables** *group.*

To name a field:
1 *Double-click in the column heading area.*
2 *Enter the field name, e.g. CategoryID.*
3 *Press* **[Enter]**.
4 *This takes you to the field name area for the next field (if it doesn't, double-click in the next column heading area).*
5 *Repeat steps 2 and 3 until all fields are named.*
6 *Click in the datasheet area in Row 1.*

Data types

By default, the ID (or CategoryID field in this example) is automatically assigned the AutoNumber data type. On data entry this field will be completed automatically, with 1 as the value in the first record, 2 in the second one, then 3, then 4, etc.

To specify a data type for a field:
1 *Click in the field, e.g. in row 1.*
2 *Select the field type from the* **Data Type** *field in the* **Data Type and Formatting** *group on the* **Datasheet** *tab.*

To set the Primary Key:
1 *Click within the field that will be the Primary Key.*
2 *Select the* **Unique Value** *checkbox in the* **Data Type** *field in the* **Data Type and Formatting** *group (AutoNumber data types are automatically assigned a Unique Value property).*

To enter data into the Category table:
1 *Type a category into the CategoryName field in record 1.*
2 *Press* **[Tab]** *until you are in CategoryName in record 2.*
3 *Repeat steps 1 and 2 until all fields are complete. Enter the following categories: Travel, Fiction, Gardening, Science, History and Cooking.*

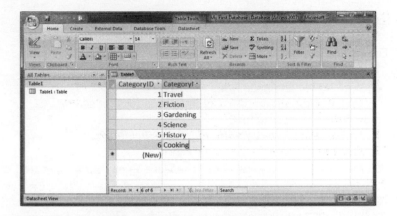

To save and close your table:

1 *Display the* **Microsoft Office** *menu and click* **Save.**
2 *Enter the table name, e.g. Category.*
3 *Click* **OK.**
4 *Close your table.*

If you try to close your table without saving, you will be prompted to do so. At the prompt, click Yes as you do want to save the changes, then complete steps 2–4 above.

Your table will be listed in the Navigation pane.

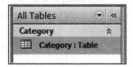

Set up the Publisher table in Design view

To create a new table:
1 *Display the* **Create** *tab.*
2 *Click* **Table Design** *in the* **Tables** *group.*

To define the table structure:
1 *In the Field Name column, key in the field name –*
   PublisherID.
2 *Press* **[Tab]** *to move along to the* **Data Type** *column and set*
   this to AutoNumber.
3 *Press* **[Tab]** *to move along to the* **Description** *column and*
   enter a field description if you wish.

Primary Key
The PublisherID field is the Primary Key for this table – each
publisher has its own code – its unique identifier.

▶ *To establish Primary Key status, click the*
   Primary Key *tool when the insertion point is*
   anywhere in the ISBN field row in the upper
   pane.

Primary
Key

Note that the Index property is automatically set to **Yes**
(**No Duplicates**) when a field is given Primary Key status.

Enter the Title details in the second row of the upper pane.

1 *In the* **Field Name** *column, key in the name – Company Name.*
2 *Press* **[Tab]** *to move along to the* **Data Type** *column and set*
   this to Text.
3 *The default field size for a Text data type is 255 characters.*
   This is more than is required for a company name, so this
   property could be reduced – 35 would be big enough.
4 *Press* **[F6]** *to move to the lower pane (or click with the*
   mouse).

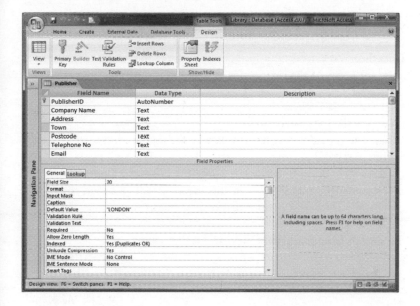

5 *Set the* **Field Size** *to* 35.
6 *Set the* **Indexed** *property to* Yes (Duplicates OK).
7 *Press* [**F6**] *to return to the upper pane.*
8 *Enter the remaining fields following the suggestions above.
   The Description is optional – anything you type in this column
   will appear on the status bar (as a prompt to the operator)
   during data entry to that field.*
9 *Save and close the table design window. Give your table a
   suitable name, e.g. Publisher.*
10 *The new table will be listed in the Navigation pane.*

Switching panes

The Design view window has two panes – an upper one
where you specify the field name, data type and description,
and a lower one where you specify the field properties.

▶ *To move from a column to the next in the upper pane,
   press* [**Tab**].
▶ *To move from one pane to the other press* [**F6**] *(once you've
   entered some data in the upper pane).*
▶ *Point and click with your mouse to move around the window.*

Create the Books table, following the guidelines in Section 7.5, using either Datasheet view or Design view. If you work in Datasheet view, you may find that you have to change to Design view for some of the properties, e.g. Validation Rule.

DATASHEET VIEW

When you create a new database, a new table is produced automatically, and it is displayed in Datasheet view. This view is used for data entry and editing purposes. You can also add new fields and specify data types in this view as well as assign the most commonly used field properties to your field.

To switch from Datasheet view to Design view:

▶ *Click the* **View** *command button in the* **Views** *group at the left of the* **Datasheet** *tab.*

DESIGN VIEW

This view is the one traditionally used when setting up the structure of your table. You can add and delete fields in this view, specify data types and assign any field properties you wish to the fields.

To switch from Design view to Datasheet view:
▶ *Click the* **View** *command button in the* **Views** *group at the left of the* **Design** *tab.*

You can also use the **View** tools at the bottom right of the screen to change views.

LOOKUP DATA TYPE

In the Book table, the value for the Category for each book will be looked up in the Category table, which contains a list of the categories we will use.

To create a Lookup field:
1. *Select* **Lookup Wizard...** *as the* **Data Type** *for the field.*
2. *Work through the Wizard, clicking* **Next** *after completing each step.*
3. *As we have the values in the Category table, choose 'I want the lookup column to look up values in a table or query'.*
4. *Select the table that contains the values, Category.*
5. *Add the field that contains the values to the* **Selected Fields** *list – click to move the field from the* **Available Fields** *list to the* **Selected Fields** *list.*

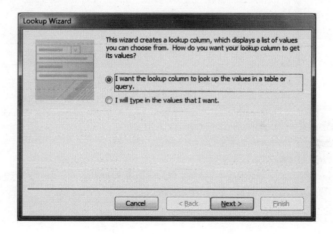

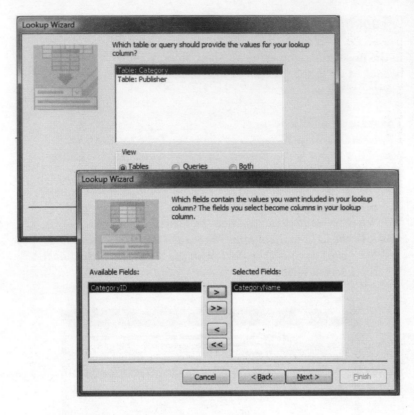

6 *Specify the sort order required (if any).*
7 *Set the column width, and select the* **Hide Key Column**
   checkbox.
8 *Give your column a name, and click* **Finish**.
9 *At the prompt, save your table.*

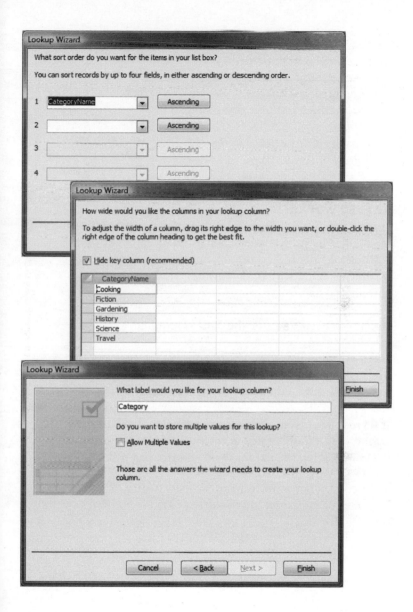

10 *Always save your table once you have changed its structure – it is not saved automatically. Access will prompt you to save if you try to do anything without first saving the table.*

11 *The tables will be listed in the Navigation pane.*

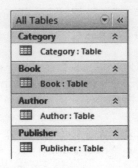

Database workers

Large databases in business are designed, created and maintained by professional database staff. In banks (with customer details and accounts); hospitals (patients, treatments and doctors); universities (students, courses, enrolments); etc.

Users then enter and edit the data as required.

Database administrators are responsible for ensuring that users get access to the data that they need and provide rights to let them enter, edit and view data as appropriate.

If there is a problem with a large company database, or it crashes, the administrator is responsible for recovering the data and getting the database up and running again.

7.7 Relationships

Once the table structures have been set up, you should establish the
relationships between your tables.

1 *Select the* **Database tools** *tab.*
2 *Click Relationships in the*
   Show/Hide *group.*

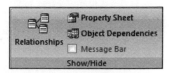

The Relationships tab will be displayed, with the Category and
Book tables related through the Category field (the lookup field).

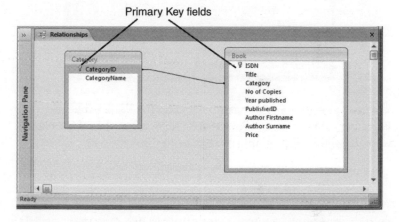

To add more tables to the tab:
1 *Click the* **Show Table** *button in*
   the Relationships group.
2 *Select the table(s) that you want to*
   add to the Relationships tab.
3 *Click* **Add***.*

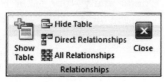

4 *Close the Show Table dialog box once all the tables have been added.*

We need to create a relationship between the Book table and Publisher table using the PublisherID field. With the tables related, we will be able to pull information from more than one table at a time if necessary.

RELATIONSHIP TYPES

One-to-many – one of the related fields is a Primary Key or holds a unique index. This is the most common type of relationship. In our example one publisher in the Publisher table can have many matching records in the Books table.

One-to-one – both the related fields are Primary Keys or contain unique indexes. Each record in the first table can have only one matching record in the second, and vice versa. These are sometimes used to divide a table that has many fields, or to isolate fields for security reasons. For example, when storing personnel data you could have general information in one table, e.g. name, address, job title, and confidential information in another, e.g. salary, bank details, etc.

REFERENTIAL INTEGRITY

These are the rules that are followed to preserve the defined relationships between tables when you enter or delete records. If you enforce referential integrity, Access prevents you from:

▶ *Adding records to a related table when there is no associated record in the primary table.*
▶ *Changing values in the primary table that would result in orphan (unconnected) records in a related table.*
▶ *Deleting records from the primary table when there are matching related records in a related table.*

To create a relationship:

1 *On the* **Relationships** *tab, click on the field you wish to relate to another table to select it.*
2 *Drag the selected field and drop it onto the field you wish to link it to in the other table.*
3 *At the* **Edit Relationships** *dialog box, select* **Referential Integrity** *(if desired) and click* **Create** *to establish the relationship.*

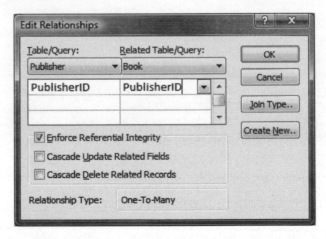

4 *Click* **OK.**

The lines between the tables are called *join lines*. These run between the fields linking the tables.

To delete a relationship:
1 *Click on the join line you wish to remove to select it.*
2 *Press* [Delete].
3 *Respond to the prompt as required.*

To edit a relationship:
1 *Double-click on the join line.*
2 *Complete the* **Edit Relationship** *dialog box as required.*
3 *Click* **OK.**
4 *Save the changes made to the Relationship window if you wish to keep them and close the Relationship window when you have finished working with it.*

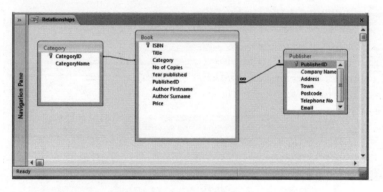

To save and close the Relationships tab:
1 *Click* **Save** *on the* **Quick Access** *toolbar.*
2 *Click* **Close** *in the* **Relationships** *group.*

7.8 Entering data in Datasheet view

We have already entered our data into the Category table.

You must complete the Publisher table before the Book table, so that you will have Primary Key fields completed in the tables at the one side of your one-to-many relationships. You will then be able to enter the appropriate PublisherID data into the foreign key fields in the Book table.

Data entry is mostly very easy. You simply open the table and key in the data – use [Tab] or the mouse to move from field to field. As you are keying in the data, look out for the features mentioned below.

To open a table:
▶ *Double-click on its name in the* **Navigation** *pane.*
▶ *To move forward through the fields press* [Tab].
▶ *To move backward through the fields press* [Shift]-[Tab].
▶ *Or click in the field you want to move to.*

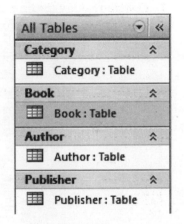

Regardless of which record your insertion point is currently in, the New Record button beside the navigation buttons, or the New command button in the Records group on the Home tab, takes you to the first empty row at the end of your table, to allow you to add a new record.

Enter some sample data into the Publisher and Book tables. There is some to get you started on the next page. Make up another half dozen or more records for each table.

In the Publisher table, notice that the Town field is completed automatically with 'London' – our default value.

▶ *Close each table when you've finished.*

Publisher table

Pub ID	Company Name	Address	Town	Postcode	Telephone No	Email
1	Hodder & Stoughton	338 Euston Road	London	NW1 3BH	020 7001 1000	hodinfo@hotmail.com
2	Westward Lock Ltd	18 Clifftop Street	London	WIX 1RB	020 7331 2000	Gill.A@yahoo.com
3	Alice Publications	4 High Street	Oxford	OX1 2QQ		a.smith@hotmail.com
4	Puffin Books	3 West Row	London	NW2 3SL	020 2222 3333	

Books table

ISBN	Title	Category	No of copies	Year Pub'd	Publisher ID	Author first name	Author Surname	Price
100-1-123-51231-1	The Snow Storm	Fiction	3	2005	2	Gill	Adamson	£7.99
200-2-210-54321-2	Indian Highlignts	Travel	2	2007	3	Peter	Smith	£9.99
300-3-321-12345-3	Elm Grove	History	1	2006	2	Andrew	Brown	£6.99
400-4-432-56789-4	Africa Trekker	Travel	2	2006	1	Morag	Dewar	£6.99
500-5-543-13245-5	The Lying Stone	Fiction	1	1954	4	Jack	Thompson	£16.99

7.9 Editing data in Datasheet view

MOVING THROUGH YOUR TABLE

We have already seen that you can move within and between records using [**Tab**] and [**Shift**]-[**Tab**], or by clicking into the desired field. You can also move through your table using the navigation buttons at the bottom left of the datasheet.

EDITING THE FIELD CONTENTS

1 *Locate the record you want to edit – use the navigation buttons or the scroll bar.*
2 *Click in the field that needs updating.*
3 *Update as required.*

To add a record:
1 *Click*  *in the* **Records** *group on the* **Home** *tab (or next to the navigation buttons).*
2 *Enter your record details into the empty row.*

To delete a record:
1 *Select the record you want to delete – click in the selection bar to the left of the first field.*
2 *Click* **Delete** *in the* **Records** *group on the* **Home** *tab.*

Confidentiality

Databases often hold personal data – names and addresses, account numbers, financial information, health records, etc. This information is of course covered by the Data Protection Act, but a lot of it is very sensitive and needs to be treated as confidential. Users should respect the confidentiality of the data that they work with and not discuss or disclose it outside their work environment.

7.10 Formatting in Datasheet view

When working in Datasheet view, there are a number of formatting options you might like to experiment with. Formatting the datasheet affects the whole table, not just the row or column the insertion point is in.

The commands in the Font group are used for most formatting options. Most are similar to those in other Office applications. Experiment with them to see the effect that they have.

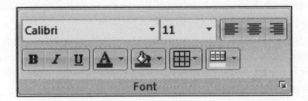

If you click the dialog box launcher in the Font group it will display the Datasheet Formatting dialog box where you can add special effects, e.g. sunken, to your datasheet, choose alternative gridline colours, and customize the border and line styles.

7.11 Changing the table structure

The table structure can be adjusted in Datasheet view or in Design view. There are a limited number of field property options available in Datasheet view – the complete range is available in Design view.

DATASHEET VIEW

To change the field properties of a field in Datasheet view, use the command buttons in the Data Type & Formatting group.

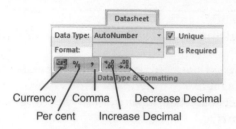

Currency / Comma / Decrease Decimal
Per cent / Increase Decimal

▶ **Data Type:** *Click the drop-down arrow to display a list where you can select an alternative data type.*

▶ **Format:** *The options in this list vary, depending on the Data Type selected.*

▶ **Currency, Per cent** *and* **Comma** *are formatting options that can be used on Number fields.*

▶ **Increase Decimal** *and* **Decrease Decimal** *are used to control the accuracy of the figures displayed.*

▶ *The* **Unique** *checkbox determines whether or not duplicate values are allowed in a field. The Primary Key field would be unique.*

▶ **Is Required** *determines whether a field must contain data.*

To change the field name from Datasheet view:
1 *Double-click in the field name at the top of the column.*
2 *Edit the field as required.*
3 *Press* [Enter].

To delete a field or record in Datasheet view:
1 *Click anywhere within the field or record.*
2 *Click the drop-down arrow by* **Delete**.
3 *Choose* **Delete Column** *to delete the field.*
Or
4 **Delete Record** *to delete the whole row.*

If you delete a field you will be asked to confirm. Click **Yes** if you are sure, and **No** if you don't really want to it.

There's no Undo here!
Take care when deleting a field. You can't use Undo to restore it – you'll have to type it back in!

To add a new field:
1. *Click into the field that will go to the right of your new field.*
2. *Click* **Insert** *in the* **Fields and Columns** *group on the* **Datasheet** *tab.*
3. *Edit the field name as required.*
4. *Press* [**Enter**].

To add a new field at the end of your datasheet:
1. *Double-click on* **Add New Field** *at the top of the next empty column.*
2. *Enter the field name.*
3. *Click in the row below the field name and enter your data.*

To move a field:
1. *Select the column – click at the top of it.*
2. *Click on the field name. Drag and drop it into its new position.*
3. *Save the changes.*

Design view
To change a field name:
▶ *Edit the field name in the upper pane.*

To change the data type:
▶ *Select an alternative data type in the upper pane.*

To adjust a field's properties:
1. *Click within the field in the upper pane.*
2. *Press* [**F6**] *or click in the lower pane.*
3. *Adjust the properties as necessary.*

To delete a field:
1. *Click within the field row in the upper pane.*
2. *Click* **Delete Rows** *in the* **Tools** *group.*
3. *Respond to the prompt as necessary.*

To add a new field at the end of the table:
▶ *Click in the first empty row and enter the field name, data type, etc.*

To add a field between other fields:
1 *Click anywhere in the row below where you want the new field positioned.*
2 *Click* **Insert Rows** *in the* **Tools** *group.*
3 *Add the field details and properties.*

To move a field:
1 *Select the row – click in the row selector area to the left of the field name.*
2 *Point to the row selector box with the mouse pointer.*
3 *Drag and drop the field in the required position.*

To change the field that has Primary Key status:
1 *Place the insertion point within the field in the upper pane that you want to take Primary Key status.*
2 *Click the* **Primary Key** *tool.*

To remove Primary Key status, and not give it to any other field:
1 *Place the insertion point within the field in the upper pane that currently has Primary Key status.*
2 *Click the* **Primary Key** *tool.*

Data Protection

The Data Protection Act (1984, updated 1998) states that users of personal data relating to living, identifiable individuals should be registered with the Data Protection Registrar. The users of the personal data should then adhere to The Codes of Practice and Data Protection Principles set out within the Act. You can check out the principles of the Act in Chapter 1.

7.12 Page layout and printing tables

You can easily print the contents of any table.

1 *Open the Microsoft Office Menu.*
2 *Choose* **Print Preview** *from the* **Print** *options.*
3 *Adjust the paper size, orientation or margins as necessary using the Preview toolbar.*

Or

▶ *Open the* **Page Setup** *dialog box and adjust the settings there.*
4 *Click* **Print** *on the Print Preview tab.*
5 *Set the print options as required.*
6 *Click* **OK***.*

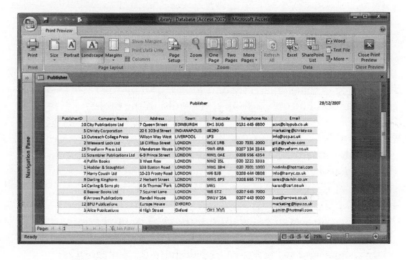

7.13 Forms

As an alternative to entering data into a table in Datasheet view, you could use a form. In Datasheet view, each record is displayed in a row, each field in a column. As many fields and records are displayed in the table window as will fit. In a form, the fields are arranged attractively on the screen (you can design forms to resemble the paper forms you actually use) and one record is displayed at a time. A form is often considered more user-friendly than Datasheet view.

To create a basic form:
  1 *In the* **Navigation** *pane, select the table to base the form on.*
Or
  ▶ *Open the table in Datasheet view.*
  2 *Click* **Form** *in the* **Forms** *group on the* **Create** *tab.*

If the form is at the many side of a relationship, it will display the first record in that table. You can move through the records using the navigation buttons, just as you would in the table.

If the form is based on a table at the one side of a one-to-many relationship, the table from the one side of the relationship is displayed at the top of the form, and the related records from the table at the many side are displayed below this.

Notice the two sets of navigation buttons. The upper ones in this example belong to the Book table (at the many side of the relationship), and the lower ones belong to the Category table (at the one side of the relationship).

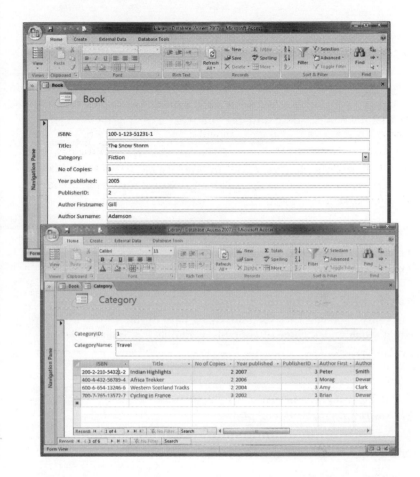

VIEW OPTIONS

Form view is where you can enter and edit data freely. The data is stored in the underlying table(s). You cannot change the structure of your form in Form view.

Layout view is new in Access 2007. It's a bit of a half-way house between Form and Design view. In Layout view, you can change the structure of your form and see the underlying data from your table at the same time. This can be useful when deciding how big you want a control to be.

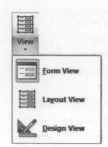

You will probably find that you can use Layout view to make most of the design changes you want on your form.

Not all tasks can be performed in Layout view and you may be prompted to switch to Design view to make a particular change.

Design view – this view gives a more detailed view of the form structure. You can't see the underlying data in this view – but there are a much wider range of controls available, e.g. images, lines, rectangles, etc.

▶ *To change from one view to another, use the* **View** *button on the* **Home** *tab, or the* **View** *tools at the bottom right of the window.*

7.14 Form Design

CONTROLS

The objects on a form are called controls. There are text boxes that display the data held in your tables or queries, labels for instructions or headings, image controls for pictures, line and rectangle controls to provide formatting and design options, radio buttons and checkboxes – and many more. We will use some of these controls in the following pages.

Controls can be bound or unbound (there are also calculated controls, but we will not be discussing them in this book).

Bound control – the data source is in a table or query.

Unbound control – one that doesn't get its data from a table or a query. They are used to display information or draw lines or rectangles, or add pictures. A label control, often used for a title on a form or report, is an example of an unbound control.

_____

7.15 Controls in Layout view

You can resize, move and delete the controls in Layout view.

To resize a control:
1 *Select it – click on it.*
2 *Move the pointer over the edge of the control – it becomes a double-headed arrow.*
3 *Click and drag to resize.*

To move a control:
1 *Select it.*
2 *Move the pointer inside the control – it becomes a 4-headed arrow when you are in a position to move the control.*
3 *Drag and drop to move it.*

To delete a control:
▶ *Select it and press* [Delete].

FORM LAYOUT TOOLS

In Layout view, the Form Layout tools are displayed in the Format and Arrange tabs on the Ribbon. The most regularly-used controls are in the Controls group on the Format tab.

Controls group

The buttons in the Controls group allow you to add and format some controls in Layout view.

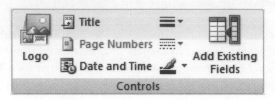

To add or replace a logo:

When you create a form, a standard logo is placed in the top left corner of the object. You can replace this with your own logo, or any picture on your computer.

1 *Click* **Logo** *in the* **Controls** *group on the* **Format** *tab.*
2 *Browse through your folders and locate/select the picture required.*
3 *Resize the picture if necessary.*

To add a title or edit a title:
1 *Click the* `Title` *command button.*
2 *Insert/edit your text.*
3 *Click outside the title area.*

To add a date or time control:
1 *Click the* `Date and Time` *command button.*
2 *Select date and/or time.*
3 *Choose the format.*
4 *Click* **OK**.

To format the border of a control:
1 *Click on a control on your form.*
2 *Select the line thickness, type and/or colour for the control border from the* **Controls** *group.*

Save the form
If you save your form, it will be listed in the Navigation pane.

To open the form again, simply double-click on it.

To print a form:
1 *Open the form in Form view.*
2 *Display the form that you want to print.*
3 *Click the* **Microsoft Office** *button and click* **Print** *to display the* **Print** *dialog box.*
4 *Choose* **Selected Record(s)** *in the* **Print what** *options.*
5 *Click* **OK**.

7.16 Sort

You can easily sort the records in a table or form into ascending or descending order.

1 *Open the table or form you wish to sort.*
2 *Place the insertion point anywhere within the field you want to sort the records on.*

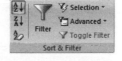

3 *Click the* **Sort Ascending** *or* **Sort Descending** *command button in the* **Sort & Filter** *group on the* **Home** *tab.*

The Book table with the records sorted into ascending order on the Title field, is displayed below.

Note the arrow at the right of the field name in the Title column – indicating that it has been sorted into Ascending order.

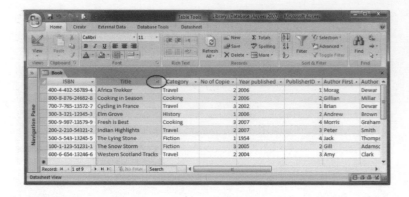

▶ To *clear a sort, click the* **Clear All Sorts** *command button in the* **Sort & Filter** *group.*

MULTI-LEVEL SORT

You can use the sort command buttons to sort your data on more than one field if you wish. Let's say we wanted to sort the *Publisher* table so that the towns were in ascending order, and in each town the company names were in descending order.

To perform this sort using the Sort command buttons, start with the lowest level sort first – the company names.

1 *Click inside the Company field and click the* **Sort descending** *command button.*
2 *Click inside the Town field and click the* **Sort ascending** *command button.*

If you look carefully at the result, you should see that the Towns are in ascending order. Where there is more than one publisher in a town, the company names are in descending order. In London we have Westward Lock Ltd, Trueform Press Ltd, Scrambler Publications Ltd, Hodder & Stoughton, etc.

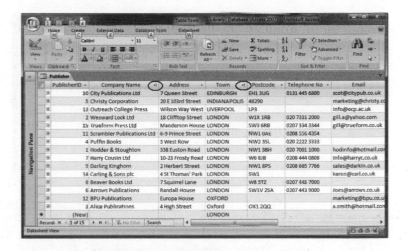

▶ *Experiment with the sort feature on your tables until you are
  sure that you see how it works.*

If you sort your records, and then decide that you want
to keep them in the new order, save your table before you
close it.

7.17 Find

To locate a record in your table, you can use the navigation
buttons, or go to a specific record number by specifying the record
number in the number field within the navigation buttons and
pressing [Enter].

To locate records using Find:
  1 *In Datasheet view, place the insertion point within the field
    that contains the text you want to find.*
  2 *Click* **Find** *in the* **Find** *group on the* **Home** *tab.*

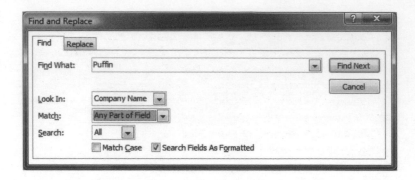

3 *Enter details of what you are looking for in the* **Find What** *field.*

4 *Set the* **Look in, Match, Search** *and other options if required.*

5 *Click* **Find Next** *to find the first matching record.*

6 *If it is not the record you want, click* **Find Next** *until you reach the correct record.*

7 *Click* **Cancel** *once you have found your record to close the dialog box.*

If Access can't find what you are looking for, a dialog box will tell you so. If this happens, check your entry in the Find What field carefully – you may have typed it in incorrectly.

7.18 Filter

There will be times when you want to display a specific group of records from a table, e.g. a list of books in a specific category. This can be achieved by filtering the records.

SELECTION

Try filtering the Book table to display those that are (or are not) in a specific category.

1 *Open the Book table.*
2 *Position the insertion point in the field that has the criterion that you are looking for, e.g. for books on travel, click in a field where the value is set to 'Travel'.*
3 *Click the* Selection *command button.*

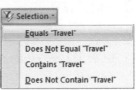

4 *Select an option –* Equals, Does Not Equal, Contains *or* Does Not Contain.
5 *You can filter your filtered list using the same technique – narrowing down your list or records as you go.*

Note the icon(s) at the top of column(s) that have been filtered.

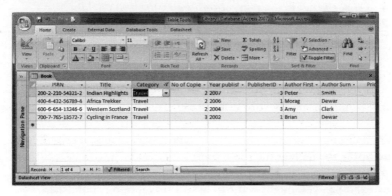

▶ *To remove the filter, click the* Toggle Filter *button in the* Sort & Filter *group.*

You can also filter your records by selecting options from the filter list.

1 *Click in the column you want to base your selection on.*
2 *Click* Filter *in the* Sort & Filter *group.*

Or
> ► *Click the arrow beside the field name you want to filter by.*

3 *Deselect the* **Select All** *checkbox.*

4 *Select the checkboxes to indicate the criteria for your selection.*

5 *Click* **OK.**

To clear your selection:
> ► *Click the* **Toggle Filter** *button in the* **Sort & Filter** *group.*

Or

1 *Click the drop-down arrow to the right of the field name.*

2 *Choose* **Clear filter from fieldname** *from the list.*

FILTER BY FORM

An alternative to filtering your data based on selection, is to use a form layout to specify your criteria.

When filtering by form, you can specify different sets of criteria and apply them all at the same time.

For example, you might want to list all travel books published since 2002.

1 *Open the Book table.*

2 *Click* **Advanced** *in the* **Sort & Filter** *group, and then choose* **Filter By Form.**

3 *Use the drop-down lists at each field to set your criteria.*

4 *Put each set of criteria on a new tab – bottom left of the window.*

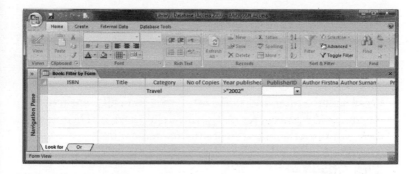

5 *Click* **Toggle Filter** *once you have all your criteria set up. The results will be displayed.*

6 *Click* **Toggle Filter** *to display all records again.*

Or

▶ *Click Filtered to the right of the Navigation bar.*

To reapply the filter:

▶ *Click Advanced, and then Apply Filter/Sort.*

To clear the filter:

▶ *Click Advanced, and then Clear All Filters.*

Save the filter

You can save your criteria as a query from the Filter by Form tab.

Just click Save and give your query a name.

If you set up a filter and then realize that you will want to use the same filter criteria regularly you should save it. Then next time, just open the query to see the filtered data.

COMPARISON OPERATORS

You can identify the range required using the following operators:

<	Less than
>	More than
. <=	Less than or equal to
>=	More than or equal to
<>	Not equal to
Between...And...	Between the first and the last value entered (including the values)

7.19 Query Design

Filtering and sorting can be done quickly and easily using the methods discussed above. However, the Query Design feature gives you many more options.

In the examples up until now, we have sorted and filtered records within one table. There may be times when you need to collect the data from several tables, and sort or filter that data. If you are working across several tables, you might find it easier to use the Query Design.

We will set up a query to display book title, author, category, publisher and year published data.

▶ *If you have a table open, close it.*

To set up a query in Design view:

1 *Display the* **Create** *tab on the ribbon.*
2 *Click* **Query Design** *in the* **Other** *group.*
3 *The* **Query1** *tab will be displayed, and the* **Show Table** *dialog box should be open, listing the tables in the database. If it is not open, click the* **Show Table** *command button in the* **Query Setup** *group.*

4 *Add the Book table and Publisher table to the* **Query** *tab. To select multiple tables: Adjacent tables – click on the first, hold down [Shift] and click on the last one. Non-adjacent tables – hold down [Ctrl] and click on each of the tables you want.*
5 *Close the Show Table dialog box.*

▶ *If you add a table by mistake, select it in the upper pane of the Query tab and press [Delete] to remove it.*

The query tab will be displayed, with the Query Design tools in the Ribbon. The tables are displayed in the upper pane and the query grid is in the lower pane.

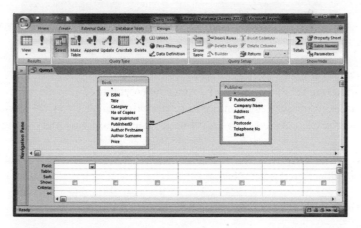

ADDING FIELDS TO THE QUERY GRID

The next step is adding the fields that you want displayed when you run your query to the query grid.

To add fields to the query grid:
▶ *Double-click on the field in the table in the upper pane.*

You should add:

Title, *Author Firstname* and *Author Surname* from the *Book* table;

Company Name from the *Publisher* table;

Category and *Year Published* from the *Book* table.

Things to note in the lower pane:

▶ *Table row – this indicates which table the field has been taken from.*
▶ *Sort – allows you to specify the sort order of a field (ascending or descending)*
▶ *Show – indicates whether or not a field will be displayed when you display the results – a tick means that it will show.*

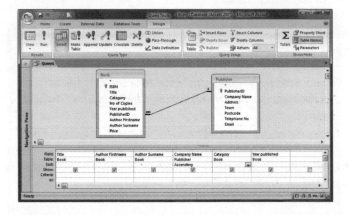

RUNNING THE QUERY

Once you have your query set up, you have to run it to display the results.

To display your results:

▶ *Click* **Run** *in the* **Results** *group on* **Design** *tab.*

When your results are displayed, you can return to the Query design by clicking the **View** command button or by selecting Design View from the View options.

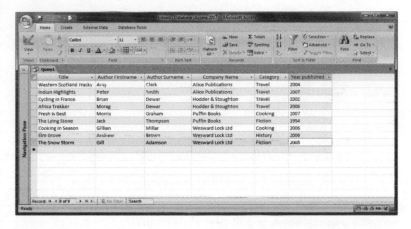

The selected fields from all your records are displayed in the result.

▶ *Save your query – click the* **Save** *tool on the* **Quick Access** *toolbar. Call it something like 'Book and Publisher details'.*

▶ *Close the query – it will be listed in the* **Navigation** *panel.*

Notice that it is displayed under each of the two tables that it takes its data from – Book and Publisher.

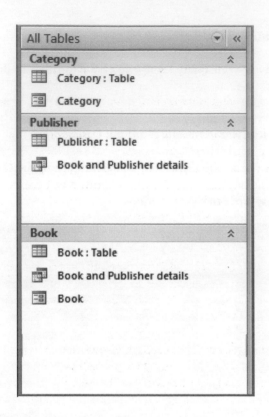

To open a query again and display the results:
- *Double-click on it in the* **Navigation** *panel.*

Or
- *Right-click on it and choose* **Open.**

To open a query in Design view:
- *Right-click on it and choose Design view.*

You can also sort your data, or specify select criteria, in Query Design view.

- **Operators** – *you can use the operators introduced in Filtering when setting up your queries. If no operator is used in the Criteria row, Access assumes that you mean equal to.*

Wildcards:

* can be used to represent a string of characters;

? can be used to represent an individual character.

For example, the criteria of EH* in the *PostCode* field would return any record whose postcode started with EH. So records with EH2 1QQ, EH24 5TT, EH1 1ZZ would all be returned.

Combined criteria

You can combine different select criteria using AND, OR or NOT

If you enter all criteria in ONE row they are combined using AND – records that match ALL the criteria will be returned when you run the query e.g. records that have a surname Stephen AND the town London.

If you enter the criteria in separate rows then records matching the criteria in any one row will be returned when you run the query. The records will match the criteria in the first row of criteria OR the second one OR the third one, etc.

If you want to exclude something, you can enter the criteria as <> or NOT. If you want all records except where the city is London, you could put "<>London" or NOT "London" in the criteria row for the city field.

If you are searching for more than one value in a single field you could join the criteria in one row using AND. In the criteria row, entering "London" OR "Glasgow" in the town field will return records where the town is either London or Glasgow – you will get both.

Books table

▸ *Extract details of all travel books published after 2004.*
▸ *Display title, category and price, sorted into price order.*
▸ *Display the book title and author of all books except those with a category of travel ("<>Travel").*

Publisher table

▸ *Extract publisher name, town and telephone number, and display details of those that you do not have a telephone number for (criteria for Telephone No = "Is Null").*
▸ *Display publisher name, town and email, in Town order.*
▸ *Display a list of the publisher names and email addresses, where you do have the email address ("Is Not Null").*

Multiple table queries

▸ *Publisher and Book table, display the publisher name, book title and price for all the London publishers.*
▸ *Extract a list showing publisher name, author name, and book title for all books priced between £8 and £12.*

Deleting database objects

You can very easily delete tables, queries, forms and reports.

Simply select them in the Navigation panel and press [Delete], then click Yes at the prompt.

Think very carefully before you delete any tables – remember, they hold your data. Once deleted the data is gone.

Queries, forms and reports can be re-created relatively easily, but a table with hundreds of records could be very time consuming and expensive to recreate.

ALWAYS have a backup of your database – just in case!

7.20 Reports

Reports are the best option when you want to generate output from your database that is easy to read and well formatted. The standard of report that can be produced is sophisticated enough to take to meetings, send to clients or give to the company's directors! Many of the terms and features used in Forms also apply to Reports. The view options in Reports are also similar to those in Forms, with the exception of Print Preview.

REPORT VIEWS

You cannot edit the data in a report – if you want to edit something, go back to the table or query.

Report view – you can filter data in Report view, in a similar way to when you are working with queries. Right-click on the column you want to filter and then select the option from the list.

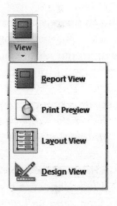

Print Preview – displays the report as it will look when printed. You can change the page set up and printing options from this view. If your report consists of several pages, you can use the navigation buttons at the bottom of the preview window to move through them.

Layout view – here you can change the structure of your report and see the underlying data from your table or query at the same time. This can be useful when deciding on the size that you want a control to be. You will probably find that you can use Layout view to make most of your design changes on a report.

Design view – this view gives a more detailed view of the report structure. You can't see the underlying data in this view, but there is a much greater range of controls to choose from, e.g. images, lines, rectangles, etc.

To change from one view to another, use the View command button or the View tools at the bottom right of the window.

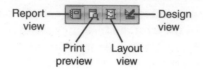

Report view — Print preview — Layout view — Design view

REPORT TOOLS

The Report tools are in the Reports group on the Create tab on the Ribbon.

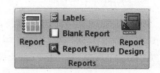

You can quickly create a simple report from any of your tables or queries using the Report tool in this group. This is useful to give you an initial idea of how your data would look in a report, or as a starting point for further development.

To create a report using the Report tool:
1 *Select the table or query that you want to create a report from in the Navigation pane.*
Or
▶ *Open the table or query in Datasheet view.*
2 *Click* **Report** *in the* **Reports** *group on the* **Create** *tab.*
3 *Your data will be presented in a basic report layout.*

The report will be presented in Layout view. This view can be particularly useful if you want to adjust any field sizes on your report as the data is displayed in the field controls.

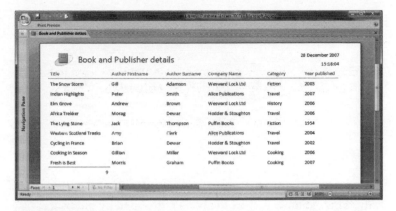

You will notice several objects on your report that enhance the presentation of the data, e.g. headers and footers, and summary data.

- ▶ *Headers and footers areas – the logo, report name, date and time are in the header.*
- ▶ *Summary data – there is a calculated field under the* **Title** *column, counting the number of items in the report.*

Report Layout tools

The Report Layout tools are displayed on the Format, Arrange and Page Setup tabs when you are in Layout view. Many of them are similar to those found in Form Layout view.

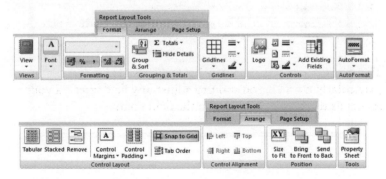

REPORT WIZARD

This can help you produce some very sophisticated reports, very easily. This example lists all the books, grouped by publisher.

1 *Click* **Report Wizard** *in the* **Reports** *group.*
2 *Select the table or query to create a report from (you can select fields from different tables as long as they are related).*
3 *Add your fields to the* **Selected Fields** *list and click* **Next**.

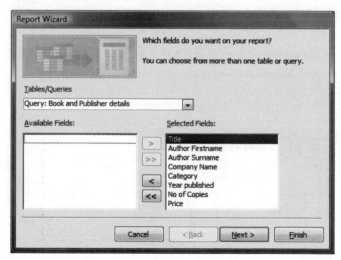

4 *How do you want to view your data – we will view it by* **Publisher.** *Click* **Next.**

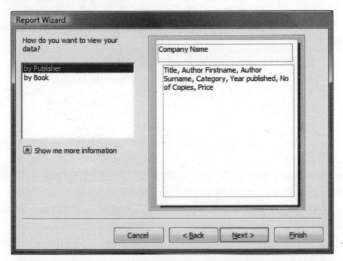

5 *Set the* **Grouping** *to* **Category** *– this will give us our books for each publisher grouped by category. Click* **Next.**

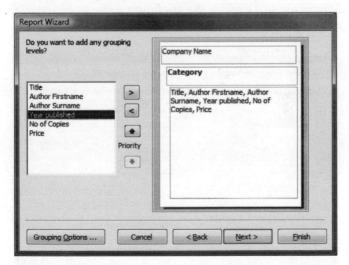

6 *At the Sorting step in the Wizard, if you have any fields in your report that contain numeric values, a Summary Options*

*button will be displayed. If you click this button you will be
presented with options that allow you to produce summary
data for your report for each group and/or the whole report.
The options include Sum, Average, Minimum and Maximum.*

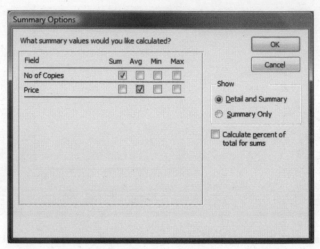

7 *Specify the sort order – the books are going to be sorted into
ascending order on Title.*

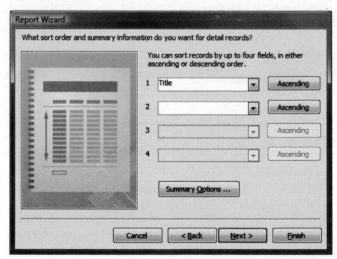

8 Choose a layout and orientation for your report (if you have lots of fields choose Landscape).

9 Select the **Adjust** checkbox if necessary – then Access will fit your fields onto the page as best it can. Click **Next**.

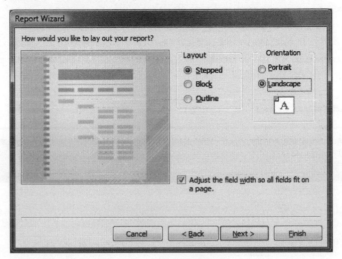

10 Select an **AutoFormat** and click **Next**.

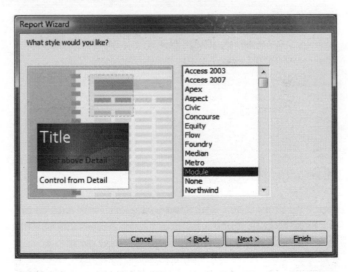

11 *At the final step, edit the report name if necessary and select* **Preview the Report.**

12 *Click* **Finish!** *Your report will be displayed.*

Check out your report in Print Preview and see if there is anything that you want to change. If you are lucky, everything will fit perfectly. If not, you may need to adjust a field size to display all of your data, or move fields closer together or further apart to get a good fit on the page.

Take your time and experiment!

Publisher				
Company Name	Title	Author Firstname	Author Surname	Year published
Alice Publications				
	Travel			
	Indian Highlights	Peter	Smith	2007
	Western Scotland Tracks	Amy	Clark	2004
Hodder & Stoughton				
	Travel			
	Africa Trekker	Morag	Dewar	2006
	Cycling in France	Brian	Dewar	2002
Puffin Books				
	Fiction			
	The Lying Stone	Jack	Thompson	1954
	Cooking			
	Fresh is Best	Morris	Graham	2007
Wesward Lock Ltd				
	Fiction			
	The Snow Storm	Gill	Adamson	2005

7.21 Exporting data

There may be times when you need to export your data to another file – perhaps so colleagues who don't have Access can use it, or so that additional operations can be performed on it.

You can easily export your data from Access in a range of formats, e.g. Excel, text, Word document, etc.

The Export options are on the External Data tab. When you select an option you will be prompted for the information required – just respond to the prompts to tell Access how to export the data. For example, to export data to an Excel spreadsheet:

1 *Click* Excel *in the* Export *group.*
2 *Verify or edit the* File name *as required.*
3 *Choose the* File format.

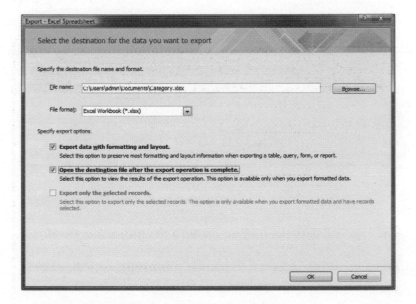

4 *Set any other export options as necessary.*
5 *Click* OK.

6 *If the export action is something that you do regularly, you could save the export steps.*

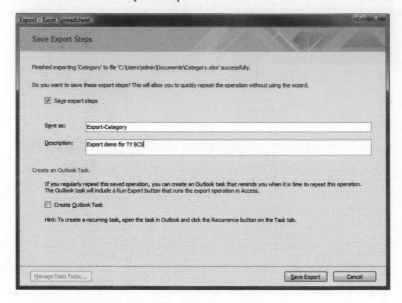

7 *Click* **OK.**

The exported data can then be viewed and processed in Excel.

If you saved your export information you can perform the same operation again from the Manage Data Tasks dialog box.

1 *Click* **Saved Exports** *in the* **Export** *group.*

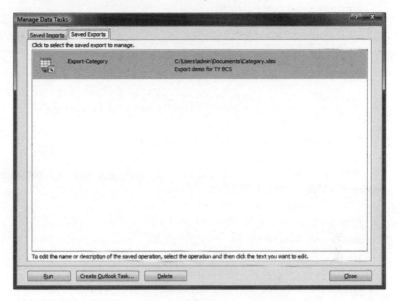

2 *Select the Export that you want to perform.*
3 *Click* **Run.**

TEST

1 Which database object contains your data?

2 Give two examples of properties that can be specified for a Text field.

3 What is meant by the terms Primary key and Foreign key?

4 Explain what a database relationship is.

5 You can enter data into a database by typing it directly into a table. What other object could you use for data entry?

6 Identify two database objects that are used to extract and display the data held in your database.

7 If you don't want to see all the records in a table, how could you show only the records required?

8 You only want to see the name and town fields out of a table that contains many fields. How could you do this?

9 What features in a report can help make the data from a database easier to read and interpret?

10 You want to manipulate some of the data from your database using Excel. What feature could you use to transfer the data?

8

Presentations

In this chapter you will learn:
- *about PowerPoint, a presentation graphics package*
- *how to create slides*
- *how to prepare and deliver a presentation*
- *how to print handouts*

8.1 Introduction to PowerPoint

You can use PowerPoint to produce:

Slides

Slides are the individual pages of your presentation. They may contain text, graphs, clip art, tables, drawings, and animation, video clips, visuals created in other applications, shapes – and more!! PowerPoint will allow you to present your slides via a slide show on your computer, 35 mm slides or overhead projector transparencies.

Notes Pages

A speaker's notes page accompanies each slide you create. Each notes page contains a small image of the slide plus any notes you type in. You can print the pages and use them to prompt you during your presentation.

Handouts

Handouts consist of smaller, printed versions of your slides that can be printed 2, 3, 6 or 9 slides to a page. They provide useful backup material for your audience and can easily be customized with your company name or logo.

Outline

Your presentation Outline contains the slide titles and main text items, but neither art nor text typed in using the Text tool. The Outline gives a useful overview of your presentation's structure.

I suggest that you choose a hobby that interests you, or any topic that you are familiar with and set up a presentation to practise on.

8.2 Getting started

When PowerPoint starts, you are presented with a new presentation displaying a blank Title slide. We'll take a tour of the PowerPoint screen, so that you know what the various areas are called.

If the Presentation file window is maximized, the file and the Application windows share one Title bar containing the Application and presentation names (initially the temporary name, e.g. *Presentation1*).

You'll find the different screen areas referred to by the names given below in the online Help and throughout this book.

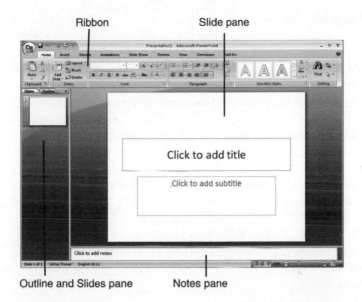

Ribbon   Slide pane

Outline and Slides pane   Notes pane

▶ *The boxes with dotted outlines that appear when you create a new slide are called placeholders.*

POWERPOINT OBJECTS

The text and graphics that you can place on a slide in PowerPoint are called objects. Objects may be:

Text	Drawings	Graphs	Clip art
Movies	Sounds	Tables	WordArt
Organization Charts or other diagrams			

Different slide layouts have different placeholders which will hold the title, text and other objects you display on your slide.

Think ahead

There is a lot to think about if you are giving a presentation.

Who is the presentation for? Why are you giving it? What does your audience hope to learn from it? How long do you have to deliver it? Where are you giving the presentation? What equipment will you have available? How big a room is it? Does the audience know anything about the subject you will be talking on? What age are they – children or adults?

Knowing the answers to questions like these will help you develop a successful presentation.

You can find some useful tips at http://www.presentationhelper.co.uk/presentationtips.htm

---

8.3 Creating a presentation

BLANK PRESENTATION

A blank presentation is just that – one with no special font formatting, background colours and effects, etc. Everything is set to the default. You can format the presentation as you wish, or add a theme to it later, once you are happy with the content.

1 *Click the* **Microsoft Office** *button.*
2 *Choose* **New...** *from the menu.*

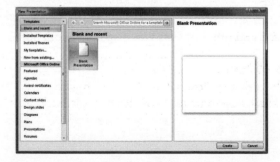

3 *At the* New Presentation *dialog box, select* Blank and recent *in the* Templates *categories.*
4 *Select* Blank Presentation.
5 *Click* Create.

Quick start

You can press [Ctrl]-[N] to create a new blank presentation file without opening the dialog box.

TEMPLATES

This option lets you create a presentation file that has already been completed with sample text and graphics. If you read the information on the slides you will get hints and suggestions on how to build a presentation using the template.

1 *Click the* Microsoft Office *button and choose* New...
2 *In the* Templates *categories, select* Installed Templates.
3 *Select a template from the list.*

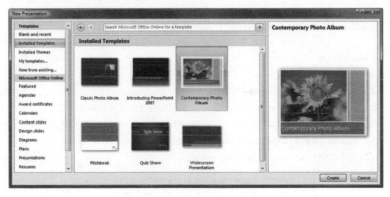

4 *Click* Create.

Help is at hand

The 'Introducing PowerPoint 2007' template gives a useful introduction to some of the features in the package.

THEMES

Themes help ensure that everything in your presentation is co-ordinated – fonts, colours, background effects, etc. If you use a theme, all you need to do is add your objects, and leave the formatting to PowerPoint! You can choose the theme for your presentation when you create it, or add it later. I prefer to use the blank presentation option so I can just concentrate on the content, and then perhaps apply a theme to finish it off.

1   *Click the* **Microsoft Office** *button and choose* **New...**
2   *In the* **Templates** *categories, select* **Installed Themes**

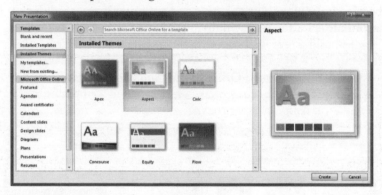

3   *Select a theme from the list.*
4   *Click* **Create.**
5   *Once a presentation has been created, you can easily add or delete slides, change slide layouts or change the theme used.*

8.4 View options

When working on a presentation, there are three view options to choose from: Normal, Slide Sorter or Slide Show view. PowerPoint displays all new presentations in Normal view.

Use the View icons at the bottom right of the screen to get a different view of your presentation.

You can also change views using the View tab. The Presentation Views group has an additional option

called Notes Page view. This displays a miniature of your slide, with the notes area below it. This is how your notes will look when printed. You can also enter and edit your notes in this view. If you wish to do this, use the Zoom command in the Zoom group on the View tab to zoom in to about 75% so that you can read the text.

In Slide Sorter view each slide is displayed in miniature – this can be used for moving slides around and to help you prepare for the actual presentation. We will discuss this view later.

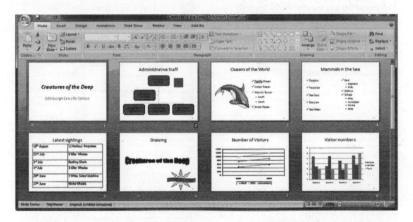

Slide Show view can be useful at any time to let you see how your slide will look in the final presentation. Press [Esc] from Slide Show view to return to your presentation file.

The view that you will use when setting up your presentation is Normal view. In Normal view, you have three panes displaying different parts of your presentation. The slide itself is in the top right pane, notes are displayed in the bottom right pane and the Outline and Slide tabs are displayed down the left.

OUTLINE AND SLIDES PANE

In Normal view the Outline and Slides pane is displayed down the left of the screen.

The Outline tab displays the text on each slide, with a slide icon to the left of each slide title. You can insert and delete text in the Outline tab just as you would on the slide itself. You can select a slide on the Outline tab by clicking the slide icon to the left of the slide title.

The Slides tab displays miniatures of the slides.

Outline tab

Slides tab

To resize the pane:
1 *Point to the splitter bar between the* **Outline and Slides** *pane and the* **Slide** *pane.*
2 *Drag the bar to make the pane wider or narrower.*

If you drag the splitter bar to the left edge of the screen (or click its **Close** button), so that the pane is hidden, you can display it again be dragging the bar to the right, or by clicking the **Normal** button in the **Presentation views** group on the **View** tab.

NOTES PANE

You may wish to add notes (to use during your presentation) to slides. They are added in the Notes pane (or in Notes Pages view).

1 *Click in the Notes pane.*
2 *Type in your notes.*

Slide titles

When creating your slides, give each slide a different title. You will find it easier to navigate your way around your presentation in the Outline pane and during a slide show if you do.

8.5 Working with slides

To move through the slides in your presentation:
▶ *Click on the slide that you wish to display on the* **Slides** *tab.*
▶ *Click the* **Next Slide** *or* **Previous Slide** *button at the bottom of the vertical scroll bar.*

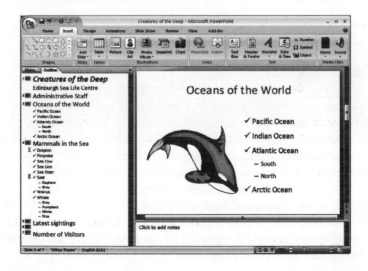

Or

▶ *Drag the elevator on the vertical scroll bar up and down.*

Once you've created a presentation, the next step is to decide on the text that you want to appear on your slides – the title and the main points that you want to discuss during your presentation.

The main text on a slide will be in the slide title or the bulleted list area.

You can determine the structure of the text on each slide (main points, sub-points, etc.), using up to nine levels if necessary.

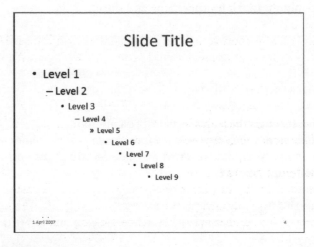

ENTERING TEXT

Follow the prompts on the slide – click within a placeholder and type in your text.

When adding text to your bullet points remember the KISS rule – Keep it Short and Simple. The bullet point should be a summary of what you are going to tell your audience, not the full script. As a general rule, you should follow the 666 rule – no more than 6 words to a bullet point, no more than 6 bullet points to a slide and no more than 6 text slides before you introduce some other layout to break your presentation up a bit.

Editing text

1 *Locate the slide you want to edit.*
2 *Click to place the insertion point inside the text to be edited.*
3 *Insert or delete characters as required.*
▶ *If you want to change the text completely, select the old text (click and drag over it) and key in the replacement text.*

Promoting and demoting (structuring the text)

The points you want to make on your slides will be structured – you will have main points (at the first bulleted level) and some of these points will have sub-points (at the second, third, fourth – up to possibly the ninth level).

Initially, all points on your slide are at level 1. You can easily demote sub-items if necessary (and promote them again if you change your mind).

1 *Place the insertion point within the item.*
2 *Click the* **Increase List Level** or **Decrease List Level** *in the* **Paragraph** *group on the* **Home** *tab.*

Moving bullet points

You can rearrange the points on a slide using cut and paste or drag and drop, or click in the item and press **[Shift]-[Alt]-[Up arrow]** (to move it up) or **[Shift]-[Alt]-[Down arrow]** (to move it down).

ADDING NEW SLIDES

You can add new slides at any place in your presentation (not just at the end).

1 *Display the slide that you want above your new one.*
2 *Click the* **New Slide** *button in the* **Slides** *group on the* **Home** *tab to add a single bulleted list.*

Or

Click the arrow beside the button and choose a layout.

3 *Enter your text – follow the prompts.*
4 *Repeat steps 1 to 2 until all slides have been added.*

Deleting slides
  1 *Select the slide miniature in the* **Slides** *pane in Normal view.*
  2 *Press* [Delete].

MOVE/COPY SLIDES

Drag and drop the slide miniatures to move the slides in either the Slides pane in Normal view or in Slide Sorter view.

You can copy or move slides from one presentation file to another using copy/cut and paste techniques.

8.6 Formatting

Most formatting options, e.g. bold, alignment and bullets, work in the same way as in all other applications. Formatting options that are unique to PowerPoint include layout and themes:

CHANGING A SLIDE LAYOUT

If you decide you have the wrong layout for a slide, it is easily changed.

1 *View the slide whose layout you wish to change.*

2 *Click* **Layout** *in the* **Slides** *group on the* **Home** *tab.*

3 *Select a new layout.*

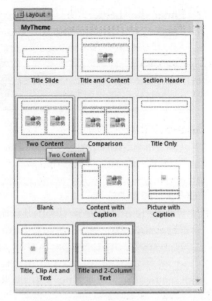

Line spacing

The line spacing of bullet points is normally set to single. You can change the line spacing to distribute the text more evenly within a placeholder if necessary.

1 *Select your text.*

2 *Display the line spacing options and click on the one required.*

Or

    Click More..., *specify your requirements in the* **Indents and Spacing** *dialog box and click* **OK.**

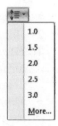

THEME

Each presentation uses a theme – a set of formatting choices that includes a colour theme (a set of colours), font theme (a set of fonts) and effects theme (a set of line and fill options) for your file. There is a wide range of professionally designed themes for you to choose from – or you can create your own. The themes are shared across the Office applications, i.e. Word, Excel and PowerPoint.

To change the theme:
1 *Display the* **Design** *tab.*
2 *Scroll through the themes in the* **Themes** *group.*

Or

    Click the **More** *button to display them all.*
3 *Select a theme.*

Mixed themes

If your presentation is divided into sections (perhaps with several slides on each topic), you could apply a different theme to the different parts so that it was clear when you moved from one topic or another. Or you could change just an element of the theme, e.g. background colour.

You can select multiple slides in Normal view using the Slides pane on the left, or you can select several slides at the same time in Slide Sorter view.

To select multiple slides:
1 *Select the first slide you want.*
2 *Hold down* **[Ctrl]** *and click on each of the other slides.*
3 *To select several adjacent slides in Slide Sorter view, click on the first one, then* **[Shift]-click** *on the last one that you wish to select.*
▶ *You can then apply a theme to, or modify a theme element on, the selected slides.*

Experiment with the other formatting options. These are found in the Font and Paragraph groups on the Home tab, and the Theme and Background groups on the Design tab.

8.7 Headers and footers

Headers and Footers can be placed at the top of Notes pages, Handouts or a printout of your presentation Outline. Footers can also be placed on slides. They can be used to display page numbers or slide numbers, the date, time or any other information you want to repeat in this area on each slide or page.

1 *Display the* **Insert** *tab in the ribbon.*
2 *Choose* **Header & Footer...** *in the* **Text** *group.*
3 *Select the appropriate tab –* **Slide** *or* **Notes and Handouts**.

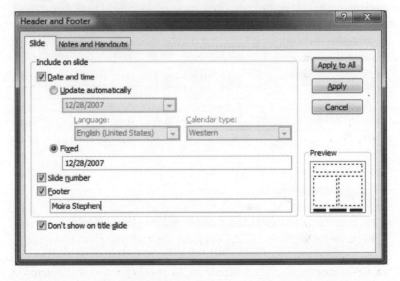

4 *Tick the items you want to appear, giving details as needed.*
5 *Click* **Apply** *or* **Apply to All**.

8.8 Charts

To create a chart:
1 *Add a slide with a Content layout.*
2 *Click the* **Insert Chart** *button.*
3 *Select the chart type you want to create in the left pane of the* **Insert Chart** *dialog box.*

4 *Choose a subtype from the right pane in the dialog box.*
5 *Click* **OK.**

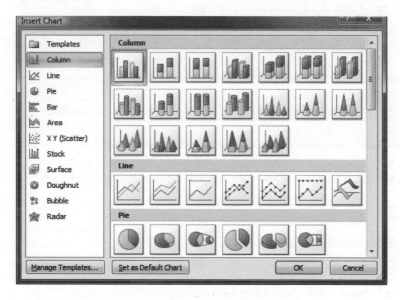

▶ *Sample chart data is displayed in an Excel window, side-by-side with your presentation file.*
6 *Edit the contents on the Excel worksheet as required.*
7 *Close Excel when you have entered your data.*
8 *Your chart will be displayed on your slide.*

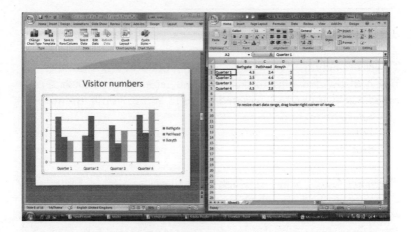

When you create a chart in this way, its data is embedded in the PowerPoint file, but you input and edit it using Excel.

You can also add a chart by clicking **Chart** in the **Illustrations** group on the **Insert** tab.

Once you have created your chart, you can format it using the same tools as when in Excel. See Section 6.24 for more details.

8.9 Organization charts

Hierarchy charts are used for organization charts or other relationships that can be illustrated in a hierarchical way.

To create an organization chart
1 *Add a chart with a Content placeholder.*
2 *Click the* **Insert SmartArt** *tool.*
3 *Select* **Hierarchy** *in the left panel.*
4 *Select the* **Organization Chart** *layout (or other hierarchy chart layout) from the right panel.*
5 *Click* **OK.**

See Section 4.12 for more information on organization charts.

8.10 Tables

Tables are arranged in a grid, consisting of rows and columns. Where a row and column intersect, you get a rectangular area called a cell. If you have created tables in Word, you'll find it very easy to create them on slides.

CREATING A TABLE

There are several ways in which you can create a table. Experiment with them to find out which method you prefer.

To create a table on a slide with a Content placeholder:
1 *Create a slide with a Content placeholder.*
2 *Click the* Insert Table *button.*
3 *Specify the number of columns and rows in the* Insert Table *dialog box.*
4 *Click* OK.

To create a table on a slide with no placeholder:
1 *Click* Table *in the* Tables *group on the* Insert *tab.*
2 *Drag over the table grid until you have the table size required.*
3 *Release the mouse button.*
Or
1 *Click* Table *in the* Tables *group and then click* Insert Table...
2 *Specify the size in the* Insert Table *dialog box.*
3 *Click* OK.

To draw a table on a slide with no placeholder:

1 *Click* **Table** *in the* **Tables** *group on the* **Insert** *tab and then click* **Draw Table**.
The **Draw Table** *command button (in the* **Draw Borders** *group on the* **Design** *tab) is automatically selected.*

2 *Click and drag to draw a rectangle the size of the table.*
3 *Draw in rows and columns where you want them.*
4 *Click the* **Draw Table** *button or press* [Esc] *to stop drawing.*

To remove lines:

1 *Select the* **Eraser** *command button.*
2 *Click on the line you wish to erase with the tip of the Eraser.*
3 *Deselect the Eraser – click the button again, or press* [Esc].

It doesn't matter which method you use to create the table, once you have it on your slide you can format it and manipulate it in many different ways.

See Section 5.15 for more information on tables.

8.11 Clip art

PowerPoint comes with thousands of clip art pictures that can be added to your slides. In addition to these, you'll find that you can access many more on the Internet.

You can easily insert clip art into any slide in your presentation.

1 *Click the* **Insert Clip Art** *tool on the Drawing toolbar.*
Or

    If the slide has a Content or Clip Art placeholder, click on the **Insert Clip Art** *tool in a Content placeholder, or double-click the Clip Art placeholder.*

2 *Enter your search criteria, e.g. food, music, animal.*
3 *Click on the picture required.*
4 *Move/resize the clip art as required.*

See Section 4.13 for more information on clip art.

Shapes and drawings

Because of the visual nature of PowerPoint, you could use the Shapes to create your own diagrams. Shapes were introduced in 4.12.

In addition to the basic skills introduced there, you should explore the Format tab in the Drawing tools to see what other features there are. In particular, try out

- ▶ *Adding text to shapes*
- ▶ *Rotate and flip shapes*
- ▶ *Group and ungroup shapes – to select more than one shape, hold down [Shift] and click on each one*
- ▶ *Move overlapping shapes backwards and forwards relative to each other.*

8.12 Masters

A template is the design on which a presentation is based. Each template must consist of at least one Master slide, and it may also contain several slide layouts. The layouts specify the position of the text and other objects that will eventually appear on your slides. The positions are set by adding placeholders to the slide master and slide layouts.

PowerPoint 2007 has several built-in standard layouts for a slide master, and you can add custom ones if you wish.

These layout elements can be added to master or layout slides:

- ▶ *Placeholders for Title, Subtitle, Body text, Headers and Footers;*
- ▶ *Background object, e.g. logo or background fill;*
- ▶ *Placeholder formatting.*

Master slides

The master slide is at the top of a hierarchy of slides in your presentation file. Below the master are the layouts, and below that are the actual slides in your presentation.

Each presentation consists of one or more master slides.

Each master contains one or more layouts. These masters and layouts make up the presentation template. Each template will also contain theme information with details of font, colour, etc.

Changes to the master slide will affect all slides in your presentation.

Changes to a layout slide will affect all slides in your presentation that use that layout.

Changes to the master or layout slides are made in Slide Master view.

SLIDE MASTER VIEW

To view the slide master and slide layouts for the presentation:

1 *Display the* View *tab in the Ribbon.*

2 *Click* Slide Master *in the* Presentation Views *group.*

The current slide master will be displayed at the top of the Slide pane, and its slide layouts will be listed below it.

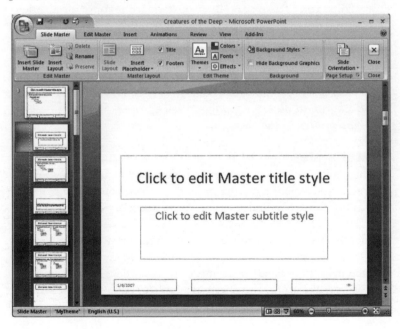

There must be at least one slide master, so if your presentation has only one (which is usually the case) the Delete option in the Edit Master group on the Slide Master tab is inactive.

If you make changes to the slide master, e.g. the colour of the main heading or the style of a bullet point, or insert a logo or clip art, this will be reflected in the slide layouts based on the master.

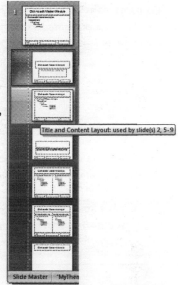

Title and Content Layout: used by slide(s) 2, 5-9

If you move your pointer over the slide layouts in the left pane, PowerPoint will tell you which slides use that layout. You cannot delete layouts that are in use.

NEW SLIDE MASTER

If you require an additional slide master for your file – perhaps because you have multiple sections, and want different layouts for each one – you can easily add it.

To add a new slide master:
▶ *Click Insert Slide Master in the Edit Master group.*

A new slide master is added, with the standard slide layouts below it.

To delete a slide master:
▶ *You can only delete a slide master if there is more than one in your file.*
1 *Select the slide master.*
2 *Click* **Delete** *in the* **Edit Master** *group.*

To format the slide master:

▶ *Choose a theme for the master, or edit the colours, fonts or effects using the* **Edit Theme** *group on the* **Slide Master** *tab.*

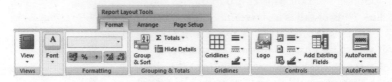

Anything you do on the slide master will be repeated on all the slide layouts that follow that master.

▶ *Click* **Close Master View** *to return to your presentation when you have finished.*

8.13 Slide show preparation

The whole point of setting up a presentation is so that you can eventually deliver it to your audience. Once you've got your slides organized, there are a number of tools that you can use to help you finalize your preparations.

HIDE SLIDE

This option can prove useful if you're not sure whether or not you really need a particular slide for your presentation. You can include the slide, but hide it. The hidden slide will be bypassed during your slide show, unless you decide you need to use it.

To hide a slide:

1 *Select the slide in Normal or Slide Sorter view.*
2 *Click* **Hide Slide** *in the* **Set Up** *group on the* **Slide Show** *tab.*

In the Slide pane, and in Slide Sorter view, the number of the hidden slide is crossed out. When you give your presentation, the slide will be skipped, and your audience will never know it was there.

▶ *If you want to show the hidden slide during the presentation, press* [H] *at the slide preceding the hidden one.*

To remove the hidden status from the slide:
▶ *Select it and then click* Hide Slide *again.*

REHEARSE TIMINGS

It is a very good idea to practise your presentation before you end up in front of your audience. As well as practising what you intend to say (probably with the aid of notes you have made using the Notes page), you can rehearse the timings for each slide. This is particularly important if you know you have a limited amount of time, e.g. a 10-minute slot at a meeting.

Whatever slide you are on when you begin to rehearse timings, PowerPoint assumes that you want to start from slide 1.

1 *Click* Rehearse Timings *in the* Set Up *group on the* Slide Show *tab. Your slide show will start at slide 1, and the Rehearsal toolbar will be displayed.*

2 *Go over what you intend to say while the slide is displayed.*
3 *Click the left button to move to the next slide when ready.*
4 *Repeat steps 2 and 3 until you reach the end of your presentation.*

DISPLAY TIMINGS

A dialog box displays the total time your presentation took and asks if you want to record and use the timings in a show. Choose **Yes** if you want each slide to advance after the allocated time.

The slide timings will be displayed in Slide Sorter view.

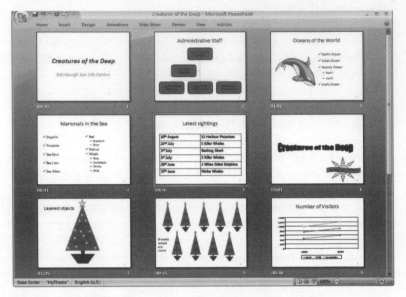

> ▶ *You can rehearse your timings as often as is necessary, until you've got the pace right to get your message across.*

Remove timings

To remove timings from your slide, go to the Animations tab and deselect the Automatically After checkbox in the Advance Slide group.

Stay in control!

Beware of Display timings or setting your slides to advance automatically after a given time.

This feature is very useful when practising or if you are setting the presentation up to run automatically at an exhibition or in a show room. However, if you are actually there delivering the presentation it is usually best to be in control. So remember to remove the timings before you give your presentation.

8.14 Animations

There are basically two types of animation effect you can add to the slides in your presentation – transitions and builds. Don't go overboard with animation effects – you'll give your audience a headache! If you are using transitions be consistent and use the same effect on each slide. The speed setting should usually be set to fast – you want your audience to concentrate on the content of your presentation rather than all the special effects!

TRANSITION

A transition is a special effect that is used when you move from one slide to another in your presentation.

To add a transition effect:
1 *Display the* **Animations** *tab.*
2 *Select the slide(s) that you want to add an effect to – the transition will introduce the slide(s).*
3 *Choose an effect from the gallery.*
4 *Set a* **Transition Sound** *if required.*
5 *Specify the* **Transition** *speed.*
6 *If you want the same effect applied to all slides in your presentation, click* **Apply to All.**

▶ *You can also set timings manually in the* **Transition To This Slide** *group on the* **Animations** *tab. Select* **Automatically After** *and set the timing in the field.*

ANIMATION

An animation is created within a slide. It is
used to build bullet points one by one, or
to bring different objects onto your slide at
different times (rather than have them all
appear at once). You have to be in Normal
view to set animations.

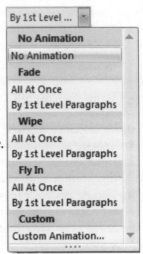

1 *Display the slide you want to animate.*
2 *Select the object you want to animate,*
   e.g. a bullet list or a chart.
3 *Select an effect from the* **Animate** *list.*

The lists of effects vary depending on the
type of object you have selected.

Builds

If you want to animate a table and bring each column or row in
one at a time, you have to create a separate table or shape for
each column or row. You can then build up the 'table', column by
column or row by row.

8.15 Slide Show

You can run your slide show at any time to check how your presentation is progressing. Each slide fills the whole of your computer screen. After the last, you are returned to the view you were in when you clicked the Slide Show tool.

1 *Select the slide you want to start from, usually the first.*
2 *Click the **Slide Show** icon to the right of the horizontal scroll bar.*
3 *Press [**Page Down**] or [**Enter**] (or click the left mouse button) to move onto the next slide.*
▶ *Press [**Page Up**] to move back to the previous slide if necessary.*
▶ *You can exit your slide show at any time by pressing [**Esc**].*

WORKING WITHIN YOUR SLIDE SHOW

When presenting your slide show, you might want to leave the normal sequence, go directly to a slide, or draw on a slide to focus attention. These, and other features, can be accessed using the popup menu or the keyboard.

▶ *Right-click anywhere on screen, or click the popup menu icon at the bottom left corner.*

To go directly to a slide:
1 *Select Go to Slide.*
2 *Choose the slide you want to go to.*

Experiment with the popup menu to see what options are available.

To draw on your screen:
1 *Press [**Ctrl**]-[**P**] to change the pointer to a pen.*
2 *Click and drag to draw.*
3 *Press [**Ctrl**]-[**A**] to change the pointer back to an arrow shape.*

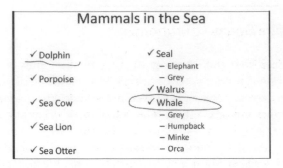

To erase your drawing:

▶ *Press* [E] *on your keyboard.*

To get more help on the options available to you while running Slide Show, press [F1]. The **Slide Show Help** dialog box lists other options you might want to experiment with.

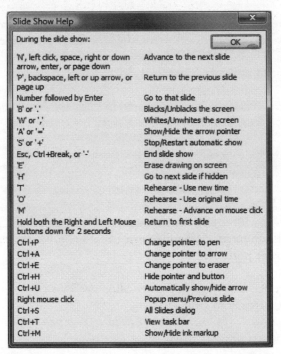

8.16 Printing presentations

The first stage to printing is to specify the slide setup, setting the slide size and orientation. The default slide orientation is landscape, and they are sized for a 4:3 ratio.

1 *Click* **Page Setup** *on the* **Design** *tab.*
2 *Select the size from the* **Slides sized for** *field.*
3 *Specify the* **Orientation** *for the slides.*
4 *Specify the* **Orientation** *for the notes, handouts and outline.*

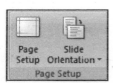

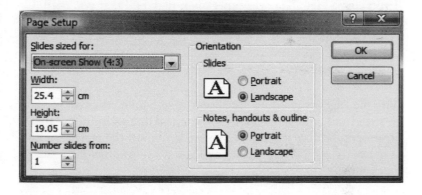

5 *Click* **OK.**

All slides in a presentation file must be in one orientation, either landscape or portrait.

These are the main options on the **Slide sized for** list (you can check the others out yourself).

Type	Width	Height	Notes
On-screen show	25.4 cm	19.05 cm	Landscape; 4:3 aspect ratio
Letter paper	25.4 cm	19.05 cm	4:3 aspect ratio
A4 paper	27.5 cm	19.05 cm	Aspect ratio between that of on-screen show and 35 mm slides
35 mm slides	28.5 cm	19.05 cm	Content will fill the slide in landscape orientation
Overhead	25.4 cm	19.05 cm	Select for OHT
Banner	20.32 cm	2.54 cm	
Custom			Set own measurements

If you change the slide orientation, you may find that you need to change the size and shape of placeholders on the Slide Master to get your objects to fit well.

PRINT PREVIEW

With the Page Setup details specified for the output required, you can go ahead and print your slides. I recommend that you preview your presentation before you print it. If you do not like the preview, adjust as necessary and preview again, until you are happy that it is ready for printing.

1 *Click the* **Microsoft Office** *button.*
2 *Click the arrow to the right of* **Print** *on the menu.*
3 *Choose* **Print Preview.**

The presentation is displayed in Print Preview and the Print Preview tab is displayed in the Ribbon.

You can move through your presentation using the elevator on the scroll bar, or the Next Page, Previous Page command buttons in the Preview group on the Ribbon or those at the bottom of the vertical scrollbar.

From left to right on the Ribbon:

Print	Displays the Print dialog box.
Options	Gives quick access to many of the options in the Print dialog box.
Print What	Choose from slides, handouts, notes or outline.
Orientation	Gives access to landscape and portrait options available for handouts, notes pages and outline.

Zoom	The default option fits the slide/page to the screen. You can increase or decrease it if you wish.
Close	Closes the preview window.

Printing from the Quick Access Toolbar

If you are confident that you want to print with the default print setting, click the Print tool on the Quick Access Toolbar. One copy of each slide will be printed on a separate page in landscape orientation.

Print dialog box

If you want to be more specific about what you print, go to the Print dialog box.

1 *Click the* **Microsoft Office** *button and select the* **Print** *option.*

In the Print dialog box you can specify:

Printer	If you can access more than one printer you can specify the printer in the **Name:** field.
Print Range	Select from All, Current slide, Selection, Custom Show or Slides.
Print what	Choose Slides, handouts, notes pages or outline.
Color/ grayscale	Choose Color, Grayscale or Pure Black and White.
Handouts	If you choose Handouts in the Print what: field, specify the number of slides per page and the order in this area.

TEST

1. *What is the keyboard shortcut that creates a new file?*

2. *Your presentation file contains the slides for your presentation. What support materials can you create for your presentation from within your PowerPoint file?*

3. *Name two view options that are specific to PowerPoint.*

4. *How do you change the slide layout?*

5. *What elements are stored in a theme?*

6. *Identify four different objects that you could put on a slide.*

7. *How can you group several shapes to create one object?*

8. *What is a Master slide?*

9. *What is the difference between a slide transition and an animation effect?*

10. *You can choose to start your slide show from two locations. What are they?*

9

···

Web browsing

In this chapter you will learn:
- *about Internet Explorer*
- *some ways to use the Internet*
- *how to keep safe online*
- *how to browse and to search for information*
- *how to copy text and pictures from the Web*

9.1 Jargon busting

Transferring information via the Internet has become in integral part of our lives, and as this comes with a considerable amount of jargon, we will start off by giving a brief definition of some of the terms you are bound to encounter sooner or later.

The **Internet** is a global network that links millions of computers together. It enables any computer, anywhere in the world, to communicate with any other – as long as they are both connected. It provides the infrastructure that many of us use (and rely on) for global communications.

The **World Wide Web** (WWW or Web) is one way of distributing information over the Internet. It displays the information on web pages, in websites (a group of web pages from the same company or individual).

You can also distribute information over the Internet using e-mail, user groups, instant messaging and file transfer.

When people think or talk about the Internet, they are usually referring to the Web and visiting websites or surfing (browsing around the Web looking for information), but it is important to realize that the Internet and the Web are not the same thing.

Internet Service Provider (ISP): A company that provides you with access to the Internet, e.g. British Telecom, Virgin, Orange.

Web browser: Software used to locate and view web pages, e.g. Internet Explorer, Netscape Navigator, Safari, Firefox.

Web server: A computer on the Internet that stores web pages or provides other services to the Web.

Website: A number of related web pages, owned and managed by one person or organization.

Web page: A web page usually contains text, graphics and hyperlinks – and often sounds and perhaps video/movie files.

Hyperlink: A 'hotspot' which could be text or pictures. Hyperlink text is normally (but not always) blue with an underline. With picture hyperlinks, the pointer changes to a hand with a pointing finger on it when you move it over the picture. When you click on a hyperlink you could be taken to another area within the page, or to another web page or a different site.

Protocol: A set of rules defining how to do something. Different sets of rules are used for different types of information, e.g.

http (Hyper Text Transfer Protocol) is used for transferring web pages on the Web.

ftp (File Transfer Protocol) is used to transfer files from one computer to another across the Internet.

smtp (Simple Mail Transfer Protocol) is used for transferring e-mails between servers.

Domain name: The name which identifies the computer on which web pages are stored.

Uniform Resource Locator (URL): The address of a file on the Internet, e.g.

http://www.hodder.co.uk/Category/8725/Computing.htm

http: this identifies the protocol.
// the slashes are used as separators – double ones after the protocol, and single ones between folders
www.hodder.co.uk/ the domain name
Category/ a folder within the domain
8725/ a folder within the Category folder
Computing.htm a document name (an individual web page)

Domain suffix: This helps you to identify the country and the type of organization that owns a domain. You may notice the following ones:

edu	US educational institution
gov	government agencies
org	non-profit-making organizations
mil	US military
com	US commercial organization
net	network organizations
ac	academic institution

Country codes

You can usually tell in what country an organization is based in from the country code.

Other than for the USA, most URLs will have country codes that identify the organization's base, e.g.

uk (United Kingdom)	fr (France);	de (Germany)
cz (Czech Republic)	dk (Denmark)	es (Spain)
ch (Switzerland)	ca (Canada)	au (Australia).

If there is no country code, it usually indicates that the domain is international or US-based.

You could try to work out the type of organization and the location of the following websites:

http://www.eastlothian.gov.uk/
http://www.virginmedia.com/
http://www.edinburghrocks.co.uk/
http://www.edinburgh.ac.uk/
http://www.washington.edu/
http://www.army.mil/
http://www.nswrno.net.au/

and then check them out to see if you were right!

Search engine: A tool that allows you to retrieve information from a system using keywords. When using the Internet a search engine will help you locate web pages that contain the keywords that you are looking for.

Cookie: A small text file that is sent from a website to your computer, and stored there. When you revisit the website, your browser will send the text file to it. The main purpose of a cookie is to allow the website to identify the user visiting the site, and perhaps customize the web page content to suit the user's interests and preferences.

Cache: A storage area in your computer's memory used for temporary storage of web pages that you visit in an Internet session. Should you revisit a web page in the same session, you may find that the page loads a lot quicker than it did the first time, as it is being loaded from cache, rather than from the Internet.

Really Simple Syndication (RSS): A Web feed format used to publish frequently updated content, e.g. blog (web log) entries, news headlines or podcasts. RSS documents, called 'feed', 'web feed' or 'channel', contain either a summary of content from an associated website or the full text. RSS allows people to keep up to date with what is happening on their favourite websites without checking them manually.

Podcast: A digital media file (or a related collection of such files) which is distributed over the Internet to portable media players and PCs using syndication feeds. The word podcast is a fusion of iPod and broadcast as the Apple iPod was the first device that used this technology. You can subscribe to podcasts, which results in you receiving new content from them automatically when it is published. Podcasts are often distributed through RSS.

9.2 Security considerations

As our use of the Internet increases, our exposure to cyber criminals also increases. It can be hard to appreciate just how vulnerable you really are to Internet crime when sitting in the comfort of your home or office, but beware – it is all around you. And there is probably a lot more cyber crime than we ever hear about, as companies prefer not to go public on it in case it affects their business, and individuals might not always report it as they think that they have been a bit naive and it is perhaps their own fault.

If you use social networking sites, e.g. Facebook or Bebo, be very careful about the information you give out and the friends you allow into your space. Think twice before giving out personal information either as part of a business transaction, or on a networking site. If the wrong people get your e-mail address or access to your Facebook area, you may become the victim of online bullying and harassment. We all hear stories in the news about people becoming victims of this – so be very selective when choosing new online 'friends'. And don't give strangers details of your home address, or arrange to meet them because they seem really friendly – anyone can claim to be anybody that they want to be when online. You have no way of checking who they really are. It just isn't worth the risk!

This section will help you become more aware of security threats, and give you some guidelines on what you can do to minimize your exposure to those risks when using the Internet.

DOWNLOADING FILES

You will find many sites that allow you to download files from them – text, image, sound and/or video. Downloading simply means you transfer the file from the website to your local computer. Downloading files is relatively easy.

Once you have found the file that you want to download, you click on its name or click on a button that says Download or Download Now. You will be asked if you want to Save the file to your local computer, or to Open it from its current location. If you opt to save the file to your local computer, you should check it for viruses before you open it.

Be careful when downloading files – they are often a source of computer viruses – so make sure that the site you are downloading from is one that you believe to be safe.

As well as the virus threat you may be breaking the law yourself when downloading music or videos – so beware!

Stay safe!

We discussed malware in Section 1.1. You might like to read the notes there again as well as the extra information given here.

And just to prove we aren't the only ones paranoid about IT security you could take a look at http://www.pcmag.com/article2/0,2817,2334856,00.asp and http://www.bbc.co.uk/webwise/askbruce/articles/security/

VIRUS

A virus is a computer program that gets loaded onto your computer without you realizing it. Once on your computer, it can spread throughout your disks, memory and files and cause all sorts of damage – and many viruses can spread across computer networks and bypass security systems.

Viruses are often spread in e-mail attachments, files that are downloaded from the Internet, and pirate copies of software.

To help protect your system from viruses you should install anti-virus software, e.g. Norton or McAfee. Once installed you must ensure that you keep it up to date (most anti-virus suppliers download updates to your system as they come available) and run it regularly to make sure that your system is clean. You can usually set your virus checker to run automatically at a specific time of day.

Some terms you may encounter when reading about viruses:

Worm: A program which actively transmits itself over a network to infect other computers.

Trojan horse: A piece of software which appears to perform a certain action, but in fact, performs another.

Malware (malicious software): Software designed to infiltrate or damage a computer system without the owner's knowingly consenting to it.

Firewall: Hardware or software device designed to prevent unauthorized access to your computer by other Internet users. The firewall will check all messages entering and leaving your system, and if they don't meet security criteria they will be blocked. Every computer with access to the Internet should have one!

A short video explaining a firewall can be found on the BBC website at http://www.bbc.co.uk/webwise/getonline/index.shtml?initialModule=firewall

Digital certificate: Identification which can be attached to an e-mail to allow the recipient to verify that the message is really from who it claims to be from. It can also be attached to a website so that the identity of the remote computer can be checked before you conduct a transaction with it (see 'Credit card fraud on the Internet' below).

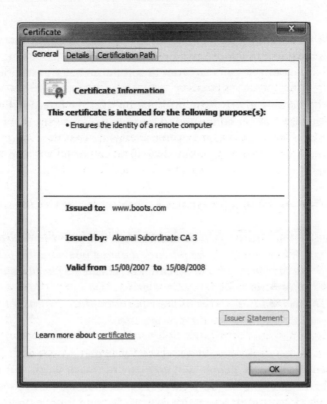

Encryption: Used to code messages that are sent electronically. The recipient must have the key to the code so that they can decode the message that they receive and read it. If you don't have the key – you can't read the message. Encryption is used when sending sensitive information, e.g. credit card details and other private information, and is routinely used by banks and companies that sell goods over the Internet.

CREDIT CARD FRAUD ON THE INTERNET

Credit card fraud on the Internet is on the increase. More and more people are buying things online – holidays, wine, tickets for everything from air travel to pop concerts, the weekly shop and car insurance. Most of these transactions cannot take place unless you pay for the service or goods there and then – using your credit card.

So it is vitally important that you are as sure as you can be that your details are going to the company you think that you are dealing with, and that no one else can read your details during the transaction.

You should only give private information over the Internet if you are sure that you are connected to a secure site. A secure site is one that takes all reasonable precautions to ensure that the connection or communication between you and them cannot be intercepted by anyone else.

There are several things to indicate that you are on a secure site:

▶ *the Security Report button to the right of the Address bar. When you click the padlock a dialog box should open giving details of who the security certificate has been issued to, by whom and what its validity period is.*
▶ *The web address in the address bar should start https:// to indicate that you are on a secure site.*

Computer networks should be secured with user names and passwords. Your IT people will take care of this at work, but you should make sure that you lock your home Internet connection and network down too. If you don't, you are leaving it wide open to abuse – at best you may find neighbours or the students on your stair piggy-backing on your connection (which could slow it down a bit) – or you may find hackers spying on you and collecting your details for their own purposes.

PARENTAL CONTROL OPTIONS

Parents are very aware of the benefits of Internet access for their children. It is a huge information resource for homework and projects, research for holidays and keeping in touch with the grandparents. But it can be a dangerous place. How can parents protect them when they are online? The main options are:

▶ *Supervision – be around when the children are online so that you can see what they are up to (easier with younger ones).*

- *Web browsing restrictions – you can restrict the websites that children can visit and thereby ensure that they visit only websites that are appropriate for their age.*
- *Computer games restrictions – you can control access to games, choose an age rating level, etc.*
- *Computer usage time limits – you can specify when children can log on, and the total hours per day/week.*

These options are in the **Tools > Internet Options > Contents** tab in Internet Explorer.

Banks and security

Several banks and building societies put security information on their websites – because they want you, the customer, to know that they take Internet security seriously. It is very bad publicity if a financial institution is found to be careless in this area.

Have a look at http://www.lloydstsb.com/security/security_learning.asp and try the quiz.

There is also a useful glossary of terms – which introduces some not covered here.

See http://www.lloydstsb.com/security/security_glossary.asp

and from the Halifax http://www.halifax.co.uk/securityandprivacy/securitydemos.asp

and the Bank of Scotland http://www.bankofscotlandhalifax.co.uk/securityandprivacy/securitytest.asp

You'll find many more if you search the Internet.

9.3 First steps...

To open your browser:
  1 *Open the* **Start** *menu.*
  2 *Click* **All Programs** *and then* **Internet Explorer.**
Or
  ▶ *Click* **Launch Internet Explorer Browser** *in the* **Quick Launch** *area of the Taskbar.*

If you have a broadband Internet connection you should have immediate access to the Internet when you launch your browser.

If you have a dial-up connection you'll be asked for your user name and password – complete the dialog box when prompted.

The page that appears on your screen when you open your browser application is your **home** page.

You can visit any page on the Web by entering the URL in the Address bar.

TABS

If you want to open more than one web page at a time, you can use the tabs that appear along the top of the browser window.

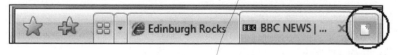

The tabs enable you to have several web pages open simultaneously in one browser window – which means that you have only one button on the Taskbar for Internet Explorer.

Address bar   Tabs   Refresh Stop
                Toolbar   Search box

The Internet Explorer screen

To open a web page on a new tab:

1 *Click* **New Tab** *to the right of the open tabs or press* **[Ctrl]-[T]**.
2 *Type the URL of the page to go to in the Address bar.*

To move from one tab to another:

▶ *Just click on the tab you want to view.*

To close a tab:

1 *Click on the tab you want to close – to bring it to the top.*
2 *Click the Close button on the tab itself.*

You must keep at least one tab open.

You could also open a new window so that you can visit another
web page without leaving the one that you are viewing.

To open a new window:
▶ *Click the* **Page** *command button and choose* **New Window** *from the options (or press* [Ctrl]-[N]*).*

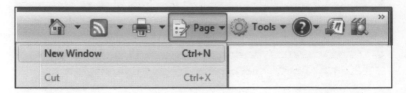

SLOW DOWNLOAD?

Some pages can take a while to download. If they have lots of graphics on them, or if your Internet connection is slow for some reason, you may find yourself – waiting – patiently – waiting – patiently… until you don't really want to wait any longer!!

When this happens, you can stop the page, and then move on to some other website.

To stop a page downloading:
▶ *Click* **Stop** *to the right of the Address bar.*

There may be times when a page downloads, but it doesn't display correctly for some reason. Bits might be missing, or you might know that something has changed but it isn't reflected on screen. When this happens, you should refresh the page.

To refresh a web page:
▶ *Click* **Refresh** *to the right of the Address bar or press* [F5].

DISPLAY/HIDE IMAGES

Most web pages have pictures on them. Some pages are slow to download because of the pictures – the files are so big it takes time to transfer them to your PC. To help speed up the display of your Web pages, you can turn the graphics off.

To switch off graphics:

1 *Click the* **Tools** *command and choose* **Internet Options.**

2 *Select the* **Advanced** *tab.*

3 *In the* **Multimedia** *area, deselect the* **Show** pictures *option (and/or* **Play animations** *in web pages, or* **Play sounds** *in web pages as required).*

4 *If the pictures on the current page are still visible after you clear the* **Show pictures** *checkbox, click* **Refresh.**

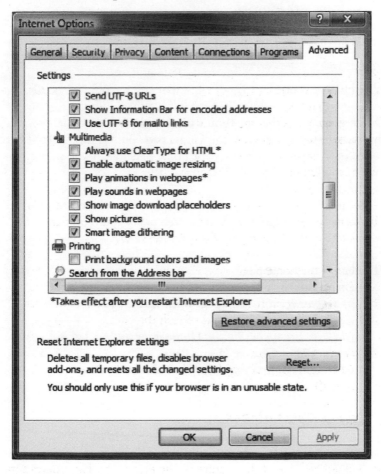

If you wish to set up your system to display pictures again, repeat steps 1–3, selecting the checkboxes required.

Viewing pictures

You can still display an individual picture or animation on a Web page even if you have deselected Show pictures. Right-click on its icon and select Show Picture.

To close the web browser
▶ *Click the* **Close** *button at the right of the title bar.*

9.4 Home page

The home page is the one that is displayed when you open your browser or when you click the Home page button on the Tool bar. You could have one page as your home page, or, if you prefer, you can have a set of pages.

You can specify the home page (or pages). You could use your favourite search engine, your own web page, your company website – or all of them – whatever you prefer.

To change the home page:
1 *Display the page you want to use for your home page (if you want more than one, open each page on a separate tab).*
2 *Click the arrow beside the* **Home** *page button.*
3 *Select* **Add** *or* **Change Home Page...**
4 *Choose the option required from the dialog box.*

- ▶ *Use this webpage as your only home page – select this option to specify the current webpage as your home page.*
- ▶ *Add this webpage to your home page tabs – if you already have a home page (or pages) use this option to add another page to them.*
- ▶ *Use the current tab set as your home page – if you have several tabs open with different web pages displayed on them, use this option to select them all as your home page setting.*

5 *Click* **OK.**

9.5 Viewing web pages offline

If you find a web page that you want to be able to view or print later, when you are not connected to the Internet, you should save it.

To save a web page:

1 *Click the drop-down arrow beside the* **Page...** *tool.*
2 *Choose* **Save As...**
3 *Specify the drive/folder that you want the page on.*
4 *Accept or edit the filename.*
5 *Specify the* **Save as type** *option – the default is* **Web Archive, single file MHT.**
6 *Click* Save.

When you are offline, you can still view and/or print the page that you saved.

To view/print the page when offline:

1 *Open the file – locate it on* **Computer** *and double-click on it.*
2 *View/print as required.*

Learn more at the BBC

You might like to have a look at the online Internet course at
http://www.bbc.co.uk/webwise/course/

9.6 Help

To open Internet Explorer Help:

1 *Click*  *on the command bar and choose* **Internet Explorer Help** *or press* **[F1]**.
▶ *The Windows Help and Support window will open, at Internet Explorer at a Glance.*
2 *You could browse through the Help pages from here.*
Or
▶ *Enter details of something you want to search for in the Search field, e.g. 'set home page'.*

Or

▶ *Click the* **Browse Help** *tool*  *and look through the contents to see what might be useful.*

9.7 Browser settings

There are a number of different settings that you can change within your browser window.

TOOLBARS

There are several bars that you can switch on or off, e.g. Links, Status bar and a Menu bar within the browser window.

To switch a bar on or off:
1 *Right-click on a blank area in the* **Command** *bar at the top of the web page.*
2 *Click on the bar that you want to show or hide in the shortcut menu.*

✓	Menu Bar
✓	Favorites Bar
	Compatibility View Button
✓	Command Bar
✓	Status Bar
✓	Lock the Toolbars
	Customize ▶

Lock the toolbars
If the toolbars are not locked in position, you will see a line of dots at the left edge of each. You can adjust the amount of space allocated to the toolbar by dragging this line – the mouse pointer changes to a double-headed arrow when it is over it.

▶ *To toggle the locked status, click the* **Lock the Toolbars** *option in the shortcut menu.*

Customize Command bar
You can customize the Command bar.

To control how the icons are displayed:
1 *Right-click on the* **Command** *bar to display the shortcut menu.*
2 *Click* **Customize Command Bar.**
3 *Select a display option* – **Show All Text Labels, Show Selective Text** *or* **Show Only Icons.**

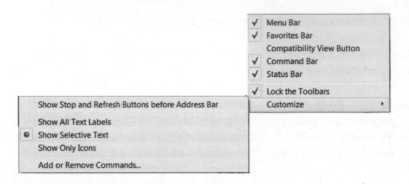

To add or remove commands:
1 *Right-click on the Command bar and select Customize Command Bar.*
2 *Click Add or Remove Commands...*
3 *Select the commands that you wish to add (in Available toolbar buttons) or remove (in Current toolbar buttons).*
4 *Click Add or Remove as necessary.*
5 *Close the dialog box.*

9.8 Web navigation

If you know the URL of the web page or site that you require you can easily go to it.

1 *Enter its URL in the Address field.*
2 *Press [Enter].*

HYPERLINKS

Many of the pages that you visit will have hyperlinks to other pages or sites that you may be interested in. As you jump from one location to another, following the hyperlinks, you are surfing the Net.

▶ *Click a hyperlink to jump to the location that it points to.*

If you want to revisit pages:

▶ *Click* **Back** *and* **Forward** *to move between the pages you've already visited.*

Or

▶ *Click the* **Recent Pages** *arrow and select the URL of the page to return to.*

Or

▶ *Click the drop-down arrow to the right of the Address bar and select the URL you want to revisit.*

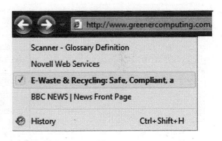

As you browse the Web, your browser will store details of where you have been in its History. Your computer will also store Temporary Internet Files so that the web pages can be displayed again quickly if you go back to them.

To display a history of where you have been:

1 *Click the* **Recent Pages** *button and select* **History** *(or press* **[Ctrl]-[Shift]-[H]**).

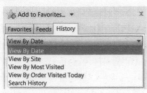

2 *Click the drop-down arrow below the History button to select the order in which to display the pages.*

3 *Click on the page that you wish to revisit.*

To clear the history list:

1 *Click* **Safety** *on the* **Command** *bar.*

2 *Select* **Delete Browsing History...**

3 *Select the items that you want to delete and click* **Delete.**

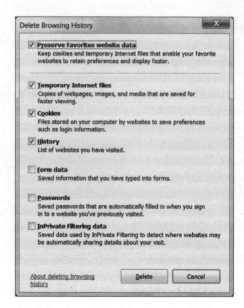

Temporary Internet Files (copies of web pages stored locally for faster viewing) can also be deleted from this dialog box.

POPUPS AND COOKIES

Popups are small windows that open up from web pages. They can be used to display additional information or services, but are mainly used to carry online advertising intended to increase web traffic or capture e-mail addresses. If you find them annoying you can block them.

To turn on the Popup Blocker:

1 *Click* **Tools** *and choose* **Internet Options**.
2 *Display the* **Privacy** *tab*.

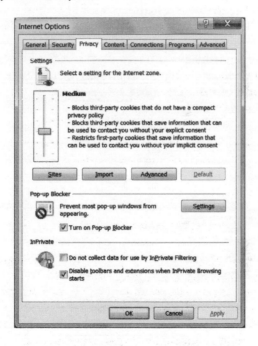

3 *Select* **Turn on Pop-Up blocker** *in the Pop-up blocker area*.
4 *Click* **OK**.

If a site uses pop-ups legitimately, you can unblock them for that site, either for that session or permanently.

Cookies are small text files that some sites put on your computer to identify you when you revisit their site. You can specify whether or not you wish to accept cookies from a website in the Settings area on the Privacy tab.

9.9 Web searching

If you don't know the URL of the page you will need to search for it. If you are looking for information on a topic you would search for it. The result of a search is a list of several (sometimes thousands) of pages or sites that you may be interested in.

To search for something:

1 *Enter a keyword or keywords into the Instant Search field on the right of the Address bar.* orkney short break

2 *Press* [**Enter**].

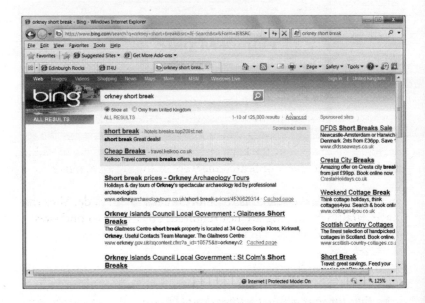

Your search results will be displayed (this search has found 125,000 results!).

SEARCH TIPS

You can specify which keywords you wish to include or omit from your search by using some basic operators.

For example, if you are looking for restaurants in Edinburgh, but not Chinese ones, you could enter into the search field:

+ Edinburgh + Restaurant − Chinese

+ means that the page must contain that word

− means that the page must not.

SEARCH ENGINES

Alternatively, you could try some of the many search engines. Try these: Google (www.google.co.uk), AltaVista (www.altavista.com), Yahoo! (www.yahoo.com), AskJeeves (www.ask.co.uk), Excite (www.excite.com).

Most search engines have a directory to allow you to locate the information you require by working through the various topics. However, if you know what you're looking for it's usually quicker to search. You can specify the keywords and phrases that you are looking for in the Search: field (or Search the web: or something similar).

In this example the search is for short breaks in Speyside. Sites that have details of camping are not required, but I want to find sites that mention skiing.

You will notice that:

▶ *Phrases are enclosed within double quotes, e.g. "short breaks".*
▶ *Words that should be included are preceded by a plus, e.g. +Speyside.*

▶ *Words that should be excluded are preceded by a minus,*
  e.g. – camping.

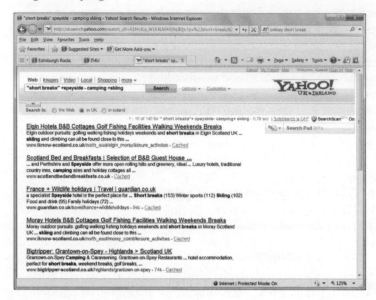

Look through the list of sites found – you may find you have
millions of them (if this is the case you need to be much more
precise in stating your search requirements).

Advanced searches

Most search engines have advanced search features that you
can use to refine your search.

In Yahoo these are under Options, Advanced Search.

You will find options to refine your search by date or file type
in here.

WEB-BASED ENCYCLOPAEDIAS AND DICTIONARIES

You may have noticed that there is quite a lot of jargon and terminology associated with computer and Internet use. As the area is developing at an ever-increasing rate new terms are always appearing. When you come across a term you don't understand you may find an explanation in an online encyclopaedia or dictionary. There are several, the best known being Wikipedia at http://www.wikipedia.org. Wikipedia is available in several languages, and contains definitions of just about anything you can think of – not just on computers or the Internet.

To use Wikipedia:
1 *Go to http://www.wikipedia.org.*
2 *Click **English** to access the English version.*
3 *Type the word you are looking for into the **Search** field.*
4 *Click **Go**.*

Beware! Wikipedia gives very accessible explanations of a huge range of words and concepts, but don't rely on it alone for information for your school or college research paper. Check out other resources to verify the information that you find before you quote it as gospel in your submissions!

> ▶ *You will also find a selection of online dictionaries that you can use – do a search for them!*

9.10 Favorites

The Favorites Center, on the Explorer bar, contains three different areas – Favorites, Feeds or History.

To display the Favorites:
1 *Click* [★ Favorites] *at the left of the bar.*
2 *Select* **Favorites.**

To pin the Center open:
▶ *Click* [◀▶]

To close the Center:
▶ *Click* [✕]

If you find a site that you know you will want to revisit, you should add it to your list of favorites. You can then access the site easily without having to enter the URL or search for it.

To add a page to your favorites:
1 *Display the page that you want to add to your list of favorites.*
2 *Click* [★ Add to Favorites... ▾] *at the top of the Favorites panel.*

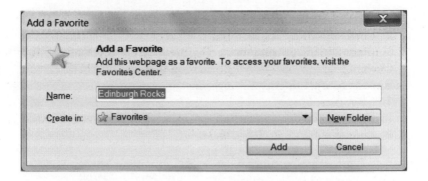

3 *Edit the page name in the* **Name** *field if you wish.*
4 *Select the folder that you want to add your page to – leave it at Favorites, or click the drop-down arrow and choose a folder from the list.*
5 *Click* **Add**.

To go to a page in your Favorites list:
1 *Display the Favorites Center.*
2 *Open the folder that contains your favorite.*
3 *Click on the page required.*

Find a jargon buster!

With so much jargon to work with it is worth putting an online encyclopedia and/or dictionary into your Favorites so you can get to it quickly to find out what something means.

You could use www.wikipedia.org or try the online dictionary at http://www.webopedia.com/ or http://www.bbc.co.uk/webwise/course/jargon/a.shtml

As you use the Internet your list of favorites will probably get larger. If necessary you can set up folders to help you organize your favorites, and move or delete them to tidy up the list. You can perform these tasks in the Organize Favorites area.

To open the Organize Favorites area:
1 *Click* 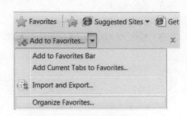 .
2 *Click* **Organize Favorites...**

To create a new folder:
1 *Click* **New Folder.**
2 *Give your folder a name.*
3 *Press* [Enter].

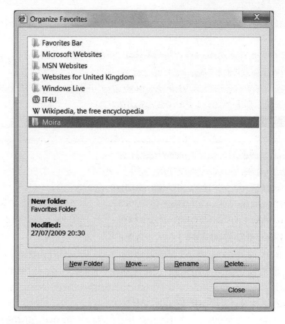

To rename a folder or favorite:
1 *Select it.*
2 *Click* **Rename.**
3 *Type in a new name and press* [Enter].

Move a folder or favorite:
1 *Select it.*
2 *Click* **Move...**
3 *Select the folder you wish to move it to.*
4 *Click* **OK.**

To delete a folder or favorite:
1 *Select it.*
2 *Click* **Delete.**
3 *Click* **Yes** *to confirm the deletion.*

To view the properties of a favorite:
1 *Select the favorite.*
2 *Read the properties in the lower part of the dialog box.*
3 *Close the* **Organize Favorites** *dialog box when you've finished.*

Get organized

It really is worth taking the time to organize your favorites into folders. If you are house-hunting or job hunting you could put all the websites you want to revisit into a folder so that you can find them again quickly. They can be deleted once you have finished your project!

9.11 Copying text and pictures

If you find a web page that contains information that would be useful for a report, paper or essay that you are working on you can easily collect the information into a Word document. As you work you may collect information from many different sources and add them to your document.

To copy text:

1 *Select the text that you require from a web page.*
2 *Right-click within the selected area and then click on* **Copy**.
3 *Go to or open Word.*
4 *Open or create a document to paste your text into.*
5 *Position the insertion point where you want the text to appear.*
6 *Click the* **Paste** *tool.*

You can add more information to your document as you find it, edit the text, save the document and print it as required.

To copy a picture:

1 *Right-click on the picture.*
2 *Click on* **Copy**.
3 *Go to the file that you want the copy to appear in.*
4 *Paste the picture.*

Plagiarism

Be aware of plagiarism when using information from the Web (using other people's work and passing it off as your own, without giving credit to the original source). Other people's work can be a useful resource, but you should acknowledge your sources. Do a search on plagiarism to find out more. And remember, your teachers and lecturers are becoming increasingly skilled at detecting plagiarism in papers!

Have a look at http://www.plagiarism.org/

9.12 Printing

You may find a web page that you want to print, e.g. one giving confirmation of an order you have placed. There may be a Print button on the page itself – if so all you need to do is click it. Alternatively, you could check the page setup, preview the page and print in much the same way as in other applications.

PAGE SETUP

To check/change the page setup options:
1 *Click the down arrow beside the* **Print** *command button.*
2 *Choose* **Page Setup...**
3 *Edit the fields as required, e.g. change orientation, paper size or margins.*
4 *Click* OK.

PRINT PREVIEW

To preview a page before printing:
1 *Click the down arrow beside the* **Print** *command button.*
2 *Choose* **Print Preview.**

PRINT

To print a page:
1 *Click the* **Print** *command button to print one copy of the page.*
Or
2 *Click the down arrow beside the* **Print** *command button.*
3 *Choose* **Print** *to open the* **Print** *dialog box.*
4 *Set the* **Print** *options, e.g.* **All, Page range, Selection, Frame, Number of copies,** *etc.*
5 *Click* OK.

9.13 Online forms

If you are booking a holiday, placing an order for goods or signing up for membership of some group using the WWW you will be asked to complete an online form.

Completing an online form is usually very straightforward.

It will consist of:

▶ *Text boxes, so that you can type information in.*
▶ *Drop-down lists, often used so that you can choose from a longish list of options.*
▶ *Radio button and checkboxes, to allow you to select from a limited range of options.*

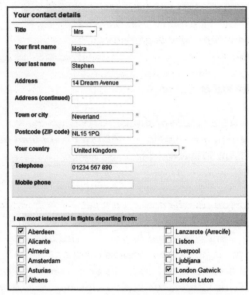

Near the end of the form there will be a button that says:

Send or **Submit** if the information is being sent over the Internet – click the button when you are finished.
Or
Print – if you are meant to print the completed form out and post or fax it.

And usually another which says:

Reset – to clear the form.

TEST

1 *What is the difference between the Internet and the Web?*

2 *Identify three different things you could do on the Internet.*

3 *What online resources may be useful if you need to find out the meaning of a new Internet/communication word?*

4 *List three ways you can help keep yourself safe online.*

5 *What do you call the page that is displayed when you launch your browser?*

6 *What does URL stand for?*

7 *If you don't know the URL of a website, what tool could you use to help you find it?*

8 *What is plagiarism?*

9 *What do you call the area on a webpage that you can click to take you to other places on the web?*

10 *What type of fields are found on an online form?*

10

E-mail

In this chapter you will learn:
* *how to use Outlook efficiently*
* *how to organize messages*

10.1 E-mail

How did we live without e-mail? It's one of the quickest, cheapest ways to communicate (once you've got yourself set up with a computer with Internet access).

The convenience and flexibility of e-mail makes it a very attractive communication media. You can send your messages, and read the ones that you've received, at a time that suits you. Even if you are in a different time zone from those you communicate with, you don't need to wake anyone up in the middle of the night to talk to them – just send them an e-mail and they'll get it when they next log on.

If you have a web-based e-mail account, you can send and receive your messages from anywhere in the world with Internet access – handy for those who globetrot! It has to be one of the best ways to keep in touch with family, friends and colleagues (next to meeting them for lunch!). There are several web-based e-mail providers to choose from, and some of these offer a free service.

E-MAIL FUNDAMENTALS

E-mail addresses
These follow the format: user@domain. You will be given an e-mail address from your ISP (Internet Service Provider), company, school, etc. Examples might be john.smith@abc.co.uk or j.f.dupleix@feic.com

E-mail systems
There are two main types of e-mail system – those that are web-based (and often free), e.g. Yahoo!, Hotmail, and those that you pay for, e.g. Outlook, Virgin, Quistanet.

The main advantages of a web-based service is that it is usually free and can be accessed easily from anywhere in the world with an Internet connection. One of the main disadvantages is often the amount of storage allocation you are given (although you can often get more if you pay for it).

Services that you subscribe to have the obvious disadvantage of cost – but they often give you a greater range of facilities and more storage space.

If you don't have an e-mail account, and would like a free web-based one, visit http://www.free-email-address.com/ to get a comparison of the current offerings.

Network etiquette (netiquette)
In all walks of life, good manners are appreciated, and e-mail is no exception. When sending e-mails you should ensure that you:

- ▶ *Complete the Subject field with a brief accurate description of what the message is about.*
- ▶ *Keep the e-mail short and to the point – no one will appreciate you using up their mailbox storage allocation with rambling messages.*
- ▶ *Spell-check the document before you send, to help ensure it doesn't contain errors.*

▶ *Consider formatting your replies so that the recipient can easily tell the difference between the original message and the reply (it might just be a case of indenting one of them).*

Digital signature

A digital signature is a type of cryptography used to identify an e-mail's sender securely. Digital signature schemes normally require two keys, the user's private key for signing and a public key for verifying signatures. They are used mainly in business where secure communications are essential.

OTHER FORMS OF ELECTRONIC COMMUNICATION

Short Message Service (SMS)

The Short Message Service (SMS) is a means of sending short messages to and from mobile phones. Most SMS messages are mobile-to-mobile text messages, though the standard supports other types of broadcast messaging as well.

Voice over Internet Protocol (VoIP)

A Voice over Internet Protocol (VoIP) is a protocol optimized for the transmission of voice over the Internet. VoIP is also known as IP telephony, Internet telephony, Broadband telephony, Broadband Phone and Voice over Broadband.

A potential benefit is cost savings due to utilizing a single network to carry voice and data, especially where users have existing underutilized network capacity that can carry VoIP at no additional cost.

Skype

Skype has become one of the most popular VoIP services. You can make free calls – voice or video (if you have a webcam) – to other Skype users.

400

You cannot use Skype to make emergency calls – so you can't really replace your normal phone with it.

Companies like Skype make their money by selling consumables, e.g. headsets and webcams and offering packages with more features, e.g. low-rate calls to normal phones and mobiles.

Instant Messaging (IM)

Instant messaging allows you to communicate with friends and colleagues in real time. When you access an IM system you can tell which of your contacts are online – you have probably heard of some IM systems, e.g. MSN, Yahoo!, Google Talk. They are low cost, and allow you to transfer files as well as messages.

Virtual communities

An online (virtual) community is one that you may join for a variety of reasons, social, study, research, etc. Social networking sites, e.g. Facebook and Bebo, have become very popular with friends and families who are geographically separate but want to keep up to date with each other regularly. Internet forums allow you to discuss topics of interest with colleagues and peers from around the globe. You can drop into chat rooms to catch up on the gossip with friends and play online computer games with people you may never meet. Sites like Second Life give you the chance to become a member of a virtual community where you have your own fictitious character and role in life.

Virtual communities

Virtual communities like Second Life have become very popular as a virtual social, cultural, educational and collaborative space for people.

However, do be careful when you are out and about in this world – just like the streets in your city, it is full of all sorts of characters!

THINK SAFE!!

E-mails are not a secure way of sending messages. They can be easily intercepted by unscrupulous Internet users! So don't send sensitive information via e-mail. Bank account details, pin numbers – in fact any information that you don't want to fall into the wrong hands – should be transmitted in some other way, e.g. a secure link to your bank.

You may receive e-mails that look like they have come from your bank or credit card company suggesting that you click here to contact them and confirm your details. Don't! Banks and credit card companies don't use e-mails to collect or confirm sensitive data! If you receive this type of e-mail you are probably being targeted by a 'phishing' scam where someone is trying to collect your details so that they can use them to their own advantage. Phishing is an attempt to criminally and fraudulently acquire sensitive information, such as usernames, passwords and credit card details, by masquerading as a trustworthy entity in an electronic communication (eBay, PayPal and online banks are common targets of phishing scams).

You are also bound to receive some unsolicited e-mail – called 'junk mail' or 'spam' – as people do mass mailings to random e-mail addresses to try and engage you in some activity and relieve you of your funds or personal details. If something looks too good to be true – it probably is. So ignore it, or try to contact the organization some other way to check things out. You will often find that a search on the Internet for information on some offer that looks suspicious will confirm that you were right to be cautious!

Spam

Have a look at the information on Spam at
http://www.bbc.co.uk/webwise/askbruce/articles/e-mail/spam_1.shtml

and a news report at
http://news.bbc.co.uk/1/hi/technology/7988579.stm

E-mail attachments are another possible danger! If you don't recognize the sender of the message, be very wary of opening any attachments the message contains. It is a favourite way of distributing computer viruses. Many virus checking systems will scan incoming e-mails and block any that are suspect. But be careful!

If you work for a company, you may find there are guidelines and rules that you must follow when using their e-mail system. So make sure that you know what they are – and follow them. They are there for a reason – to try to ensure the safety and security of the company's staff and systems.

E-mail is no more dangerous than any other activity – just keep your wits about you! You wouldn't write your pin number on a piece of paper, store it beside your bank card – and leave them lying on the table in your bank (would you?) – so don't be careless online either.

Whatever e-mail system you use, set your security settings to their limit and/or ensure you have up-to-date anti-virus software checking your incoming e-mails.

If you are part of a virtual community, remember to be careful with your real personal details!

10.2 Introducing Outlook

The e-mail service discussed here is Microsoft Outlook.

To open Outlook:
  1 *Click the* **Start** *button.*
  2 *Select* **Microsoft Office Outlook** *at the top of the* **Start** *menu.*
Or
  ▶ *Click* **Microsoft Office Outlook** *in the* **Quick Launch** *area of the* **Taskbar.**

Navigation pane   Message headers

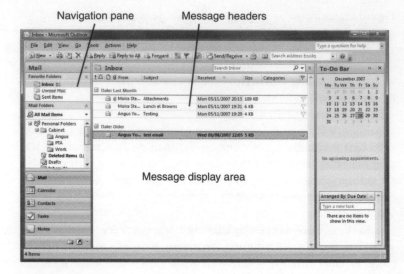

The Outlook window.

10.3 Send e-mail

To send an e-mail:

1 *Select the* **Mail** *option.*
2 *Click* **New** *on the toolbar.*
3 *Enter the address of the recipient in the* **To:** *field.*
4 *If you wish to send a copy of the message to someone else, enter their address in the* **Cc:** *field.*
5 *Type in a* **Subject.**

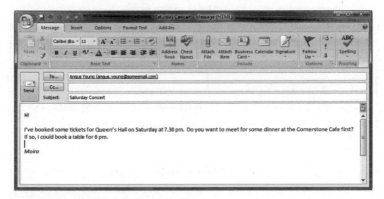

6 *Key in your message.*

7 *Spell check it – click the* **Spelling** *tool on the* **Message** *tab.*

8 *Most messages have normal priority but you can mark a message as High priority (or Low priority) if required – the feature is in the* **Options** *group on the* **Message** *tab.*

9 *Click* **Send.**

Messages that you send will be saved automatically in your **Sent Items** folder.

You can save an e-mail message – perhaps because you haven't finished it – and then complete it at a later date. When you save an e-mail, it is put in the *Drafts* folder. To complete the message just open it from the *Drafts* folder, update and send.

To: Cc: and Bcc:

Type the address of each recipient into the appropriate field (if there are more than one, separate them with a semicolon ;).

▶ *The To: field is for the main recipient(s).*
▶ *The Cc: field is for those that you want to send a copy so that they know what's going on.*
▶ *The Bcc: field is for sending blind copies. Only the message sender and each individual in the Bcc field know that they have been sent a message. Those who have been sent a Bcc will not know who else has been sent a copy.*

To show the Bcc field for a message:
1 *Create a new message.*
2 *Display the* **Options** *tab.*
3 *Click* **Show Bcc** *in the* **Fields** *group.*

Subject field
Type the message title in the Subject field – this will be displayed in the Inbox of the recipient, so they have an idea what the message is about.

Message area
Type your message in here.

▶ *You can use the tools in the* **Basic Text** *group on the* **Message** *tab to format your text.*
▶ *The Spelling checker is in the* **Proofing** *group on the* **Message** *tab.*

E-mail message formats

Outlook allows you to format your e-mail messages as HTML, RTF or Plain Text. The default format is HTML.

Both HTML and RTF allow you to format your messages using different fonts, colour, bullet points, etc. Plain Text just allows – well – plain unformatted text.

Not all e-mail applications allow their users to view formatted messages. So you should format your e-mail messages using a format that your recipient's e-mail system supports. All e-mail applications support unformatted text – if in doubt Plain Text is a safe option. It also keeps the mail message smaller.

If you know your recipient is using Outlook (or an application that supports formatting) then the best option to use is HTML. You can then format the text with the usual formatting options.

Outlook RTF is a format that is only supported by earlier versions of Outlook (97, 98, 2000 and 2002), Office Outlook (2003 and 2007) and Microsoft Exchange Client 4.0 and 5.0.

Outlook will automatically convert RTF to HTML when you send it to an Internet recipient.

The format can be changed on the Options tab, in the Format group.

Practise sending messages to some of your friends and family. You can copy and paste text from other e-mails or documents into your e-mail using normal copy and paste routines.

You can preview and print a message in the normal way – using the Print Preview tool and the Quick Print tool on the Quick Access toolbar (or the options in the Microsoft Office menu).

10.4 Attaching a file

You can easily attach files to your e-mail message. You may want to send someone a report or spreadsheet to have a look at, or a picture that you took on holiday. Beware when sending large attachments, e.g. pictures – they can take a while to transmit and fill up your recipient's mailbox!

To **attach a file to a message:**
1 *Enter the address(es) and Subject fields as usual.*
2 *Click* **Attach File** *on the* **Message** *tab.*
3 *Locate the file you wish to attach.*
4 *Click* **Insert.**
5 *Repeat 2–4 for each attachment.*

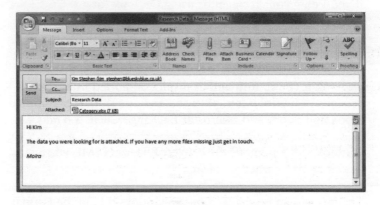

▶ *Your attachments will be displayed below the Subject field.*

6 *Enter your message (if you haven't already done so).*
7 *Spell-check your message.*
8 *Click* **Send.**

Things to remember when sending attachments:

▶ *Attachments will make your e-mail larger and so it will take longer to send.*

- *If an attachment is too big, the recipient's mailbox may not accept it, or not have room for it. The files are converted into a different format for sending by mail, and become about 50% larger. So, a 100Kb document will produce a 150Kb message.*
- *The attachment should be of a file type that your recipient can open. There is no point sending them a Word 2007 document if they are using WordPerfect 5.1! You may need to convert the file to a suitable format before you send it (use File > Save As... in the application).*
- *Anti-virus software may stop your attachment from reaching the recipient's mailbox – many will not allow an Access database file through.*
- *Network software may also stop your attachment – perhaps because it is too big or of a file type it won't permit.*

10.5 Inbox

Messages that you receive will be displayed in your Inbox.

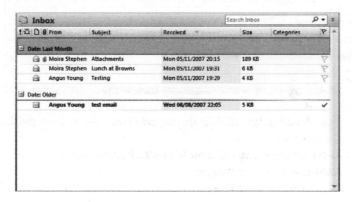

Things to note about your Inbox:

- *Unread messages have a closed envelope icon beside them, read messages have an open envelope.*

- *If you have read a message, then want to mark it as unread again (perhaps to remind yourself to have another look at it), with the message open, click* **Mark as Unread** *in the* **Options** *group on the* **Message** *tab. Alternatively, right-click on the message in the Inbox and click* **Mark as Unread.** *The envelope icon will appear closed again.*
- *You can sort the messages in your Inbox into ascending or descending order. Click the column heading,* **From, Subject, Received** *or* **Size,** *to sort your messages.*
- *A message with an attachment will have a paperclip icon beside it.*
- *To open a message to read it – double-click on it.*

Saving addresses

You can save the address of the sender from an open message. Right-click on the address and choose Add to Outlook Contacts from the menu.

ATTACHMENTS

If the message has an attachment:

- *Double-click on the attachment to open it.*

Or

1 *Right-click on it.*
2 *Click on* **Save As...**
3 *Specify where you want the file saved and what you want it called.*
4 *Click* **Save.**
- *Beware of attachments from sources that you do not recognize. If in doubt, do not open them or save them.*

Blocking senders

If you get e-mails from someone that you don't want to receive them from, click the Block Sender tool in the Junk E-mail group on the Message tab.

10.6 Print a message

You can print a copy of an e-mail if required.

1 *Open the message.*
2 *Click* **Print Preview** *if you want to preview it.*
Or
▶ *Click* **Quick Print** *to send one copy of the message to the default printer.*

If you wish to set any printing options, e.g. number of copies, display the Print dialog box and select the options required.

▶ *To close messages without replying to it click the* **Close** *button.*

10.7 Reply to/forward a message

You will often want to reply to an e-mail message, or perhaps forward it to someone else.

1 *Open the message.*
2 *Click* **Reply** *(to reply to the sender only) or* **Reply to All** *(to send your reply to everyone that the message was sent to).*

3 *Type in your reply/message and attach any files required.*

4 *Click* Send.

To forward a message to someone else:

1 *Click Forward.*

2 *Enter the recipient's address details.*

3 *Carry on from step 3 above, when replying.*

10.8 Productivity options

CUSTOMIZE FIELD DISPLAY

To customize the list of fields in the folders:

1 *Right-click on the column headings.*

2 *Choose* Customize Current View.

3 *Click* Fields...

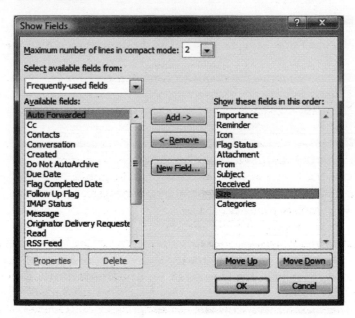

4 *Add, remove or re-order the fields as required.*
5 *Click* OK.

REPLY AND FORWARD OPTIONS

Do you want to include the original message when you send a
reply? It's normal to include it in business e-mails, but not in
private ones.

At the Inbox/Outlook window:

1 *Open the* Tools *menu and choose* Options.
2 *Select the* Preferences *tab and click* E-mail Options.
3 *Set the* Replies *and* Forwards *options as required.*
4 *Click* OK.

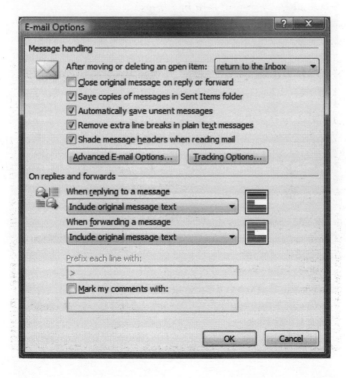

FLAG A MESSAGE

There may be times that you receive or send a message and you know that you want to return to it, perhaps to follow it up or do something else that needs to be done.

To stop you losing track of the message, you can flag it so that your attention is drawn back to it.

▶ *Click the flag in the last column in the* **Inbox** *or* **Sent Items** – *the message will be red flagged.*

To see the options available for flagging messages:
1 *Right-click on the flag.*
2 *Explore the options available.*

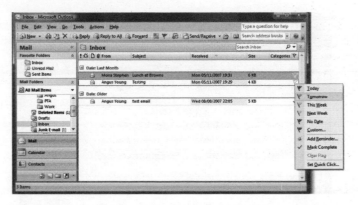

To mark the message as dealt with:
▶ *Click on the flag again – the flag will become a tick to indicate it is finished with.*

To remove the flag from a message:
1 *Right-click on the flag.*
2 *Click* **Clear Flag.**

10.9 Contacts

It is a good idea to put addresses that you will use again into your Contacts area. You can add addresses when you send or receive a message, or you can enter them manually.

To add an address manually:
1 *Open the* **Address Book** *– click on the* **Address Book**  *on the toolbar in the Inbox.*
2 *Right-click in the Contacts list.*
3 *Click on* **New Entry...**
4 *Select* **New Contact** *and click* **OK.**
5 *Select* **General** *in the* **Show** *group.*
6 *Complete the contact details.*
7 *Click* **Save & Close.**

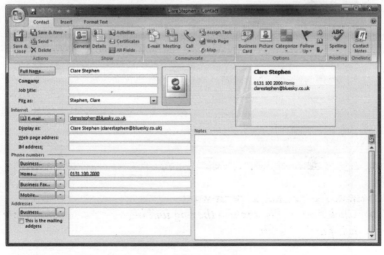

To add an address from incoming mail:
1 *Open the mail message – double-click on it.*
2 *Right-click on the sender's e-mail.*
3 *Click on* **Add to Outlook Contacts.**
4 *Complete the details as necessary and click* **Save & Close.**

DISTRIBUTION LISTS

You can set up distribution lists or groups, so that you can quickly add a number of recipients to your e-mails. This option is useful if you will be sending e-mails to the same group of people regularly, e.g. your friends, social club or team at work.

1 *Open the Address Book.*
2 *Right-click in the list of addresses.*
3 *Click* **New Entry...**
4 *Choose* **New Distribution List** *and click* **OK.**
5 *Click* **Select Members** *in the* **Members** *group on the* **Distribution List** *tab in the Ribbon.*

6 *Double-click on a name to add it to the* **Members** *field.*
7 *Click* **OK.**

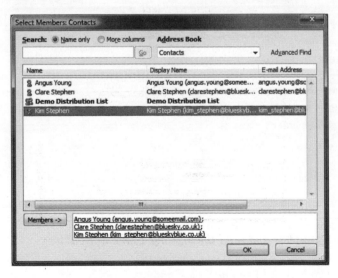

8 *Enter a name for your group.*
9 *Click* **Save & Close.**

To send an e-mail to the group:

1 *Select the group name from the Address Book. This opens the* **New Message** *window, with the group in the* **To:** *field.*

Or

2 *Create a new message.*

3 *Type the group name into the* **To:** *field in your message.*

Or

4 *Click* [**To...**] *then in the* **Select Names** *dialog box, double-click on the group name to select it and click* **OK.**

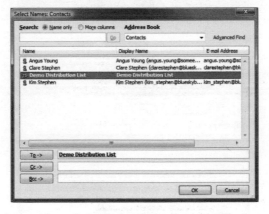

5 *Complete and send the message in the normal way.*

10.10 Signature

An Outlook signature allows you to append your standard closure to an e-mail automatically.

You might like to finish your e-mails with something like:

With best wishes

Moira

Rather than type this into every message, you can store the text in a signature and get Outlook to add this to every e-mail.

To display the Signatures and Stationery dialog box:
1 *Open the* **Tools** *menu and choose* **Options.**
2 *Display the* **Mail Format** *tab.*
3 *Click* **Signatures...**

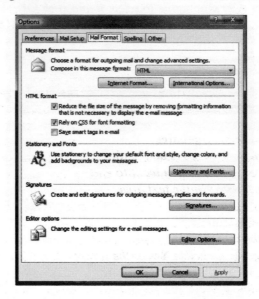

To create a new signature:
1 *At the* **Signatures and Stationery** *dialog box click* **New**.
2 *Give your signature a name.*
3 *Click* **OK**.
4 *Enter your signature text in the text area.*
5 *Format it as you wish using the tools available.*
6 *Repeat steps 1–5 for each signature (you may have one for new messages and a different one for replies/forwards).*
7 *Select the default signature for* **New messages** *and/or for* **Replies and Forwards**.
8 *Click* **OK**.

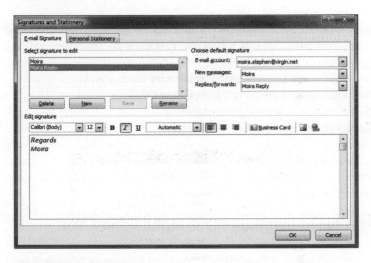

To edit an existing signature:
1 *Display the* **Signatures and Stationery** *dialog box.*
2 *Select the signature you want to edit.*
3 *Update the text in the text area.*

To delete a signature:
1 *Select the signature.*
2 *Click* **Delete** *and click* **Yes** *at the prompt.*

To rename a signature:

1 *Select the signature and click* **Rename**.

2 *Enter a new name at the dialog box and click* **OK**.

10.11 Message management

Once you've started using e-mail, you will probably find that it becomes one of your main ways of communicating with family, friends and colleagues. The number of e-mails that you send and receive will increase substantially. Eventually, you will get to the stage where you need to sort your e-mails out – perhaps get rid of some, and put others into folders. You need to get organized!

In a work environment the number of e-mails can become quite overwhelming if you don't stay on top of things.

Rather than be constantly distracted by e-mails, it is best to set aside a time to look at them. Depending on the volume you receive and the urgency of them you could do this twice a day – in the morning and afternoon, or every couple of hours. That way you can get some other work done too.

Tips for managing your e-mails – the 4 D's

▶ *Do It – if it is easily dealt with, just do it – immediately – job done!*

▶ *Delete It – anything not work related or spam that got through*

▶ *Defer It – if you can't deal with it immediately, mark it as closed, or flag it, or put it in your To Do folder (whatever system you have decided to use) – and set aside time to come back to these and work through them*

▶ *Delegate It – if someone else can deal with it (and you have the authority to delegate) – pass it on*

SEARCHING FOR MAIL

You might need to search through your e-mails to find the one that you are looking for, or if you receive a lot of e-mails from the same source, or about the same topic, you might want to organize the messages into folders so that you can find them easily.

To search for a message by sender, subject or e-mail content:
▶ *Type the text you are looking for into the* **Search** *field at the top of the list of messages.*

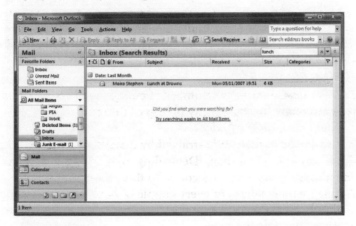

To clear the search:
▶ *Click the* **Close** *button (the cross) at the right of the search field.*

To set your search options:
1 *Click the down arrow to the right of the search field.*
2 *Choose* **Search Options...**
3 *Complete the dialog box as required.*

To sort your e-mails:
▶ *Click the column heading that you wish to sort on.*

The first time you click on the heading, the list will sort in ascending order on that column. Click again and it will sort in descending order.

USING FOLDERS

To create a new folder:

1 *Right-click on the folder that will be the parent of the one you are about to create, e.g.* **Personal Folders.**

2 *Click* **New Folder...** *to open the* **Create New Folder** *dialog box.*

3 *Give your folder a name e.g. Cabinet.*

4 *Click* **OK.**

You can create additional folders within this, if you wish to store the messages you send and receive from different individuals or on different topics. Just remember to right-click on the folder that will be the parent of the new folder you are creating.

To move messages to a folder:

1 *Right-click on the message – probably one in your Inbox or Sent Items folder – and click on* **Move to Folder...**

2 *Select the folder to move the message to and click* **OK**.

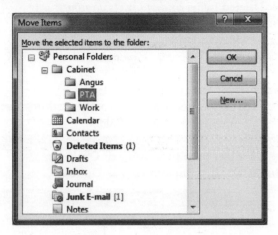

To manage folders:

1 *Right-click on the folder to open the menu then...*

2 *To rename, click on* **Rename** *folder name then type the new name and press* [Enter].

3 *To move, click on* **Move** *folder name, then select the folder you want to move it to and click* **OK**.

4 *To copy a folder, click on* **Copy** *folder name, then select the folder you want to copy it to and click* **OK**.

5 *To delete a folder, click on the* **Delete** *folder name or select it and press* [Delete].

DELETING MESSAGES

When you deleted a message, it is put in your Deleted Items folder. If you delete accidentally, you can recover it from here (provided the folder hasn't been emptied). The Deleted Items folder should be emptied regularly.

To delete a message:

1 *Select the message in a folder and press* [Delete].

Or

    If the message is open, click **Delete** *in the* **Actions** *group.*

To restore a deleted message:
1 *Select* **Deleted Items** *to display its contents.*
2 *Right-click on the item you want to recover.*
3 *Click on* **Move to Folder...**
4 *Select the folder (or create a new one) and click* **OK.**

To manually empty the Deleted Items folder:
1 *Right-click on* **Deleted Items** *in the Navigation panel.*
2 *Click on* **Empty Deleted Items Folder.**

To empty the folder each time you exit Outlook:
1 *Open the* **Tools** *menu and choose* **Options.**

2 *Display the* **Other** *tab.*
3 *Select* **Empty the Deleted Items on exiting.**
4 *Click* **OK.**

TEST

1 *What is netiquette?*

2 *Identify two other ways of communicating electronically (other than e-mail).*

3 *What is phishing?*

4 *The subject and To fields in an e-mail are an example of:*
   (a) Attachments   (b) Headers   (c) Spam   (d) Contacts

5 *Where will you normally find messages that you have sent?*

6 *How can you identify a Read or Unread message in your Inbox?*

7 *Where can you customize your Reply and Forward options?*

8 *What is the Contacts area used for?*

9 *If you send e-mail to the same group of people regularly what feature will help you select all recipients at the same time, without having to identify them all individually?*

10 *What feature allows you to organize our e-mails so that you can keep e-mails relating to the same subject/project together?*

Answers

Chapter 1

1 *System performance; Information; Technology.*
2 *The message asks you to invest in something or tries to sell you something. You didn't ask for information on what has been sent. It sounds too good to be true!*
3 *Delete it; forward it to your IT security person (or whoever deals with ICT security in your organization).*
4 *You don't – it installs itself without you knowing.*
5 *Install anti-virus software; don't install pirate software; don't open e-mail attachments from unknown sources.*
6 *They are easily stolen, lost or left behind because you forget to take them with you.*
7 *Secure it – with a password. You could also set up a list of authorized devices.*
8 *Guidelines on the use of ICT; privacy policy.*
9 *Theft; accidental damage, e.g. user deletes a file by accident; data corruption as a result of hardware failure.*
10 *It gives you another copy – so the data is not lost altogether if it gets stolen/corrupted, etc.*

Chapter 2

1 *To ensure that no-one can access your files while you are away from your computer. Start, click arrow to right of Shut Down, Lock.*
2 *Varies with machine.*
3 *Press PrintScreen. Paste into a document, e.g. WordPad or Word. Print the document.*

4 Recycle Bin; Shortcut to Paint application; Folder called Win7text; File called Contents; Printer
5 USB pen; CD.
6 Provide an off-site backup of data; allows for data sharing.
7 Image file; Word 2007 document; Portable document file (Acrobat); Access 2007 database; Web page.
8 A way of reducing the size of a file on disk.
9 A = WordPad button; B = Quick Access toolbar; C = Ribbon.
10 Press [Delete] to delete the character to the right of the insertion point, or press [Backspace] to delete the character to the left of the insertion point.

Chapter 3

1 Back-up files; Empty Recycle Bin; Clean screen/hardware.
2 The printer that you will normally print to – unless you choose a different one.
3 Adjusting the brightness of the screen; Using uplighters rather than overhead lights; Use blinds on the windows; Anti-glare filters for the screen.
4 Sufficient desk room and leg room to allow for posture changes; Movable keyboard – positioned and tilted to ensure operator comfort; enough desktop space for documents as well as the computer.
5 Ensure data is removed (in line with requirements of DPA); ensure software is removed so that licensing agreements are not breached; ensure that hardware meets safety standards if it is being re-used; if it is being disposed of ensure that it goes to an ICT recycling site.
6 They help identify and authenticate the user. This ensures that only authorized user have access to the data on the system.
7 Both a and b are weak.
8 Use the Bcc field rather than the To or Cc. That way no-one else knows who else has received the message.
9 Install, keep up-to-date and run anti-virus software regularly. Do not open e-mail attachments that you are not expecting.

10 *Virus checker; Firewall; anti-spam software.*
11 *Copyright means acknowledging the owner of published material. Software, music, images.*
12 *Shareware – you are usually given it free for a limited period. You must then pay a licence fee to continue to use it. Freeware is free.*

Chapter 4

1 [Ctrl]-[F1].
2 *True – hold down* [Alt] *to display the key tips, then follow the prompts on the buttons*
3 *Right-click on a command and choose* **Add/Remove** *from Quick Access toolbar.*

Or

 Right-click on the Quick Access toolbar and choose **Customize Quick Access Toolbar...**
4 [F1].
5 *To save a file that has already been saved, but using a different location, name or file type.*
6 **Save As...** *dialog box,* **Tools, General Options.**
7 [Ctrl]-[Z] *or click the* **Undo** *button.*
8 *Spell checker and Grammar checker.*
9 *SmartArt, clip art, Shapes (also charts and pictures).*
10 *Status Bar.*

Chapter 5

1 *Paragraph mark, tab, space.*
2 *Click the* **Show/Hide** *button in the* **Paragraph** *group on the* **Home** *tab.*
3 *Word – double-click.*
 Sentence – [Ctrl]-[Click].
 Paragraph – double-click in the selection bar.
 Document – [Ctrl]-[A].

4 [Ctrl]-[Enter] *or* Insert *tab,* Pages *group,* Page *break.*
5 *A pattern/layout on which a document is based.*
6 *Styles.*
7 *Header or Footer area.*
8 *Press* [Tab] *when you are in the last cell.*
9 *Main document and data document.*
10 *Link it.*

Chapter 6

1 [Ctrl]-[Home].
2 *Currency/accounting, percentage, comma.*
3 *Freeze panes and Split Screen.*
4 $=(A7+B24)/D10.$
5 *Max – returns the highest value from a range of cells.*
   Min – returns the lowest value from a range of cells.
   Count – counts the number of numeric entries in a range of cells.
6 *Formula tab, Show Formulas (Auditing group).*
7 $=IF(C8>500,C8*10\%,0).$
8 *A sort on more than one column (maximum 64), e.g. sort on surname, and then on firstname.*
9 *The cell address will not change when the formula is copied or moved.*
10 *Legend, axis, title, data series, etc.*

Chapter 7

1 *Tables.*
2 *Size, Index, Required, Default value, etc.*
3 *Primary Key – a field that uniquely identifies a record, e.g. StudentID, Car Registration, Staff Number.*
   Foreign Key – a field in a table that contains a value that is actually a Primary Key in another table.

4 *A link that joins two tables – usually the Primary key in one table to its corresponding Foreign Key in another Form.*
5 *A form.*
6 *Query and Report.*
7 *Filter by selection, filter by form, or create a query.*
8 *Create a query and add just the fields you want to see.*
9 *Grouping, report headers/footers, page numbering, formatting, subtotals and grand totals.*
10 *Export.*

Chapter 8

1 [Ctrl]-[N].
2 *Notes and Handouts.*
3 *Slide Sorter, Slide Show.*
4 *Home tab, Layout (in the Slides group).*
5 *Colors, fonts and effects.*
6 *Title, bulleted list, table, clipart, chart, shape.*
7 *Select the objects ([Shift]-[Click] on each). Then* **Drawing** *tools,* **Format** *tab,* **Group** *(in the* **Arrange** *group).*
8 *The slide at the top of the slide hierarchy that contains the various slide layouts, colours, etc. for your presentation.*
9 *Slide transition is an effect as you move from one slide to the next; Animation is an effect that builds up the objects on the slide.*
10 *From beginning or from current slide.*

Chapter 9

1 *The Internet is a network of computers. The Web is a series of pages that can be viewed on the Internet.*
2 *Visit web pages, send e-mail, transfer files.*
3 *On online encyclopedia or dictionary.*

4 *Don't disclose personal information, use a virus checker, install a firewall, ensure you are on a secure site if giving sensitive information.*

5 *Home page.*

6 *Uniform Resource Locator.*

7 *Use a search engine.*

8 *Using someone's work without their permission, and trying to pass it off as your own.*

9 *Hyperlink.*

10 *Text, checkboxes, radio buttons, combo boxes, lists, etc.*

Chapter 10

1 *Netiquette is a set of rules to help that you communicate effectively without offending and annoying people.*

2 *SMS, IM and VoIP.*

3 *Phishing is when someone tries to find out your username, password or other sensitive information by conning you!*

4 *Headers.*

5 *Sent Items.*

6 *Read – open envelope icon; Unread – closed envelope icon.*

7 **Tools** *menu,* **Options, Preferences** *tab –* **E-mail Options.**

8 *Storing details of people, e.g. email addresses, names – so that you can find their details again quickly.*

9 *Distribution list.*

10 *Folders.*

Index